PENGUIN BOOKS
JAPAN VERSUS THE WEST

Endymion Wilkinson is head of the Southeast Asia department at the Commission of the European Communities. He was born in England and educated at Gordonstoun School and King's College, Cambridge. On going down in 1964, he continued research on East Asia in Peking and Tokyo, gaining a Princeton PhD in 1970. After four years as lecturer in the history of the Far East at the University of London, he became a European Community diplomat in 1974 and served for six years in Tokyo and for six years in Southeast Asia.

Japan versus the West: Image and Reality is based on an earlier book (*Japan versus Europe: A History of Misunderstanding*) which was a best-seller in Japan and was translated into four languages. The present edition has been completely revised. He is the author of *The History of Imperial China: A Research Guide* (Cambridge, 1975) and *Studies in Chinese Price History* (New York, 1980) and has translated from the Chinese *The People's Comic Book* and *Landlord and Labour in Late Imperial China*.

ENDYMION WILKINSON

JAPAN VERSUS THE WEST

IMAGE AND REALITY

PENGUIN BOOKS

PENGUIN BOOKS

Published by the Penguin Group
Penguin Books Ltd, 27 Wrights Lane, London W8 5TZ, England
Penguin Books USA Inc., 375 Hudson Street, New York, New York 10014, USA
Penguin Books Australia Ltd, Ringwood, Victoria, Australia
Penguin Books Canada Ltd, 10 Alcorn Avenue, Toronto, Ontario, Canada M4V 3B2
Penguin Books (NZ) Ltd, 182–190 Wairau Road, Auckland 10, New Zealand

Penguin Books Ltd, Registered Offices: Harmondsworth, Middlesex, England

First published in Japan by Chuokoron-Sha Inc. 1980

English language edition published under the title *Misunderstanding: Europe vs. Japan*, 1981
First published in Great Britain in a revised edition under the title *Japan versus Europe: A History of Misunderstanding* by Penguin Books 1983
Newly Revised edition published under the present title 1990
Reprinted with revisions 1991
1 3 5 7 9 10 8 6 4 2

Copyright © Chuokoron-Sha Inc., 1980, 1981
Copyright © Endymion Wilkinson, 1983, 1990, 1991
All rights reserved

Printed in England by Clays Ltd, St Ives plc
Filmset in Linotron Times

CONTENTS

LIST OF FIGURES, MAPS AND TABLES

Figures

Maps

Tables

List of Tables in Annex

PREFACE

I first went to Japan in 1968 to work on a doctorate and spent an industrious year living in a 'four and a half mat' room next to Tokyo University.

Five years later, returning on academic study leave, I found that my income only allowed me to rent a small apartment in a noisy student quarter. It was next to a railway line. There were cramming schools (*yobikō*) nearby from which came the droning of students memorizing the answers to university entrance exams. And then came the oil shock of October 1973 and rapid inflation. I began to live like a church mouse, even worse than I had done as a graduate student.

That was the final straw. In the bleak winter of 1973 I decided to change my profession. My chance came the following spring when I joined the Commission of the European Communities and, as my first task, helped set up the Commission's diplomatic representation in Tokyo. I settled down for a long stay, which in the event lasted for six years and involved me full-time in the fascinating story of Japan's rise to great wealth and influence in the world.

So this book reflects my various experiences of Japan – as a graduate student in the sixties; as an EC diplomat in the seventies and as a frequent visitor on both official and private business in the eighties.

It is based on an earlier one (*Japan versus Europe: A History of Misunderstanding*) which was revised and updated six times between 1980 and 1983 and was translated into four languages. The new book has been rewritten to take account of recent changes in the relations between Japan, Europe, and the USA and is therefore published under the new title *Japan versus the West: Image and Reality*.

Main Themes

The main themes are introduced with a sketch of the shift in the balance of economic power between Japan, the USA and Europe, and of the major role now played by Japan in East Asia.

Next, these changes are placed in a broader context by tracing the development of Japanese and Western attitudes towards each other. I have not attempted to write a history of Japan's relations with Europe, still less with America. Instead, I have outlined the development of the mutual prejudices which from time to time have obscured a clear understanding of the changing power relations, and which have also exacerbated the economic, trade and technology frictions between Japan, the USA and Europe.

The story has its harsh as well as its light moments.

The Europeans have found it exceedingly hard to adjust to the rise of Japan and to their own diminishing role on the world stage. At the same time, Europe has become more inward-looking, concentrating ever larger amounts of its trade and investments in markets closer to home. One expression of this trend, which has also acted as a stimulus, is the shift towards regional integration in the European Community. Another is the creation of new links with Eastern Europe and the Soviet Union.

In the USA too, there is difficulty in adapting to the arrival of a new player on the world stage who appears to be winning at games, such as being successful, making money or constructing automobiles and semiconductors, which were felt to be quintessentially the things which Americans did best. And all on the basis of such traditional US values as the family, hard work and thrift.

The Japanese, on the other hand, have found it equally hard to alter an understated self-image as a poor and defeated people still 'on the make', nervously grabbing at every rung on the international status ladder and, having made it in this or that field, acting with what others perceive as arrogance.

While awaiting the outcome of these essentially internal adjustments of self-perceptions, Europe and the USA find it particularly hard to talk to Japan, as does Japan to them, for none of the three is sure where it or the other stands.

Part I sets the scene by showing the extent to which Japan has become a major economic and financial power, and how its arrival has affected its neighbours in Asia as well as the other two main centres of wealth and power in the world, the USA and Europe.

In Part II, I sketch the evolution of Japanese attitudes towards the West. Because they have seen themselves as learners, the Japanese have been able to form more timely and accurate images of Europe and the USA than those which the Europeans and Americans, who saw themselves as teachers, formed of Japan. I have deliberately quoted at length from all sorts of sources so that the reader may enjoy the authenticity of the originals.

Part III completes the picture by tracing the European and US images of Japan. Until recently they were composed of an arsenal of stereotypes founded on the shifting sands of indifference, ignorance, prejudice and fear, rather than based on the results of a serious effort to understand Japan.

Part IV turns to the most lively form of dialogue between Japan and the West in recent years, namely economic, trade and technology frictions.

In Part V, I suggest various measures both to avoid frictions as well as improve communications.

ACKNOWLEDGEMENTS

Many people taught me all sorts of things about Japan. It is impossible to list them all by name, but I would like to thank my old friend Hiroshi Hayakawa. It was he who gave me the practical encouragement to sit down and start writing. My Japanese publisher, Chuokoron-Sha, launched the first version of the book with tremendous verve, and Masazumi Kikkawa of TV-Man-Union and his team transformed it into a television documentary series. Both the launch and the making of the documentary were novel and fascinating experiences which incidentally taught me something about marketing in Japan.

My former colleagues at the EC Delegation in Tokyo, in addition to the daily round of office work, helped me in innumerable ways. In particular, my thanks to Hajime Takahashi for his continued advice and good judgement, Natsuo Taku and Takuro Tsukatani for trying to nudge me in the right directions, and Kyoko Tanaka for her mastery of many sources of information. While translating the book into Japanese, and on many later occasions, Takao Tokuoka gave me a great deal of advice and encouragement.

Fred and Simone Warner and Georges Berthoin steered me towards the EC Commission, and thereafter continued a conversation begun in Tokyo. Wolfgang Ernst, Horst Krenzler, Michael Hardy, Roy Denman and Leslie Fielding, all in their different ways, set the tone for a stimulating and friendly work environment, mainly in Tokyo, but also in Brussels.

I am most grateful to Michael Finger, Andrew Horvat, Jorn Keck, Jean-Pierre Lehmann, Pornchai Mahaisavariya, Giles

Merritt, Maurice Miodownik, Philippe Pons, Choosak Rata-
nachaichan, Johannes Van Rij, Yoichi Shibasaki, Adrian
Thorpe and Masaru Yoshitomi, and many others who, over the
years, have shared their views and provided much information,
comment or advice. Ron Dore gave sage guidance on the entire
manuscript.

As anyone who has ever tried to write a book in their spare
time will know, it cannot be done without the understanding of
able secretaries. My thanks therefore to Marion Chapman,
Kiyoko Furusawa, Hiroko Deguchi, Patricia Quinn, Yoshiko
Masuko, Annette Allard-Graf, Elsie Van Ocken, Angie
Cheang, Christine Asker and Argiro Ioannidou. In the final
stages of revision, Jennifer Munka was able to impose order and
grammatical consistency.

The views expressed here are my own. They are in no sense
intended to represent those of the EC Commission.

PART I

THE RISE OF JAPAN

1

CHANGES IN THE WORLD BALANCE OF POWER

One hundred years ago, Europe was the centre of the world's wealth and power. Today the situation is very different. Europe contains no more than a quarter of world product. The remaining three quarters are unevenly divided between the other three centres of wealth which have developed over the last one hundred years.

After Europe came the USA, then what is today the Soviet Union and its former European satellites) and Japan (and its Asian neighbours).

The rise of each new centre inevitably led to realignments in the balance of power accompanied by wars, the formation of hostile blocs, migrations, social upheavals and, at the very least, frictions and recriminations.

But the arrival of new players created new opportunities; indeed, without their inventiveness and competition, it is doubtful if the older centres could have increased their absolute wealth as rapidly as they did even as their relative shares of world product declined.

The emergence of East Asia, with Japan at its core, marks the most recent shift in the balance of world economic power, the consequences of which for the other three are still far from clear.

Japan has scored the largest surpluses in history in merchandise trade, and in the process cut a swathe through some of the key industries of the USA and Europe. As other countries, particularly those in its region, followed a similar course, Japan has transformed itself into a financial and technological superpower.

From 1848 to 1914 Great Britain was the leading creditor nation; then the USA assumed that role for the next seventy years. In 1985, it became the turn of Japan. It is the largest creditor and the largest net investor in the world, and its surplus on current and capital accounts is the highest ever recorded. Its banks, stock markets, brokerage houses and insurance companies are among the world's largest. Its postal savings system has assets of over $1 trillion – considerably more than the sum of the assets of the top five US banks.

Its overseas investments have grown so rapidly that it will soon be a larger investor in the USA than all the European countries put together. It is the top donor of development aid.

As Japan came to play an increasingly large role in the world economy, its impact, first in the form of exports then in investments and in other uses of its new financial power, began to be strongly felt in the USA and Europe. It is this shift in economic power that has been the principal cause of frictions in the bilateral relations between Japan and the USA, as well as between Japan and Europe.

One of the main themes of this book is that these long-term changes in the relative wealth of the three main players in the world economy have not yet led to an adjustment of the US, European or Japanese views of themselves or of each other. Old images have persisted, thereby impeding communications and exacerbating frictions.

The speed and scale of the rise of Japan can be seen in Table 1, which compares its growing share of world product over the last

Table 1. Shares of World Product, 1960–2000 (per cent)

	1960	1980	1990	2000
USA	33	23	25	23
EC (12)	21	24	23	20
Japan	3	9	13	14
USSR	15	13	13	12

Source: Based on Economic Planning Agency, Tokyo (1983, 1987).

Table 2. GNP per Capita ($)

	1960	1970	1980	1988	1990*
Japan	400	1,600	9,900	23,100	24,175
USA	2,500	4,520	10,700	19,480	21,970
EC(12)	1,000	2,300	8,350	14,580	15,550

Source: IMF(IFS), 1989; *Estimate.

forty years of the twentieth century with the shares of the other three poles of the world economy.

The most striking change is the rapid rise of Japan and the relative decline of the USA, from its high point in 1960 to a shared pre-eminence with Europe in 2000. In that year the USSR will have a smaller percentage of the world economy than Japan. The European share remains more or less stable, considerably larger than Japan's, but slightly smaller than the USA's. Expressed in per capita terms, the rise of Japan is even more striking (Table 2).

By 1978, Japanese GNP per capita had overtaken the average of the EC(12), and by 1987 had overtaken the USA. By the year 2000, it will be 25 per cent higher than the USA and 40 per cent higher than the EC. These estimates are based on market exchange rates. If the real costs of living in each country were taken into account, then Japan would rank after the USA but ahead of the EC.[1]

Add the estimated GNP of Japan and its neighbours, China, the Asian newly industrializing countries (NICs) and the Association of Southeast Asian Nations (ASEAN)[2] for the year 2000, and the total would come to 22 per cent of world product, but per capita it would be well below the other main poles of wealth, the USA and Europe, because of the huge population of China.

Rapid economic growth in Japan and the Asian NICs has rightly caught the attention of the world and it has already acted as a stimulus and as an opportunity to economic development in the USA and Europe.

For example, take merchandise trade, the old-fashioned measure of economic flows between nation states. Since 1984,

Japan exported more to the USA than did the EC and from 1985, more than Canada, making it the USA's top supplier. It is also the USA's second largest market in the world for merchandise exports, and it has become a major market for the EC. Its exports there have increased to the extent that both the EC and Japan now have larger shares in each other's markets than ever before in history.[3]

But in examining the economic flows between post-industrial societies such as the USA, Japan, and the European countries, in which service industries now play such an important role, it is not enough to look at the merchandise or 'visible' trade. Trade in 'invisible' items such as financial services, the income from overseas investments, royalties, shipping, insurance and tourism now amount to a significant percentage of total US and EC trade balances (see Fig. 1 and Table 3). Furthermore, about one-quarter of the merchandise trade of the USA, the EC and Japan is trade between subsidiaries and affiliates of the same transnational corporation (intra-firm trade) which set their own transfer prices according to the accounting requirements of the group. For these reasons the oft-repeated remark that the USA or Canada does more trade across the Pacific than across the Atlantic is not very useful, because it ignores the huge transfers in the 'invisibles' account, the profits of manufacturing subsidiaries in overseas markets and the difficulties of measuring intra-firm trade.

Table 3 shows that the service trade between the EC and the USA is 80 per cent as large as the merchandise trade; and that the volume of cross investments between the two is larger than the total trade in goods and services. The level of US–Japan trade in goods and services or the level of US–Japan cross investments lags far behind. The most developed side of the US–EC–Japan triangle measured in these terms, or indeed in terms of the cross holdings of total assets, is therefore the US–EC side.

This state of affairs could change; the US–Japan link grew rapidly in the eighties. Japan exports more goods to the USA than does the EC. Japanese direct investments in the USA have been increasing at a faster rate than European since 1985, although from a much lower base. There are also greater dependencies than in the US–EC link. A much larger share of Japan's exports and investments go to the USA than to Europe. Washington is also more dependent on Tokyo to finance its foreign debt than it is on London or Bonn.

Whether the Japanese will wish to continue to subsidize the USA while taking a secondary role in international affairs, or whether US financial dependence will lead to a political backlash against Tokyo, are open questions. But whatever the outcome of the ongoing adjustments in US–Japan relations, already bilateral deals between the two in trade and in currency realignment, for example, or the increase in high-tech corporate alliances across the Pacific, are important straws in the wind. At the very least, so long as Europe fails to develop a single voice, many of the decisions affecting the management of the world economy will by default be taken initially by the USA and Japan acting together as the Group of Two, or G-2 for short, on the basis of their shared stake in the emerging '*Nichibei* economy'.[4]

The weakest side of the US–EC–Japan triangle is the EC–Japan side. Not only are the economic ties between the USA and Japan more developed than between Europe and Japan, but there are also many other links which are totally lacking in Europe's relationship with Japan.

While Japan has political, economic, cultural and security interests linking it to the USA, and while the USA has similar links with Europe, the same is not true of the Japan–Europe side of the triangle. There is no direct security linkage, and the quantities of trade and cross-investments are much smaller than those with the USA, or between the USA and Japan. Likewise, Europe's cultural influence over Japan is today diminished.

This is in striking contrast to the situation one hundred years ago, when both Europe and America were much more powerful than Japan. Then it seemed only natural for the Westerners to teach and for the Japanese to learn. Today the roles are reversed. For a start, Western involvement in East Asia, especially during the nineteenth century, now seems merely a one-time intervention in the full sweep of the region's history.

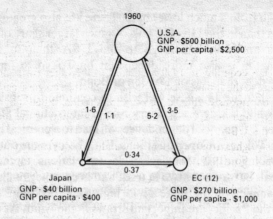

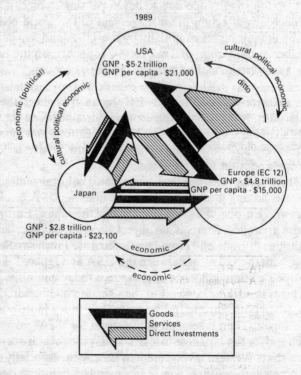

Fig. 1. The USA, Japan and the EC, 1960 and 1989

Comments on Fig. 1

The circles are drawn to scale and represent the relative size of each of the three economies in 1960 and 1989. Note the comparatively large size of the US economy in 1960 compared to the other two, and the very small size of the Japanese economy. By 1989, the Japanese economy had grown enormously. Indeed, in per capita terms, it had outgrown both the USA and the EC. The EC economy was almost the same size as that of the USA.

The straight arrows represent only trade in goods (merchandise trade) for 1960. For 1989, they are drawn to scale and represent trade in goods, services and quantity of direct investment. Note that in 1960 the USA had a comfortable surplus in merchandise trade with both Japan and the EC (it also had a surplus on invisibles and invested more in them than they did in the USA). EC–Japan trade was more or less balanced. By 1989 the picture had changed completely. The USA had deficits on current account (goods and services) with the EC and Japan, and both of them invested more in the USA than did the USA in them.

Japan's merchandise exports to the USA were more than to the EC. But US–EC two-way trade in goods and services and volume of investments was much larger than either's trade or investments with Japan. Conversely, Japan's exports of goods and its direct investments in the other two were larger than those of either the EC or the USA in Japan. But the USA had a much better showing in Japan under all three heads than did the EC. The thinnest arrow of all was from the EC to Japan. The curved arrows are explained in the text.

Table 3. Economic Flows between the USA, Japan and the EC, 1989 ($ billion)

	Merchandise Trade	Services	Direct Investments (cumulative)
USA→ EC	87	72	150
USA→ Japan	45	31	19
EC→ USA	85	87	235
EC→ Japan	23	44	3
Japan→ USA	93	49	104*
Japan→ EC	51	35	42*

Note: Exports and services based on exporting country's statistics; on direct statistics, see Part IV, note 43.
Sources: US Commerce Department, *Survey of Current Business* (Cumulative to December, 1989); *Bank of Japan, *Balance of Payments Monthly*; Ministry of Finance (cumulative to April 1990); *Eurostat*.

In many ways the situation today has reverted to pre-nineteenth-century patterns. China is again almost united, Japan is vastly strengthened (sufficiently to replace China as the dominant regional economic power), the European presence in East Asia is once more marginal and the influence of the USA is on the wane. In line with these changes it is only natural that European and US trade with the region is less important to many countries there than it was in the nineteenth century.

One hundred years ago it was the Japanese complaining of sudden influxes of Western goods disrupting domestic industries. Today the boot is on the other foot, and it is the turn of the Europeans and Americans to complain of Japanese 'adversarial' trade, 'laser beam targeting' of markets or predatory pricing, and to plead with the Japanese to restrain their exports. The only difference is that today the Japanese do not send gunboats to keep European and US markets open, as was the practice in the nineteenth century, when the Western powers were in the habit of taking Japanese protectionist moves as a *casus belli*. As the prime minister of Singapore summed up this passage in his address to the US Congress in 1985: 'The irony is that it was the USA and Europe that forced a reluctant China and the hermit-like Japan to open up their countries to trade with the West. Now it is the Japanese and the Chinese instead who have to come knocking at the US's door to get in to trade. What a bitter-sweet irony of role reversal.'

The roles have been reversed in other spheres, too. In the nineteenth century, Europeans and Americans regarded Japan as an exotic playground, while the Japanese regarded Europe and the USA as disciplined, group-oriented societies possessing the secrets of efficient industrial production. Today, it is the Japanese who flock to the USA and Europe for exotic tourism, and it is the Americans and Europeans who regard Japan as a disciplined society with amazingly efficient industries.

In the nineteenth century the West was felt to be the very embodiment of progress, the home of political liberty and the world centre of innovation and new ideas. In short, powerful, dynamic and outward-looking. The East, on the other hand, including Japan, was regarded as stagnant, despotic, nonscientific and superstitious; as weak and inward-looking. Today, most of these simplistic contrasts have been stood on their head. Neither the USA nor Europe is any longer the world centre of new ideas and the natural sciences, and in social and economic organization it is often Europe which seems slow to change and parts of East Asia which seem dynamic. The wheels of capitalism hum with energy in Japan (or in Singapore or in South Korea), while in Europe they merely tick over. People even walk more slowly in London or Paris than they do in Tokyo or in Singapore.[5]

It is often hard to escape the feeling that Europe has become the home of an elegant stagnation, and that the USA is on the decline, while Japan, and the other East Asian countries following its lead, throb with a fresh dynamism.

Such impressions are not new. Europe has gone through bouts of 'Euro-pessimism' on and off since the 1890s because it has been in the unique and unenviable position that, as each new world industrial centre emerged and started to go into rapid catch-up growth – first the USA, then Russia, then Japan – Europe by comparison appeared to have slowed down and to have lost its lead, not once but repeatedly.

These thoughts were already explicit in the comparisons between the 'New World' and the 'Old World'; and later, in the metaphor drawn from nineteenth-century geopolitics, when sea power was regarded as the key to the balance of world power and the rise of the Pacific was linked to the decline of the Atlantic. One of the first to make such a linkage was the historian Lord Macaulay. In 1840, in a speculative mood stimulated by the scientific voyages to the Pacific, he imagined 'when some traveller from New Zealand shall, in the midst of a vast solitude, take his stand on a broken arch of London Bridge to sketch the ruins of St Paul's'.[6]

As the Americans and Russians expanded across their respective continents towards the Pacific, they were overcome with excitement at the prospects which the Pacific held out – not the least being a chance to get away from Europe and to carve out their own new spheres of interest. 'The Ocean of Destiny,' rhapsodized Lincoln's secretary of state; 'the Mediterranean of the Future,' echoed Alexander Herzen. Or, as Theodore Roosevelt put it after Japan's defeat of the Qing and Russian Empires, 'The Pacific era, destined to be the greatest, is just at its dawn.'

Many others have taken up the same theme, including practically every US secretary of state from Seward in the 1840s to Baker in the 1990s, often declaring the dawning of the Pacific, but also linking the rise of the Pacific with the decline of the Atlantic. This kind of rhetoric is, of course, misleading and out of date because we live in a multipolar world economy where growth in one of the three main centres depends upon growth in the other two.

At the beginning of the nineties European, US and Japanese GNP accounted for over 60 per cent of world product, but their combined populations were only 13 per cent of world population; their exports accounted for 60 per cent of world exports and their investments accounted for 90 per cent of the world total. The bulk of these flows were between each other.

Over the coming years, the volume of trade and of capital flows between the three will intensify and will account for ever larger shares of their exports and direct investments. Their combined share of world product may have declined slightly by the year 2000 as a result of growth in a handful of NICs in Asia, in southern and eastern Europe and in Latin America.

One of the first to moot the idea of a trilateral relationship between the USA, Western Europe and Japan was the Japanese prime minister, Mr Ikeda, during a trip to Europe in 1962. 'The free world,' he proposed, 'should be supported by three pillars, that is, North America, Western Europe, and Japan and East Asia.' The initiative was not taken up by the European governments; the remark made by General de Gaulle, the French president, comparing Ikeda with a transistor salesman was not forgotten, at least in Japan.

Ten years later in 1972 on a visit to Europe, another Japanese prime minister, Mr Tanaka, proposed holding a trilateral summit. The proposal was rejected, either because Japan was not yet regarded as being on the same level as the Western powers or because memories of the Pacific War were still too fresh.[7]

In the private sector, trilateralism received some encouragement, in 1973, with the foundation in Tokyo of the Trilateral Commission, which brings together distinguished figures from the private sectors of the trilateral countries to discuss public policy issues. The idea for the Commission was formulated by Dr Brzezinski, who later became national security adviser to President Carter; it was financed by David Rockefeller.

Because of the weight of the USA, Europe and Japan in the world economy, any move by the newcomer (Japan) to the triangle, in its relations with one of the other two, immediately affects the third. This is seen clearly in the growth of protected markets and the decline of free trade.

The pattern is usually the same. Because of the stronger ties between Japan and the USA, Europeans suspect, often rightly, that a deal is being cut between Washington and Tokyo which leaves them in the cold. Thus, any agreement by Japan to voluntarily limit its exports to the USA is immediately followed by a similar request from the EC, to prevent the US industry enjoying more favourable treatment and to stop further diversion of Japanese exports. Subsequently, such bilateral agreements have been globalized at the request of Japan's other trade partners. It started in this way with textiles in the sixties, with steel in the seventies, and with automobiles, electronics, and semiconductors in the eighties. A similar pattern emerged during the yen–dollar realignments.

Over the years there has been much talk of trying to make up for the weakness of the EC–Japan side of the US–EC–Japan triangle. In the early days, Japanese initiatives were rebuffed by the Europeans; during the recession in the seventies there was little spare energy for such an enterprise. Since then, from time to time when Tokyo's relations with Washington were under heavy strain, the Japanese underscored the need to reinforce their political links with Europe. Despite similar rhetoric on the European side, these intentions have not yet been translated into effective action. Moves towards the creation of a single market in Europe by 1992 have aroused considerable interest in Japan. Many have seen the opportunity. Some have used the threat. One result has been to accelerate plans to relocate Japanese export capacity to production in Europe. Nevertheless, although the Europeans like to think they are on an equal footing with the Japanese, the Japanese do not for the most part see it that way; they continue to regard the USA as their only partner and rival worthy of full attention.[8]

The most recent rise of Japan came at a time of crisis and uncertainty in the world economy. The industrial heartlands of Europe and the USA were under severe pressure to adjust to new technologies and the new growth centre in East Asia; they found it a slow and painful process, made all the more difficult throughout the seventies by stagflation and unemployment at home, and by the end of the era of cheap raw materials and energy supplies abroad.

In the eighties, foreign trade and foreign investments accounted for a growing share of world product. Capital markets became global, so what happened in one centre could immediately affected the other two. Uncertainties in the world economy centred on the huge external imbalances between the main industrialized countries, plus the debt burden of many developing countries, as well as the violent fluctuations in foreign exchange, stock and bond markets. The post-war institutions for managing the world economy were bypassed or discarded, and the USA was no longer able or willing to act as the lead manager. Often the three main players (the USA, Europe and Japan) were unable to agree on how to coordinate their separate policies, and the stresses and strains between Japan and its two principal partners took the form of almost continual economic, trade and technology frictions.

In each of the main poles of the world economy the already existing trends towards regionalism are being strengthened. Whether this takes the form of exclusive and protectionist trading blocs (a real danger) will depend on whether or not solutions can be found to the problems of managing the world economy, especially the interfaces between the three main players (see Chapter 25). Interdependence not only increases the potential areas of friction between industries and between countries, but it also means that now, more than ever before, decisions taken for domestic political reasons have an immediate external impact. So, the frictions between the main players will continue until there are more effective means, not only of resolving conflicts over international trade, but also of coordinating domestic economic policies.

Much depends on how Japan, the epicentre of the third pole of the world economy and now the world's largest creditor nation, will seek to translate its new wealth into political gains, and how it will use its power to help sustain and manage the world economy. The biggest unknown is how Japanese society and the political system will adjust to these new responsibilities. A key variable will be how the relations of Japan (the banker) develop with the USA (the policeman). Much also depends on whether Europe can develop a single voice. In the meantime, part of the answer lies nearer to Japan, in East Asia itself, because it is here that some of the first indications of Japan's new leadership role are emerging.

2

JAPAN AND THE RISE OF EAST ASIA

In 1910, Great Britain, France, Germany, Holland, the USA and Russia were all colonial powers in East Asia with extensive territories in the countries which are Japan's neighbours and which were the sources of raw materials for its new industries. Japan, too, had just become active as a colonial power. International relations in East Asia were therefore inevitably influenced by the rivalries and shifting alliances of the Great Powers, including the new member of the club – Japan.

Largely as a result of the rapid growth of the Japanese colonial empire and the weakening of Europe in two world wars, Japan defeated the colonial powers, one by one, in Asia. First came the staggering victory over the Russians in 1905. Next, the Germans were forced to withdraw from Shandong in 1914 as well as from the last of their Pacific possessions – the Marianas and the Bismarck islands. A generation later, like the Americans at Pearl Harbor, the British and Dutch were caught completely by surprise and defeated in their colonies in Southeast Asia in 1941 and 1942, at which time the French administration in Indo-China was also brought under Japanese control (see Map 1).

Since before World War I the Japanese had been encouraging Asian nationalists to overthrow 'white imperialism', and preaching 'Asia for the Asians'. But it was only after 1931 and during the Pacific War that the enemies of the Asian nationalists and the Japanese became the same for a short while.

The Japanese trained anti-colonial armies and deliberately recruited from strata which had not served under the previous

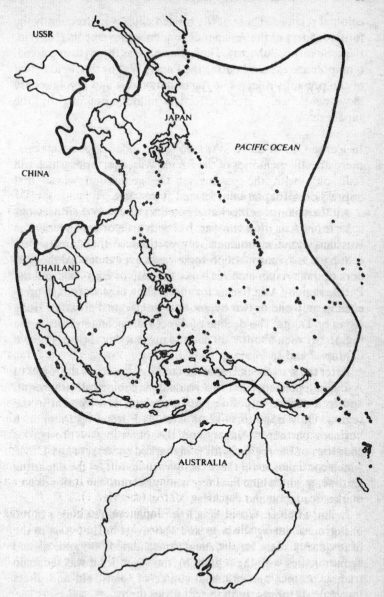

Map 1. The Japanese Empire at its Height, 1942

colonial regimes. These newly trained élites were frequently the future leaders of the Asian independence movements (Ne Win, Park, Sukarno, Suharto). Thus, not only was the myth of colonial omnipotence exposed during the Pacific War by the rapid defeat of the previous rulers, but Asian nationalist and revolutionary movements were given effective military training by the Japanese.

In Europe, as in the USA, among the older decision-makers, there are still memories of the Pacific War, memories which will fade only with the passing of the generation whose first impressions of Japan were formed at this time.

All the colonial powers attempted to return to their previous colonies in Asia after the war, but with little or no success. The Russians alone maintained vast portions of their nineteenth-century acquisitions, and in some cases even extended the borders of their Asian empire. Now, the map of East Asia and the Pacific region (Asia Pacific for short) shows the European presence in only one or two exceptional or marginal areas: in Hong Kong or Tahiti. The decline of direct European interests in the region between about 1910 and the present day is clearly shown in Maps 2 and 3.

After the war, the defeat of the colonial powers by the forces of Asian independence led to a gradual psychological withdrawal, and to a decline in political and economic involvement in the region. Only now, forty years later, is Europe returning as a business partner to Japan and the other newly prosperous countries of the region. This is in marked contrast to the USA, which continues to fill the security vacuum left by the departing Europeans and which has increasingly become the major export market for Japan and the Asian NICs.

Japan, although adopting a low profile and remaining in the background during the wars and upheavals in East Asia in the fifties and sixties, nevertheless consolidated its political and economic ties with the region; by the seventies it was the main trading partner and principal source of loans, aid and direct investments for nearly all the countries there.

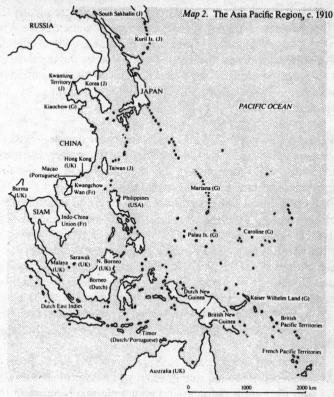

Map 2. The Asia Pacific Region, c. 1910

Hong Kong (leased to UK 1841; 1860; 1898)
Kwantung Territory (leased to Japan 1905–45)
Korea (J)
Kuril Is. (J)
South Sakhalin (J)
Taiwan (J)
Kiaochow (leased to Germany 1898–1919)
Kwangchow Wan (leased to France 1898–1945)
Macao (Portuguese)
Indo-China Union (Fr) (Tonkin, Annam, Cochinchina, Laos, Cambodia)

Burma (UK)
Malaya (UK)
Dutch East Indies (Indonesia)
Sarawak (UK)
Borneo (Dutch)
N. Borneo (UK)
Philippines (USA)
Timor (Dutch/Portuguese)
Dutch New Guinea
British New Guinea (Papua)
Kaiser Wilhelm Land (German)
Palau Is. (German)
Caroline (German)
Mariana (German)
French Pacific Territories
British Pacific Territories

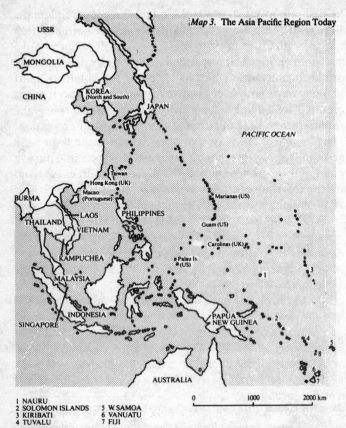

¡Map 3. The Asia Pacific Region Today

1 NAURU
2 SOLOMON ISLANDS   5 W.SAMOA
3 KIRIBATI   6 VANUATU
4 TUVALU   7 FIJI

0   1000   2000 km

Note: In 1990, the situation was the reverse of what it had been in 1910. Then there had been only four sovereign states in the region. Now there are two dozen and only a handful of dependent territories.

British dependent territory:
Hong Kong

French overseas territories:
French Polynesia
New Caledonia
Wallis and Futuna

Portuguese territory:
Macao

US trust territory of the Pacific Islands
Palau Is.
Carolinas
Marianas
Guam

Soviet possessions:
Sakhalin
Kuril Is.

The first important step was the establishment of diplomatic relations with South Korea in 1965. Next was the normalization of relations with China in 1978, which touched off something of a 'China boom' in Japan. It was stimulated partly by relief that the abnormal circumstances which had kept the two countries apart for so long were now over, and partly by the prospect, often exaggerated, of huge new markets opening up just when the USA and Europe were filled with the sour grapes of protectionism. The bubble of false expectations was only pricked when the Chinese unilaterally postponed Japanese contracts in China in 1979 and, if that was not enough, did the same again in 1981 and then slammed shut open-door economic policies in 1989. But Japan is now playing a key role in the modernization of China, and this will continue despite the violent ups and downs of Chinese politics. It does more business with China than does the USA or all the European countries put together. It is also China's largest supplier of concessional loans, direct investments and development aid.

Today this causes no particular surprise, but at the turn of the century the very possibility of the Japanese entering into competition with the West, which held a predominant position in China, gave rise to the first wave of fear of a 'yellow peril': of Chinese brawn led by Japanese brain, threatening the West either with military force or with cheap exports. Such fears have been all but forgotten.

Only the Soviet Union, in retaining many of its nineteenth-century conquests, seems also to have retained many nineteenth-century attitudes, including the old fears of a 'yellow peril'. Thus, it was the Soviet Union which, as late as 1978, greeted the signing of the Japan–China treaty of peace and friendship with warnings of the dangers that this implied for the rest of the world. It was not until 1986, and again in 1988, that the Soviet leader, Mr Gorbachev, announced a more forward looking East Asia policy.

The Russians clearly cherish the old idea of developing Soviet Asia and one way of doing this would be to open up business with Japan and South Korea, and increase Soviet economic and trade links with the rest of the region. But there are still formidable stumbling blocks including the territorial dispute with Japan over the Northern Territories, and with China over the demarcation of the Sino–Soviet border. For the businessman, there is also the unenticing prospect of trying to do business with the Soviet bureaucracy.

Closer links with Southeast Asia were somewhat prematurely sought by the then prime minister, Mr Tanaka, during a tour of the area in 1974 which was marred by anti-Japanese riots. This unfortunate episode was set right by his successors, who paid many visits to the region bearing impressive gifts (in the form of soft loans). At the ASEAN summit in 1976 Mr Fukuda announced a loan of $1 billion, and at the next ASEAN summit in 1987, Mr Takeshita, the only outside head of government invited, offered a loan of $2 billion. Between these visits Japanese loans, aid and private investments were on a very large scale. So far had the Japanese image improved that, in the late seventies, Malaysia and Singapore declared 'Look East' policies to learn from Japan (and South Korea).

In the age of *endaka* (the high yen), from 1985 on, a new wave of Japanese manufacturing investment has gone to Southeast Asia; much of the output is exported back to Japan. The degree to which the economies of Southeast Asia now depend upon Japan will no doubt continue to lead from time to time to occasional, usually stage-managed, outbursts of economic nationalism.

Anyone who travelled in the region in the early sixties, and again in more recent years, will have noticed the strikingly visible signs of the replacement of Europe – first by the USA, then by Japan, and now by those coming after Japan.

Today, over the whole region in both the towns and the villages, practically everything that moves on powered wheels – the cars, the trucks, the tractors, the motorcycles, even the bicycles – as well as the neon lights, the radios, the stereos and the TVs, the sewing machines, the clocks, the watches and all the other visible paraphernalia of modern life, are made in Japan, in the Asian NICs, or in China. Not, as they once were, in

Europe or in the USA. These consumer durables are the most striking signs of the massive flow of Japanese and East Asian exports and investments which now pour into the region. The only European products are limited to snob symbols for the rich – Mercedes Benz or BMW; expensive low-volume goods.

The increasing role of Japan, not only in Southeast Asia but all over the Asia Pacific region, shows in the changing flows of merchandise trade, direct investments and development aid.

In 1960, the USA did more trade with the region than either the EC (the present twelve member states) or Japan. By 1970, Japan had caught up with the USA, the only difference being that Japan exported far more than it imported. The EC came third. With the high dollar in the first half of the eighties, US imports rose dramatically, as did Japan's with the rise of the yen at the end of the decade. When the currencies of the Asian NICs began to revalue against the dollar, and as their governments started to stimulate their domestic economies and open their markets to imports, Japan, the EC and the USA began to export even more to them, with Japan taking the lion's share.

By 1985, Japan already had three to four times more invested in South Korea, Taiwan, Indonesia, the Philippines and Thailand than did all the countries of the EC. In Hong Kong, Japan had one and a half times more invested than the EC, and in Malaysia and in Singapore slightly more. The USA invested a fraction more than the EC in these countries, but much less than

Table 4. Trade with the Asia Pacific Developing Countries, 1960–90 ($ billion)

	Exports								Imports							
	'60	'70	'80	'85	'86	'87	'88	'89	'60	'70	'80	'85	'86	'87	'88	'89
Japan	1.0	4	30	43	49	59	73	74	0.9	2	34	36	34	45	56	62
EC (12)	0.6	2	16	21	25	30	38	42	0.9	2	22	22	30	42	52	55
USA	1.0	3	20	25	27	33	47	53	1.1	3	24	58	65	80	90	96

Note: Asia Pacific refers here to the 26 developing countries of East and Southeast Asia and the Pacific. It does not include the Middle East or South Asia or Pacific Latin America.
Source: IMF (DOT), 1990; Exports, FOB; Imports, CIF.

Table 5. Aid to the Asia Pacific region, 1976–89 ($ billion)

	1976–80 annual average	1981–85 annual average	1986	1987	1988	1989
Japan	0.6	1.1	1.4	2.3	3.0	3.8
EC (12)	0.4	0.5	0.8	0.9	1.2	1.8
USA	0.3	0.3	0.7	0.4	0.3	0.4

Note: Asia Pacific refers here to the 26 developing countries of East Asia and the Pacific. It does not include the Middle East, South Asia or Pacific Latin America. EC refers to European Community aid as such, plus that of each of the twelve member states. The figures (from OECD) are for net ODA disbursements. About 30 per cent of the EC's aid is accounted for by French assistance to its overseas territories of New Caledonia and French Polynesia.

Japan. After the revaluation of the yen in 1985, the Japanese lead in direct investments in the region increased even faster.[9] Soon the number two investor after Japan will be the Asian NICs.

Until 1986, Japan gave only slightly less aid to the developing countries of the Asia Pacific region (to which it sends 50 per cent of its bilateral assistance) than the EC and the USA combined. Thereafter it stepped up its programmes so rapidly that by 1988 it was donating two and a half times as much as the EC and ten times more than the USA. Not only is Japan now the major donor by far, but its programmes, taken together with its direct investments, have become an important influence on industrial and macro-economic planning throughout the region, as influential in their way as the US military assistance programmes.

Stimulated by Japan, the Asian NICs first began catching up in the late seventies in external markets, especially the USA. Next, they began putting direct pressure on the Japanese market itself in consumer durables, textiles, steel and ships. By 1989, the four Asian NICs held almost as large a share of world markets as did Japan. Led by Taiwan, they have also become a major source of direct investments in East Asia, in some cases more important than the USA or Europe.

The rise of the Asian NICs has not always been welcome in Japan, especially in those sectors which feel directly threatened, and lobbies have emerged demanding protection. For example, successful efforts were made to secure an agreement from Korea to voluntarily limit exports of textiles to Japan.

On the other hand, now that labour costs are high in Japan, and there is a need to switch away from energy-intensive, high-pollution industries, it makes better sense to import such goods rather than manufacture them domestically.

The change from a vertical to a horizontal division of labour with the Asian NICs was greatly speeded by the high yen. Speciality stores even began to open in the late eighties in Tokyo, selling low-cost consumer durables manufactured in East Asia. Many of these products were from Japanese subsidiaries who had moved part of their operations offshore to Asia, including to those newcomers with low labour costs such as Thailand and Malaysia, and this in turn speeded the development of export-oriented industries in these countries.

At a time when Japan is shifting to domestic-led growth and its imports are increasing rapidly, the Asian NICs are gaining ground on the Japanese market and their share of the imported manufactured goods will soon be similar to that of the USA (whose share has declined since the seventies) and the EC (whose share has increased, see Table 6).

Despite the very rapid increase of Japan's imports from its Asian neighbours, the USA still imports far more manufactured

Table 6. Japan's Imports of Manufactured Goods, 1970–90

	1970	1980	1985	1986	1987	1988	1989	1990
Japan's imports of manufactured goods ($ billion)	6	31	40	53	66	92	106	114
Per cent of total imports	30	23	31	42	44	42	50	49
Per cent shares of Japan's imports of manufactured goods held by:								
Asian NICs	5	14	14	15	19	20	22	17
EC	18	21	19	25	23	23	23	26
USA	47	33	36	33	27	25	25	30

Note: Manufactured goods = SITC 5–9 (excluding gold and non-ferrous metals). Figures have been rounded to the nearest whole number.

goods from them than does either Japan or the EC (see Annex, Table 4).

This is not the place to enter into a more detailed discussion of the trade flows, the quality of the aid or the nature of the different investments. Already the balance of the multipolar world economy has been altered fundamentally by the rise of Japan and its Asian neighbours as the third main concentration of wealth in the world. Japan's own economic development has been one of the principal stimuli for these changes. Japan will also be one of its main beneficiaries.

Europe is still a major player in the region but now comes in third place after Japan and the USA.

The ties, especially the economic ones, between Japan and the other countries of East Asia will grow much closer as regional economic integration is stimulated by the huge investment flows from Japan itself as well as from Korea and Taiwan. The emerging pattern of the region is Japan at the apex, followed at the next level by the four Asian NICs and China; at the third level, the rest of the ASEAN group (Brunei, Indonesia, Malaysia, the Philippines and Thailand), and at a fourth level, the East Asian 'failures' which have hardly started to be integrated into the new regional economic system – North Korea, Vietnam, the rest of Indo-China and Burma.

Not the least of the attractions of the region for Japan is that emphasis on integration with Asia no longer necessarily implies a weakening of its links with the West. On the contrary, it is one of several distinguishing features of the new age that the old, false dichotomy between 'East' and 'West', between the Orient and the Occident, is less sustainable than ever before.[10]

Both East and West have fragmented here and there to coalesce into new combinations, or to be absorbed into the new homogenized global culture. Nowhere is this seen more clearly than in the East Asia region itself, whose dynamism today derives precisely from the successful blending of many cultural traditions, including some of the best from both East and West. It is now too late to switch the clock back to the days of the Meiji intellectuals, even if anybody wanted to, when it was possible to envisage a stark choice between two mutually exclusive categories, 'East' and 'West'; between 'dissociating from Asia' or 'Pan-Asianism'.

In spite of the trend towards regional economic cooperation in other parts of the world, it is unlikely that a tightly organized trading bloc will emerge in the Asia Pacific region in the near future. The region is too large; its political systems, economies and cultures too heterogeneous. Bitter memories of the war are also still not far from the surface: witness the angry reactions, throughout East and Southeast Asia in 1982, to the revision of Japan's history textbooks to downplay its wartime attack on the region by describing it as an 'advance' rather than as an 'invasion'.

Other controversial statements from time to time raise the spectre of belligerent Japanese nationalism, giving the impression that the Japanese are still not prepared to acknowledge their responsibility for the suffering they caused during the Pacific War. The comments of Okuno Seisuke, a member of the Japanese cabinet, became notorious and forced his resignation. In 1988 he said that Japan was not an aggressor in the Pacific War but merely defending itself against 'the white race that had turned East Asia into a colony'. Remarks like this should not be taken too seriously. They are the public expression by elderly conservative politicians of the usually unspoken views of only a minority. But they do arouse intense feelings, especially when other slips of the tongue seem to indicate not only a wilful forgetfulness of Japan's own record as a colonial power, but also arrogance tinged with racism. A notorious example was Nakasone's off-the-record remark about the mental level in the USA (see Chapter 8). Another sensitive issue was the prime minister's attendance at the annual service in commemoration of the war dead at Yasakuni shrine, a controversial matter because the shrine houses the remains of fourteen Class A war criminals.

Like Germany in Europe, Japan is the major agent of peaceful change in its region, but unlike Germany, Japan has no European Community 'umbrella' to cover its growing regional influence.

Not wishing to be isolated and fearing the formation of regional blocs in other parts of the world, Japan has a clear interest in strengthening its relations with the countries around it. All the more so because the region is rich in food and raw materials including oil, has plentiful supplies of manpower and growing consumer markets. But too hasty a Japanese assumption of leadership could easily awaken the fears and resentments of the past. Another complication is that neither the USA nor Japan would like to see the other take the lead in any regional grouping; the smaller countries fear that too overt a role for the big powers could dilute their own efforts at sub-regional cooperation in established groups such as the ASEAN. Nor is there any consensus as to whether countries such as China or the USSR should be included.

So, the numerous efforts made by Japanese prime ministers and others to foster the growth of regional cooperation have been deliberately rather vague and cautious. There are a number of informal annual get-togethers of businessmen, academics and officials from the Asia Pacific countries; from time to time calls are heard for the formation of a 'Pacific OECD' or some trade policy forum for the region.[11] For the time being, Japan will continue to support the existing groups, such as ASEAN, while avoiding the articulation of a full-blown Asia Pacific policy. It will seek to advance more ambitious plans using the proposals of minor players such as Australia. In addressing other Asian nations, there will be soft talk about a spiritual and cultural heritage common to the region, about a shared lifestyle (in the words of Mr Nakasone) that 'values harmony over differences, cooperation over confrontation and humility over assertion'.

Much depends on what happens in Japan's most important markets, the USA and Europe. If either, for whatever reason, should significantly increase existing levels of protection against Japan, Tokyo will be faced with two enormous trade blocks; it will then no doubt step up its own not inconsiderable level of protection and more actively seek some kind of defensive groupings with certain of its Asian and Pacific neighbours.

The rise of Japan has already led to a fundamental shift in the balance of world economic power and will lead to many further changes. At times such as these, it pays to step back and take a long cool look at the illusions which Europeans and Americans have held about Japan, and to question the assumptions upon which our relations have been based. Only by tracking down past images can we begin to understand present-day actions and the full range of metaphor available today as we seek to rid ourselves of old prejudices.

3

OUT-OF-DATE IMAGES

What disturbs and alarms man are not things, but his opinions and fancies about things.

Epictetus

When I first became directly involved with some of the controversies surrounding Japan's emergence as a major economic power, I began reading up on the subject. The more I read, the more I found the same things about Japan and the Japanese appearing over and over again. Even the examples used were often the same. Observations of the amateur European or American Japanologists of the nineteenth century would suddenly pop up in late twentieth-century works. Intrigued, I pressed my inquiries further back to the earliest Western writers on Japan – the missionaries of the sixteenth and seventeenth centuries. The same thing: their comments appeared to have been echoed, not entirely or even clearly, but echoed nevertheless, in the nineteenth and twentieth centuries. I decided then that I would jot down the most often repeated stereotypes and see if any pattern emerged.

Several years passed; my reading was spasmodic but broad. Also, while I was stationed in Tokyo, I had the opportunity to listen to the comments about Japan made by numerous visitors of every kind: diplomats, politicians, businessmen, journalists, university professors, and tourists. My net was trawled through many waters – the astonishing thing was that at the end of the day my catch was usually composed of the same fish. I concluded that in the collective European and American mind there has formed a limited stock of images, both positive and negative, about Japan and the Japanese from which, depending on the mood of the day, the relevant image can be recalled any number of times.

So I have devoted considerable attention to images which were formed in the past because, even though they may seem to belong to a remote age, they have not been discarded. On the contrary, they are still part of the basic vocabulary, the inherited scripts, as it were, by which logic a European's or American's view of Japan is deeply and often unconsciously influenced. Here and there I found characteristics attributed to the Japanese which bore a striking resemblance to what the Europeans and Americans have thought about other 'Oriental' peoples. This is not surprising. Japan, for example, has consistently been confused with China for at least five centuries. I have attempted to note this deeper layer in the Western stock of images about Japan whenever I have been able to identify it for what it is.

During my stays in Japan, I had many occasions to learn at first hand about Japanese popular images of the West. Even after my identity as a European had been established, I was constantly reminded that I fell into the larger category of *gaijin* – 'outside person', a word used for Westerners (but not, for example, for Chinese foreigners). Over the years I can count on the fingers of one hand the Japanese I met who reacted to me as just another human being. More usually, in the politest possible way, one was continually put in one's place, reminded that one was an outsider by incredulous questions and naive comments such as 'What do you think of Japan?', 'Oh, how skilfully you use chopsticks!' or 'How fluently you speak Japanese!', as if it was amazing that a foreigner could be expected to use chopsticks or speak even a few words of Japanese after many years in the country. Such comments are made, no doubt, with the best possible intentions. Foreign tourists are certainly flattered. It is also true that such remarks are now heard less from the better educated and the younger generations which do not necessarily see 'foreign' and 'Japanese' as exclusive categories, and pride themselves on being 'international'.

In the end I became used to being regarded as something of a curiosity. After all, I had been warned. All the textbooks, both Japanese and foreign, had drummed home the point that the Japanese had been isolated and regarded themselves as uniquely unique, therefore it was only natural for them to draw a very sharp line between themselves and 'foreigners'. And no doubt they found it as hard to distinguish one Westerner from another, as most Westerners have difficulty in telling the difference between a Chinese, a Japanese and a Korean. Indeed, in 1968, when I first went to Japan, it was so commonly assumed that all 'foreigners' were Americans, that I was often asked as a first question, 'What State are you from?' Later, when I went back in the mid-seventies, the US influence had sufficiently waned for one to be greeted by the more broadminded question, 'Excuse me, but what country are you from?' By the late eighties foreigners had become so numerous that, although not yet anonymous, they enjoyed much less attention than in the past.

In general, just as with European images of Japan, it seems that in the collective Japanese mind there has formed a limited stock of images, both positive and negative, about Europe and the USA from which, depending on the mood of the day, the relevant image can be recalled any number of times.

The key difference is that Japanese images of Europe and the USA have tended to be more positive and closer to reality than European and US images of Japan. The reasons are clear: at the formative period of modern Japan, Westerners were regarded with a mixture of fear and respect, two excellent reasons for wanting to learn from somebody else. Westerners, on the other hand, until recently regarded the Japanese with indifference; sometimes with scorn and sometimes with fear, but seldom with respect.

Had I been writing about the best available Western knowledge of Japan or Japanese knowledge of the West, I would have concentrated on the works of Japanologists and academic experts on Europe and the USA and on the findings of specialists in international relations, the social sciences and comparative literature. Such was not my aim. Nations conduct their foreign affairs on the basis not of what is but of what they perceive it to be. People are disturbed and alarmed not by things but by their 'opinions and fancies' about things.

Despite both more opportunities for travel and direct contacts, and television and instant communications, the grip of inherited prejudices appears to be as strong today as in the past. Even with the rapidity of modern communications, it still appears to take at least one generation to absorb and encapsulate perceptions of another country in a memorable stereotype. *Idées reçues* are not formed overnight in the minds of individuals; still less so in the collective unconscious of a country. By the time the stereotype has become embedded in the literature and the elementary textbooks, and passed down to the following generation, the reality which inspired it originally is likely to have changed. To take a trivial example, decades after Paris had ceased to be a centre of European painting, would-be Japanese artists were making their way to Montparnasse. In a similar fashion, Western visitors to Japan frequently express surprise on arriving in high-cost, high-rise, high-tech Tokyo. This is because they expected it to be either exotic, in which case their image of it was a hundred years out of date, or unbearably polluted, in which case the image was only twenty-five years behind the times. In the following pages many examples are given of such out-of-date images which hamper understanding – and not all of them are as trivial.

So, I wanted to understand the inherited scripts, the range of metaphor available to decision-makers as they considered each other's countries – a level of basic attitudes, even prejudices, sometimes held unconsciously and derived not from the reading of academic monographs, but learnt from parents, at school, and later enforced by early formative experiences. As illustrations of these popular images I frequently quote from such diverse sources as opinion polls, light operas, textbooks, fiction and the mass media. For example, I have used best-seller lists as a handy index to the attitudes of an age or generation. Scholars are as prejudiced as anyone else; their ideas can occasionally influence the popular mind. When that has happened I have quoted them.

A second reason which led me to focus on popular images is

that today they play a more direct role in international relations than in the past. It can matter very much what particular illusion about a foreign country is uppermost in this or that segment of society or pressure group. Politicians are aware of this and, although demagoguery is certainly not always the outcome, decision-makers ignore popular prejudices at their peril. It also goes without saying that the policy-maker himself may hold popular images or be influenced by them.

I have used the word 'image' loosely to cover two broad ranges of meaning. In the first sense, the emphasis is on the emotional attitudes – whether positive or negative – prejudices or illusions which colour or even determine the pictures that we form of reality. In the second sense, an image is merely a picture of reality which may or may not have congealed into a stereotype, and may be either true or false.

When there is no necessity felt to learn about another country, then knowledge of it will be slight, and the images which are held of it will be subjective, emotional and extreme. In general, this has been true until recently of Western images of Japan. Conversely, in Japan where there was once a strongly felt necessity to learn about the West, images were formed which were less emotive and closer to reality.

In talking of 'the Western image' or 'the Japanese image', I am guilty of a gross over-simplification, whose only excuse is that these are a convenient shorthand. For a start, not all European countries have held the same images of Japan, and the US images of Japan have sometimes differed from the European. Also, the terms 'West' and 'East' are ambiguous and give the false impression of complete opposites.

The same applies to the Japanese terms for East and West. They normally use the phrases seiyō (literally 'Western ocean', that is, the Occident or the West) as opposed to tōyō (literally 'Eastern ocean', that is, the Orient or the East). Another common expression for the West is OuBei ('EurAm' or 'Europe–America' for which there is currently no opposite).

Second, consider the images which two individuals hold of each other: they may be simple or complex, they may change as the years go by, or, more frequently, they congeal into stereotypes, but their formation and content are relatively easy to grasp when compared with the images which are held in one country of another. In the case of a country, many people are involved, so there are numerous channels of communication and many images. Different age groups will hold different images of the outside world, as will different social and work groups. Thus, a tourist will usually have a more rosy view of a country than a businessman working there, and a successful businessman will form a more positive view than a less successful one, and so on. Each individual forms his own personal, and often contradictory, mix of images of another country.

This is not to deny there are certain images, often passed from one generation to the next, which seep into every level of a country's imagination and form, as it were, a sediment of commonly held prejudice. During the colonial period, racial prejudice was of this kind, and images which emerge at a time of war are also of a similar nature.

The relationship between image and reality is subtle, often complicated by the fact that images, whether true or false, take on a life of their own, first vigorous and demanding attention, then fading away, only to reappear when least expected. And always, suddenly or slowly, influencing reality.

As he glances through these pages, the reader will come across images of his country held by foreigners which will probably strike him as absurd or funny, perhaps even insulting; certainly very far from the realities which he himself knows so well. When this happens, I would ask him not to form too hasty a judgement of the stupidity of foreigners. First, because even the most exaggerated caricatures usually contain a kernel of truth. Second, if there is a communications gap, it is not always as a result of the recipient of a signal not receiving it correctly. Sometimes the originator of the signal may not be sending it clearly.

So, I would ask the reader to bear in mind a simple question – who is responsible for what other people think of you? You yourself, or the people who form an image of you?

PART II

THE WEST AS SEEN BY JAPAN

4

LEARNING FROM ABROAD

For centuries, the Japanese were accustomed to situating themselves on the cultural periphery of great powers. First China, then Europe, then America. They even developed useful slogans to encapsulate the process: *Wakon Kansai* ('Japanese spirit, Chinese techniques') during the period of learning from China, and *Wakon Yōsai* ('Japanese spirit, Western techniques') during the period of learning from Europe and America.

Like all such simplistic dualisms, the slogans did not so much describe the reality of the learning process as provide a comforting reassurance that, no matter how much was brought in from abroad, there was always an essential core of integrity at home which retained its 'pure Japanese' character. This core of integrity could always be redefined as the need arose. To some it meant aesthetic sensibility, to others martial spirit. The slogans legitimized the learning process which itself came to be regarded as one of the strong points of the national character.

Europeans, too, have at many periods of their history turned to other, more advanced cultures for models and inspiration. But these cultures, notably Greece and Rome, were dead and therefore could be claimed as part of the 'European' past itself, not external to Europe. The pressures for change in the fourteenth and fifteenth centuries may have been largely external (Islam), but the cultural inspiration in the Renaissance was based on classical models which had long since come to be regarded as part of the European tradition itself. In the twentieth century the USA has been the greatest source of rejuvenation for Europe, as indeed it has also been for Japan. But the USA is an offshoot of

Europe and therefore less of an alien influence than it was for Japan.

There is a fundamental difference, then, between the conditions under which Europe and Japan have renewed themselves. For the Europeans it has usually been an internally generated process, even if triggered by external threats. For the Japanese in the nineteenth century, the necessity was to adopt an alien model, and adopt it at the point of a gun. Again in the twentieth century, another alien culture, the US, was adopted following the defeat in the Pacific War and occupation by the victors.

These differences were summed up by the great novelist Natsume Sōseki:

The enlightenment in the West . . . is inner-directed, while the enlightenment in modern Japan is outer-directed. By the phrase 'inner-directed' (*naihatsu-teki*) I mean spontaneous growth like the process by which a flower blossoms with its bud opening and its petals growing outward. By 'outer-directed' (*gaihatsu-teki*) I mean the moulding of a shape by means of external forces imposed from outside.[1]

If you have to learn a matter of life and death under strong external pressure, there is bound to be a sense of nervousness, if not downright panic.

One of the traditional strong points of Japan has been a timely ability to learn from other cultures. Even if this meant situating themselves psychologically on the periphery of those cultures, there was always a core of Japanese identity jealously guarded, as such mysteries tend to be, from the profane eye of the foreigner. Indeed, the corollary of learning so effectively from abroad was the intensely strong feeling in Japan itself that it was unique. This feeling more than made up for being situated, as it were, at the edge of a culture area, and for accepting the world view of the culture upon whose periphery it had placed itself.

There is a persuasive interpretation of the roots of Japanese individual behaviour by the psychiatrist Dr Dōi Takeo that holds that the fundamental characteristic of the Japanese is his desire, his need, to be loved (*amae*) by an understanding and respected parental or big brother figure on whom he can depend.[2] To extend Dōi's concept of the role of *amae* to Japan as a nation: in the past Japan felt not only unique but also isolated. In looking to China, to Europe and then to America as models it derived a sense of belonging. If Japan acted in consonance with the patterns laid down by these models, it would win their approval and affection. Conversely, the parental model figure was expected to play its role in extending understanding to Japan.

Although there are plenty of signs that Japan has begun to break out of this role playing, nevertheless, the pattern persisted until recently. For example, for many years the government's aid programme was not seen primarily as an obligation to the recipient developing countries, but rather as a burden-sharing exercise with the other advanced countries in the West.[3] Likewise, the opening of the Japanese market in the 1960s and 1970s was seen as an unavoidable means of reducing foreign pressure (*gaiatsu*) and not so much as a desirable step in itself.

To take another example, it is not enough for individual Japanese artists to win the esteem and affection of the domestic audience, but they must seek recognition and awards from Europe and the USA. The pursuit of fame beyond one's own country is common, and in today's global markets almost automatic, but for a Japanese, unless you first gain recognition outside Japan, you will find it harder to be accepted at home (a phenomenon known as 'reverse imports', *gyaku yunyu*). Writers such as Mishima or Kawabata went to extraordinary lengths to win the Nobel prize for literature. And to the man in the street, the prize is like a first-class badge of foreign approval. Even politicians have been affected by this desire for foreign approbation. Witness the former prime minister Mr Sato's single-minded but fruitless pursuit of the Nobel peace prize.

In an earlier age, the entire government and elite of Tokyo succumbed to the craze for swallowtails, bustles and ballroom dancing in the Rokumeikan period as part of an all-out effort to win foreign approval. The irony is that these efforts have often been rewarded with the opposite of the expected results. Westerners acted with indifference or even scorn; this inevitably led in Japan to a revulsion against the West.

Another important consequence of the habit of taking an

external culture as a model has been that the Japanese held over-idealistic images of the model culture. At the time of the war with China in 1894–5, many Japanese were shocked to find that China, whose culture had been revered for centuries, turned out to be a weak country riddled with corruption and racked with poverty. Esteem quickly turned to scorn.

Likewise, the image of Europe or the USA has often been an ideal cultural image based on books rather than on observed realities. Time and again young Japanese would report their disappointment at finding that actual Europeans or Americans did not live up to the ideals of freedom, humanism, love of truth or whatever qualities they had associated with Europe or America and which they therefore expected the people of these countries to embody. Many preferred simply to hold an ideal image of the 'West' rather than to adjust to the complex, confusing and inevitably disappointing flux of reality.

In line with the habit of identifying with the expected wishes of a parental figure, Japanese saw the world in terms of the model country of the day, whether the USA, Europe or China. In the seventies, it was often said that Japan still accepted a US map of the international scene. Having accepted it, Japan 'took for granted' US goodwill, and therefore felt shock and disappointment when the Americans suddenly changed their world view and recognized China without prior warning.

It was the same in the nineteenth century when Japan, with all the fervour of an aspirant member of a club, sought to adopt the European view of the world, including the European colonial view of the rest of Asia. It did so, and was understandably hurt when the Europeans and Americans failed to fully acknowledge the fact.

In the sixteenth and seventeenth centuries, when the first European merchants and missionaries arrived in Japan, they were regarded as outside the pale of civilization as defined in the Chinese world view, and dubbed 'southern barbarians' (*nanbanjin*). The term itself was originally Chinese.

Japanese tradition and the Chinese model prevailed: the Europeans except for the Dutch were expelled. As we trace this and later contacts with the West, a second pattern begins to emerge: a zigzag course between revulsion and attraction.

In the nineteenth century, it was a much more powerful Europe which came to trade and colonize in the Asia Pacific region. At the same time, China had entered into one of its long periods of decline. When these two tendencies became clear, particularly after the shock of China's defeat at the hands of the British in the Opium War (1842), the Japanese gradually began to abandon those elements of their own tradition derived from China, as well as the centuries-old view of China as the centre of the civilized universe, and to turn to the West as a new model.

By the 'West', the Japanese, of course, meant Europe and America. And in Europe, interest which had been focused on the Dutch during the period of isolation shifted to Britain, France and the newly emerging state of Prussia. Soon the Dutch joined the Spaniards and Portuguese in the limbo reserved for cultural contacts of a past age.

First the reaction was totally negative; then, on the old Chinese principle of 'know yourself, know your enemy', it became the overriding objective of patriotic Japanese from the mid nineteenth century onwards to learn the strong points of the West, to catch up with it and to surpass it, and thereby defend their country, saving it from further encroachments and possible subjugation. The Japanese wanted to learn about the West because they were convinced it was a dangerous threat to their country.

After the domestic political upheavals of the Meiji Restoration, Japan in the 1870s and 1880s entered into a feverish effort to adopt Western ways. This was the period of Europe's greatest influence. The copying of guns and armaments industries was no longer felt to be sufficient to establish a strong army and a rich and powerful country (*fūkoku kyōhei*). European and US institutions, laws, even ideas, were widely adopted. And soon there was the inevitable rejection.

In the twentieth century as Europe's role in the world declined, it was replaced by the USA as the model and guide for Japan, especially following the US victory over Japan in the Pacific War. Thereafter, Europe, with the possible exceptions of Austria, Switzerland, Sweden and Germany, joined the Dutch, the Spaniards and the Portuguese as models of a bygone age.

Today, it is the turn of the Americans to be downgraded in Japanese eyes.

Glancing back rapidly over Japan's contacts with the West over the last five hundred years, we can detect a pattern of initial revulsion, followed by assimilation and then rejection. An external presence or threat, particularly if it coincides with, or is in part the cause of, a major domestic, social and political upheaval, is followed by a period of openness to Western ideas, including, in the nineteenth century and after, such novel ideas as individual liberty and parliamentary democracy. An idealized version of Western culture is held at such times; the China model, or the Asian roots of Japan, even Japanese tradition itself, are downplayed if not completely rejected.[4]

Next, often following a rebuff by the Western powers, Japan turns back to its own roots and to a militant nationalism. There is a spate of books seeking to define the nature of 'Japaneseness' at such times. The West is seen chiefly as a threat and the negative aspects of its culture are emphasized. Externally Japan stresses its role as the leader of Asia and seeks a more active role there.

The pattern can be summarized schematically:

Table 7. Japan and the World

1543–1639	Superficial contacts with Europe
1639–1853	Country closed; traditionalistic reaction
1868–87	Opening to the West (Europe and America) ('dissociating from Asia', *Datsu-A ron*); individual liberty stressed
1887–1914	Nationalistic reaction; state power and Japanese tradition stressed; external adventures in Asia ('Pan-Asianism', *Ajia ichi*)
1920s	Opening to the West (the USA and Europe); democracy and liberty stressed
1931–45	Nationalistic reaction; state power stressed; external adventures in Asia ('Greater East Asia Co-prosperity Sphere', *Dai Tōa Kyōeiken*)

1945–60s	Opening to the West (the USA); individual liberty and parliamentary democracy stressed
1970s	Transitional period
1980–90s	Development of a new self-confidence; search for a new role in Asia and in the world; 'internationalization' (*kokusaika*)

Many other countries have followed a similar zigzag course as they felt the pressures of external models from the West competing with their own traditions, but few have done so with the intensity experienced by the Japanese. Some of the reasons have already been suggested why this should be so. Some obvious ones remain to be added.

First, Japan was in a unique position – it was the first Asian country to Westernize, therefore there was no clear pattern to follow. But the Japanese saw themselves in the world as outsiders, as a unique minority both in Asia and in the West. So, just like other innovating minorities, much of their energy was devoted to catching up in an effort to win acceptance from the more established powers.

Second, there was an acute sense that time was running out and that the country was in grave danger for the first time since the Mongol invasion six hundred years previously. The Iwakura mission in the 1870s drew the conclusion that the West had taken fifty years to reach the stage of its development at that time. So Japan had a massive lead to catch up with – or be swallowed. Ever since that unpleasant realization Japan has been running feverishly to draw level, crowding social and economic changes which Europe had achieved in two centuries and America in one, into two or three generations. And after the Pacific War, Japan moved in one generation from being an agricultural to an industrial to a post-industrial society.

The results were dramatic, with every decade producing world headlines, as Japan pulled and pushed to win its place in the international system and to be accepted by the West. This remorseless climbing of the international status ladder has had its rewards. It has become almost second nature, like the motorist who automatically drives in the 'fast' lane of a motorway, regardless of whether or not there is other traffic on the road or coming up behind.

All countries are familiar with the stereotypes of youth as questioning tradition, in the shape of the previous generation, only to sink back into traditional patterns of thought and behaviour as they grow old, curiosity replaced by nostalgia. But the speed of the switch-back process between the West and Japanese tradition in early modern Japan meant that the differences between the outlooks of different generations were unusually extreme; indeed, within the course of the life of an individual, the changes must have seemed totally confusing.

People have often been torn between philosophical interest in the West and nationalistic imperatives – the desire to be modern and accepted by the West, yet at the same time to retain their identity as Japanese, even as the very definitions of what was acceptable in Western terms and of Japanese tradition were constantly changing. Small wonder that the term 'identity crisis' seems to have been coined to describe modern Japanese intelligentsia, and that attitudes towards the West and Westerners have been ambivalent.

In the past, as they looked to China, to Europe and then to America, it became second nature for the Japanese to see themselves in the role of a learner or student. It was easy to accept the self-image of the Chinese, the Europeans and the Americans, who all in their different ways, and for their different reasons, saw themselves as teachers. The foreigners, on the other hand, found it easy to adopt the Japanese self-view of student, which reinforced their own self-image as teacher.

One important and fruitful result of this pattern of role playing remains to be noted. The Japanese have learned ten times more about the Chinese, the Europeans and the Americans than any of these three peoples have ever learned about the Japanese. Japanese images of Europe and America are based, therefore, upon a rich tradition of knowledge.

5

FIRST IMPRESSIONS

The Spanish and Portuguese missionaries and traders, who came to Japan in the sixteenth century, provided the first direct contacts between Japan and Europe. They came from the south, from Macao or Luzon, and they were given the name 'southern barbarians' (*nanbanjin*). The phrase had been adopted from the Chinese, who used it to describe the non-Chinese people in the South China seas and the Indo-China peninsula. The first Japanese people to meet the *nanbanjin* had no clear idea where they came from originally. Typical was the daimyō of Kagoshima and his mother who, when they met Francis Xavier in 1549, probably thought that he was an itinerant priest propagating a new sect of Buddhism from India.[5]

Gradually, as a more accurate idea of Europe took shape, the adjective '*nanban*' shifted to mean 'Southern Europe': it was widely used in such phrases as '*nanban* food' (for example, *tempura*), '*nanban* wine', '*nanban* hats', '*nanban* paintings' and so on. There were even, from time to time, what might be called '*nanban* booms'. Thus, when Xavier's successor, Valignano, was received by Hideyoshi in 1591 in Kyoto, his procession was said to have caused a great stir and longing for foreign exotica. Next year the same thing happened again when Hideyoshi set up his headquarters for the Korean campaign at Hizen near Nagasaki. There was a '*nanban* boom' throughout the army; both officers and men began sporting Portuguese clothes and trinkets and it became the fashion, at least for a short time, to wear amber balls, gold chains and buttons. Some even went so far as to experiment with eating eggs and beef.[6]

Was there a particular image of Europe associated with such booms? Probably not. The *nanbanjin* were truly exotic – neither fitting Japanese tradition nor stemming from India or China. As such they naturally aroused considerable curiosity and sparked off a short craze for foreign exotica, crazes which are characteristically, but not exclusively, Japanese. There was a further and practical interest in the new arrivals. They brought with them arquebuses and cannon. Their huge ocean-going vessels were novel and awe-inspiring. Their medicine too was potent. All these were more attractive than gold chains or amber balls, or Christianity, or even the *nanbanjin* themselves.

Eventually, fears that the missionaries were the vanguard of predatory soldiers from Europe, and fears of the subversive influence of Christianity itself, led to the exclusion of the *nanbanjin*, the proscription of Christianity and the closing of the country to foreign intercourse in 1639. Such fears are today almost totally forgotten, but the word *nanbanjin* still probably carries negative connotations.

Actual knowledge of the southern barbarians faded fast and, during the remainder of the seventeenth century, the little that had been known and diffused about the *nanbanjin* was also forgotten. As one of the leading opponents of extreme Westernization in the Meiji period, Shiga Shigetaka summed it up in an amusing comment reminiscent of Voltaire's celebrated remarks on the results of Columbus's discovery of America:

After nearly a hundred years of Christianity and foreign intercourse, the only apparent results . . . were the adoption of gunpowder and firearms and weapons, the use of tobacco and the habit of smoking, the making of spongecake, the naturalization into the language of a few foreign words, and the introduction of new and strange forms of disease.[7]

The most vivid images today of those first far-off contacts between Europe and Japan are the intricate and brightly coloured screen paintings of southern barbarian themes – Portuguese and Spanish galleons in the harbour and tall strangers disembarking, in exotic clothes and conical hats, to trade, convert or conquer.

The first encounter with the Europeans sparked curiosity,

mixed with anxiety, and it led eventually to a firm and complete rejection of the potentially dangerous foreigners, and an effort to purify and strengthen Japanese tradition itself, during a long period of introspection conducted behind closed doors. Not for the last time intellectuals busied themselves with elucidating the fundamentals of the Japanese tradition.

The next serious encounter with the West took place in the nineteenth century. The initial reaction was to reject Westerners and their 'barbarian' ways, but the conditions both within Japan and outside the country were different in the nineteenth century from what they had been in the sixteenth. Eventually it became clear that outright rejection of the West and continued closing of the country were impossible.

But this is to anticipate somewhat because, from the seventeenth to the nineteenth centuries when Japan was closed, not all contact with the West was lost. The court made efforts to keep itself informed about events in the world, including Europe, which knowledge it kept secret to itself. Individual scholars also studied from the Dutch and learned new perspectives and practical knowledge.

As part of the policy of closing the country (*sakoku*), not only were all foreigners forbidden to enter Japan, but also Japanese were forbidden to go abroad or to teach the Japanese language to foreigners. There was also a strictly enforced censorship on importation of Western books. During this period of self-imposed isolation the only foreigners who had a limited intercourse with Japan were the Chinese and the Dutch, who were permitted to maintain small trading stations in Nagasaki. The Dutch won this privilege for their proclaimed lack of interest in propagating Christianity. Over the next two centuries Westerners (the Dutch, and to a lesser extent the British) were called 'red-hairs' (*kōmōjin*). Japanese public knowledge of Europe was limited to what a few enthusiasts of 'Dutch studies' (*Rangaku*) were able to glean through the haphazard mediation of the Dutch trading station and the officially appointed hereditary interpreters attached to it.[8]

No matter how strict the censorship on foreign affairs and

knowledge, information did filter in. The thin edge of the wedge, as in so many other countries, was European medicine and astronomy, both of which proved themselves to be more effective than the traditional (Chinese) techniques which had been in use until then. Such Western sciences had an additional point in their favour: they were not political and they had no connection with Christianity. Furthermore, it is worth recalling that doctors, along with Confucian scholars and Buddhist priests, were one of the three major intellectual professions in Tokugawa times. In general, doctors were the most pro-Western, while Confucian scholars, because they saw their 'rice bowls' threatened, were the most anti-Western.

From at least the early years of the eighteenth century, the Shōguns had retained among their physicians practitioners of 'Dutch medicine', usually specializing in surgery, the internal medicine being conducted by doctors of Chinese medicine. How much these doctors actually knew is open to question, since no work of Western medicine had been translated at that time into Japanese. But already two court doctors in the mid eighteenth century had observed dissections and noted that the traditional Chinese manuals of anatomy bore no relation to their actual observations. To justify to themselves this discrepancy, they concluded that Japanese were anatomically different from Chinese – a striking example of the tyranny of inherited perceptions. It was not until the 1770s that, by a series of accidents, a Japanese practitioner of Dutch medicine was able to compare a Dutch illustrated manual of anatomy (the *Ontleedkundige Tafelen*, 1731) with observations made at a dissection.

The story is extremely interesting because it symbolizes the beginnings of a massive shift that was at the very heart of Japanese cultural dilemmas for most of the nineteenth century: disenchantment with China and a turning towards the West.

It was in 1771 that a medical practitioner, Sugita Genpaku, attended the dissection of the body of an executed female criminal with the nickname 'green tea hag' (*aocha baba*). Sugita and his other friends present were unable to identify the lady's organs with those which were listed in the old Chinese medical textbooks. On the other hand, when they compared her organs with those illustrated in the charts in the *Ontleedkundige Tafelen*, they were amazed to find perfect agreement between the two. So, the following day, the group of friends decided to translate the work into Japanese. No easy undertaking since they had only a slight knowledge of Dutch and no dictionary. 'After two or three years' hard work and as we gradually learned how to deal with it, we began to find pleasure in it like chewing on a sugar cane and tasting its mellowness. We also came to realize what wrong ideas we had been fettered to for many long years in the past.' Writing of his own motivation, Sugita recorded in 1803, 'All I wanted was to show somehow to the people that the real structure of the human body was different from the one described in Chinese books.'[9]

The scholars of Dutch learning – the *Rangaku* scholars such as Sugita – concentrated their efforts, apart from language studies, mainly on European medicine as well as on other practical sciences such as astronomy, navigation, geography, natural history, physics and mathematics.

There was also something of a 'Dutch boom' at the end of the eighteenth century. In the words of Sugita, 'People somehow began to be enamoured of anything Dutch. They would treasure imported vessels and other curious things. A dilettante, if worthy of the title, never failed to have a collection, large or small, of Dutch things . . .' These included barometers, thermometers, Leyden jars, hydrometers, magic lanterns, sunglasses, megaphones, timepieces, telescopes, glass handiworks and numerous other objects. 'People wondered at their delicate workmanship and the subtlety of their mechanism. People swarmed every spring around the hotel where the Dutch party was staying [in Edo for the annual visit to the Shōgun's Court].'[10] One is reminded of the '*nanban* boom' of the sixteenth century and the later crazes for Western 'exotica' in the nineteenth century or the craze for *Japonaiserie* in Europe in the 1870s.

We have already seen that contact with European medicine and astronomy led to a certain amount of questioning of traditional learning of Chinese origin. In the late eighteenth and early nineteenth centuries, some of the *Rangaku* scholars even began to dispute China's claim to be the centre of world culture and

model for Japan. They did so by asserting the greater age of
Europe (citing ancient Egypt). The picture they painted of
Europe was as idealistic as the European *philosophes* were
painting of China at the same time. And for the same reasons. A
conveniently distant and little-known culture was held up as
possessing those features which the writer wished to see introduced into his own country. In other words, just as the European
philosophes used China as a supposedly 'objective correlative'
with which to belabour obscurantism at home, so the *Rangaku*
scholars used Europe.[11]

Several of the *Rangaku* scholars were remarkable men who
advocated policies far in advance of their age. Some of them paid
with their lives – for example, the thirty-eight people implicated
in the so-called 'Siebold incident', who were executed in 1828 for
having passed maps and other information about Japan to a
foreigner. Some pursued their studies along unexpected lines.
Shiba Kokan (1747–1818) studied Western techniques for creating the illusion of space by the use of shadow and relief and
perspectival lines leading into the back of the composition. His
paintings had a considerable influence on Hokusai and the early
ukiyo-e print makers. Thus, in the nineteenth century when
French painters 'discovered' the Japanese print, they were unconsciously drawn to a form of Japanese art which had in part
already been influenced by Western perspective.[12]

Among the population at large, Westerners were regarded as
exotic, if not peculiar. Even the word 'Oranda' (Dutch) had long
since evoked the sense 'eccentric' or 'odd' as in the charming
little verse of Sōin, who on a visit to Nagasaki towards the close of
the seventeenth century wrote: 'Is that Dutch writing? Across
the heaven stretch a line of wild geese.'[13]

In the nineteenth century as news of the Western advance
towards East Asia began to reach Japan, and as European,
Russian and US ships, and sometimes small fleets, began to
cruise off Japanese waters, fear, dislike and even hatred of
Western 'barbarians' and Western studies began to mount. A
warning by a conservative scholar, Aizawa Seishisai, was made in
1825:

Recently, there has appeared what is known as Dutch Studies, which had its inception among our official interpreters at Nagasaki. It has been concerned primarily with the reading and writing of Dutch, and there is nothing harmful about it. However, these students, who make a living by passing on whatever they hear, have been taken in by the vaunted theories of the Western foreigners. They enthusiastically extol these theories, some going so far as to publish books about them in the hope of transforming our civilized way of life into that of the barbarians. And the weakness of some for novel gadgets and rare medicines, which delight the eye and enthral the heart, have led many to admire foreign ways. If someday the treacherous foreigner should take advantage of this situation and lure ignorant people to his ways, our people will adopt such practices as eating dogs and sheep and wearing woollen clothing. And no one will be able to stop it.[14]

Fear and suspicion of Europe, particularly England, redoubled following the Opium War (1840–42) in which China was defeated by the British. The image of China, the age-old model for Japan, also suffered a heavy blow as a result of the war. Many Confucians who made their living by expounding Chinese learning hated the West, but could only express an impotent fury, like Shionoya Tōin (1810–67), who described Western writing as

confused and irregular, wriggling like snakes or larvae of mosquitoes. The straight ones are like dog's teeth, the round ones are like worms. The crooked ones are like the forelegs of a mantis, the stretched ones are like the slime left by snails. They resemble dried bones or decaying skulls, rotten bellies of dead snakes or parched vipers.[15]

Others, while just as anti-foreign as Shionoya or Aizawa, nevertheless recognized the practical necessity of learning from one's enemies, or as one statesman put it, 'the necessity of defence against the barbarians requires that we know them and know ourselves; there is no other way to know them than through Dutch learning'.[16]

Many drew a distinction between the Dutch, whom they could learn from, and even admire, and the English, who were regarded as intrepid, crafty and calculating with a national character deeply rooted in militarism. All would have agreed that the barbarians (banjin, for that was what Westerners were now called) were crafty, fox-like and on the lookout to seize Japan. In the popular mind it was even rumoured that the Westerners concealed bushy tails in their pants and urinated like dogs.[17]

On the eve of the arrival of Commodore Perry's 'black ships' in Yedo [Tokyo] Bay in 1853, despite the fear and suspicion of the West, or perhaps because of it, not only did the Japanese know far more about the outside world than the outside world knew about Japan, but they had also made themselves better informed about Europe and America than any other non-Western people. There is, therefore, a remarkable contrast between the enthusiasm and effectiveness of the early Japanese students of the West, the *Rangaku* scholars, as well as government efforts to gather intelligence about the West, and the almost total indifference of the Europeans, even in the shape of the Dutch, towards Japan. It is a contrast which we shall find repeated again and again.

The demands of Commodore Perry that Japan open its doors to foreign trade and thereby bring to an end the two-century-old Tokugawa policy of isolation were soon known throughout the country: 'the appearance of the US fleet in Yedo had already made its impression on every remote town in Japan', as one of the reformers later recalled of the year 1854, and 'the problem of national defence and modern gunnery had become the foremost interest of samurai'.[18]

Two consecutive reactions to the foreigner may be observed in these years: complete rejection or partial assimilation. Each reaction was grounded on a different domestic political programme. At first, the debate divided between those who advocated keeping the country closed and expelling the barbarians completely ('reverence the Emperor, expel the barbarians', *sonnō-jōi*), and those who felt that the only way to make the country strong enough to resist foreign pressures was to open it partially to learn Western science and military technology while maintaining traditional values ('Japanese spirit, Western techniques', *Wakon Yōsai*).

This second formulation is notable for fitting snugly into one of the basic stereotypes of each other shared by both East and West: the East is spiritual, the West material. There were precedents for such a dualism in Confucian thinking, and in the Japanese tradition which explicitly sanctioned adopting and making use of the strong points of other countries. The old phrase *Wakon Kansai* was easily adapted to *Wakon Yōsai*. The formulation was a useful transitional one, allowing those who propounded it to maintain their pride in adverse circumstances and at the same time to justify extensive borrowing from the West. But the rigid dualism which it implied very soon proved impossible to maintain. Eventually, after 1868, it was to be temporarily replaced by a third option: imperial restoration coupled with out-and-out Westernization.

As Western pressure mounted in the 1850s and 1860s, it began to look increasingly impractical simply to keep Japan closed. Despite waves of anti-foreign violence, and resentment at the bullying and arrogant behaviour of the foreign envoys, the government had little option but partially to open the country. In 1854, it signed a treaty with Perry. Immediate efforts were made to learn more about the new enemies. An Institute of Barbarian Letters was set up in 1856 to train interpreters and make translations, and seven diplomatic-cum-study missions were sent to the United States and Europe between 1860 and 1867. Extensive records of these missions were kept, both public and private, and they afford a fascinating insight into Japanese attitudes towards the West at the time.

The first mission abroad, that to America in 1860, was astonished to find how politely the foreigners treated them, whereas in Japan, 'seven or eight out of ten people think of Europeans as dogs and horses. Some even have killed them . . .'[19]

People in the wave of anti-foreignism in Japan in the 1860s 'simply hated the foreigners because all foreigners were "impure", men who should not be permitted to tread the sacred soil of Japan'.[20]

Fukuzawa Yukichi, who later became one of the leading proponents of out-and-out Westernization, managed to join no less than three of the Bakufu diplomatic missions to Europe and America. Recalling the atmosphere in his hometown of Nakatsu in Kyushu in the 1850s, he later wrote, 'All the men in town, including my near relatives, hated anything Western . . .', adding that 'it was still the age of Chinese studies and anything Western was to be frowned upon. But since the Perry expedition, one subject in the culture of the West, the gunnery, came to be recognized as a necessity. This was one way of escape to study the civilization of the West.'[21]

Fukuzawa made his escape from the stifling atmosphere of his lower samurai family, and eventually studied Dutch and medicine in Osaka. There he learnt much the same lesson as Sugita Genpaku had learnt three generations before him: for Japan to advance, it would first have to throw off the influence of China, or, as he put it in a description of his student days: 'The only subject that bore our constant attack was Chinese medicine. And by hating Chinese medicine so thoroughly we came to dislike everything that had any connection with Chinese culture. Our general opinion was that we should rid our country of the influence of the Chinese altogether.'[22]

A contemporary who stopped in Hong Kong in 1863, on the way back from one of the Bakufu missions to Europe, reached the same conclusions for different, but typical, reasons: 'They [the Chinese] are all rude and deceitful . . . After having been a very great country, they are now the slaves of the English barbarians, who beat and drive them out.'[23]

For Fukuzawa, and others like him, China was to be replaced by 'the West'. And the West meant for them not just guns and scientific inventions and industrial machinery, but different social customs and ways of thinking. After his third trip abroad, Fukuzawa wrote a short book called *Conditions in the West* (1866). It was the first book on the West which attempted to explain in simple language what the West was like to live in. The book was modern Japan's first best-seller: some 250,000 copies were sold in the year of publication alone. Fukuzawa's reputation was made and, within a few years after the Meiji Restoration in 1868, Japan entered into a frenzy of out-and-out Westernization.

6

OUT-AND-OUT WESTERNIZATION

After the Meiji Restoration in 1868, the state launched the policy of 'reverence the Emperor, open the country' (*sonnō-kaikoku*) and inaugurated a period of rapid Westernization with the aim of completely renovating Japan's government and economy along Western lines to catch up with Europe and America, particularly in military power.

Between 1868 and 1900, some 2,400 foreign experts, the largest number from Britain, were invited to work in Japan as advisers to the new government ministries, including the armed forces, and as teachers in the new schools. In 1875 there were about five hundred such experts; by 1885, their numbers had declined to less than a hundred. Large study missions and dozens of students a year were also sent to the West by the government. Many of the students, on their return to Japan, became prominent in their different fields and, from that day to this, returned students have acted as the main body of mediators introducing the USA and Europe to Japan. The practice of sending hundreds of students abroad reached a peak in the 1920s. Today, young men and women are sent abroad by their company as well as by the government, or by their university, but many thousands more go under their own steam.

For a brief time in the 1870s and 1880s the imitation of European manners became all the rage in the new capital of Tokyo. European influence on Japan reached its height at this time. 'Foreign countries are not only novel and exotic for us Japanese,' wrote Fukuzawa in 1875, 'everything we see and hear about these cultures is strange and mysterious . . . a blazing brand has been thrust into ice-cold water. Not only are ripples and swells ruffling the surface of men's minds, but a massive upheaval is being stirred up at the very depths of their souls.'[24]

The urge to catch up with the West was inspired by the fear of being overcome by the Western powers. Another motive was the desire to wipe out the shame of the unequal treaties by which foreigners in the treaty ports enjoyed extra-territoriality and the Japanese government had no tariff autonomy. To show, in other words, that Japan too was a modern (Western) civilized state which should be treated as an equal. Many ardent Westernizers were also no doubt influenced by their own rapid advancement on the basis of their knowledge of the West.

Nor should one underestimate the attractiveness in themselves of such new ideas as 'freedom'. J. S. Mill's *On Liberty* was a best-seller in 1872. Political ideas were also introduced through popular translations of novels such as Disraeli's *Coningsby* or Bulwer-Lytton's *Ernest Maltravers*. During these years of 'Progress and Enlightenment', 'Magna Charta was circulated in facsimile reprints; the name of Rousseau was repeated as if it were a saviour; Patrick Henry was well known to many, and his words, "Give me liberty, or give me death", became a slogan.'[25]

All nine 'best-sellers' between 1866 and 1878 were translations of Western works or books about the West. The list shows the extraordinary influence of Fukuzawa, indeed works about the West at this time were known popularly as 'Fukuzawa books' (*Fukuzawa-bon*).

Table 8. Early Japanese Best-sellers

1866	Fukuzawa Yukichi	*Conditions in the West*
1871	Samuel Smiles	*Self-Help*
1872	Fukuzawa Yukichi	*The Encouragement of Learning*
1872	J. S. Mill	*On Liberty*
1875	Fukuzawa Yukichi	*An Outline of a Theory of Civilization*

1877	Taguchi Ukichi	*A Short History of the Opening of Japan*
1878	Jules Verne	*Around the World in Eighty Days*
1878	Bulwer-Lytton	*Ernest Maltravers*

Fukuzawa's *The Encouragement of Learning* appeared in seventeen parts over the years 1872–84. Some 200,000 copies of each part were printed and sold, making a total sale of 3,400,000 copies!

By far the most popular of Western books during the Meiji period was *Self-Help*, by the Scottish moralist Samuel Smiles, who argued that the qualities needed to get ahead in industrial society were not rank or status, but hard work and self-improvement, perseverance and thrift. His teaching was thoroughly absorbed in Japan and has remained influential long after it was abandoned in Europe and the USA.[26]

The popularity of Samuel Smiles was matched by the influence of the Social Darwinist Herbert Spencer (1820–1903), who argued that the survival of the fittest applied as well to nations and to the rise and fall of Great Powers as to individuals. There was no immutable law making one nation more powerful than another, he taught, it only required efforts and effective political and economic policies to boost a nation up the path to progress.

The desire to learn about and to emulate the West was not limited to government officials and intellectuals. It was also matched by a wave of popular enthusiasm and curiosity stretching down to the illiterate, as the following excerpt by the contemporary writer Hattori Busshō (1842–1908) indicates:

The Western Peep Show

The viewing parlours are for the most part small painted shacks, the fronts of which have been given a hasty coat of whitewash. The rear, however, is neglected, suggesting nothing so much as a slattern who powders her face but leaves her back dirty . . . Inside the building, at intervals several feet apart, are arranged a number of machines, and one goes from one machine to another peeping at its display . . . Some machines contain pictures of the scenery of countries all over the world;

others are of completely imaginary subjects: the steel bridge of London is longer than a rainbow; the palace of Paris is taller than the clouds. An enraged Russian general pulls out a soldier's whiskers; a recumbent Italian lady kisses her dog. They have bought an American conflagration to sell us; they have wrapped up a German war to open here. Warships push through the waves in droves; merchant ships enter port in a forest of masts. A steam engine climbs a mountain; a balloon flies in the sky . . . You look at a picture of a museum and despise the pawnshop next door; you peep at a great hospital and lament the headaches of others. As the spectator approaches the last peep show he becomes increasingly aware how cheap the admission price has been.[27]

During these years the wearing of Western clothes and the sporting of Western hairstyles were taken as signs of cultural openness. Just as in the sixteenth century, it was the army which first switched to a Western uniform. Next, the government bureaucracy and the Court adopted Western clothes. Controversy raged. Some argued that Western clothes should be for practical use, while Japanese dress should be reserved for aesthetic delights, thereby making a sartorial application of the slogan 'Japanese spirit, Western techniques'. Even now this reasoning is often advanced to explain why men and women wear kimonos outside their place of work: men at home, and women away from home. Others pointed out with some justification in those days of bustles and stays that Western clothes were impractical, unhygienic and expensive.

Even the prime minister, Itō Hirobumi, held definite views on the subject, as the German doctor, Erwin Baelz, recorded in 1904:

When, a long while ago, Itō informed me that European dress was to be introduced at the Japanese court, I earnestly advised against the step, on the ground that European clothing was unsuited to the Japanese bodily structure, and especially that the corset would be most unwholesome for Japanese women. Hygiene apart, I said, from the cultural and aesthetic standpoint the proposed change was simply impossible. Itō smiled and replied: 'My dear Baelz, you don't in the least understand the requirements of high politics. All that you say may be perfectly sound, but so long as our ladies continue to appear in Japanese dress they will be regarded as mere dolls or bric-à-brac.'[28]

Itō's remark has an authentic ring. Behind the good humour is the very real sensitivity as to how foreigners regarded the Japanese and their attempts to conform to Western ways. As part of its policy to revoke the unequal treaties the government sought to convince the Western powers that Japan was not a backward Oriental country, but a modern power with a constitution (modelled on that of Bismarck's Prussia), a legal code (modelled on the French code), an up-to-date school system (part German, part American), a business code (British and American), a Central Bank (Belgian) and an army (German) and navy (British). And as Itō pointed out, clothes too had a role to play.

This purposeful and unique approach to the West, an eclectic choice of the best models available from the different countries, left the Japanese, especially in the early Meiji period, with an idealistic image of the West based on book learning and élite study missions which in their reports very naturally concentrated on the rationale of Western institutions, rather than on their functioning. Take this description of the roots of Western success by Fukuzawa (which incidentally sounds very much like the sort of thing said by some Americans and Europeans about Japan today): 'The citizens of the West are not all intelligent. However, most of what they achieve through concerted group action proves to be the product of intelligent men. The internal affairs of these countries are all agreed upon by these groups. The governments are based on group consensus . . . Westerners are intellectually vital, are personally well-disciplined and have patterned and orderly social relations.'[29]

For the intellectuals of the Japanese enlightenment, the West was a desirable collection of cultural assets representing 'civilization' and 'strength'. It was not an actual congeries of different countries each packed with its own strengths and weaknesses. The early Meiji image of the West as the source of light, civilization, and above all high culture, has been extraordinarily pervasive, and it continues as a powerful image right to the present day.

Another Meiji image of the West has continued to the present. It was derived from the image of abroad as the perfect setting for adventure and for romance. Abroad was a region of pure otherness where ordinary Japanese rules did not apply. Most of the Japanese going to Europe or the USA were young and single. Fukuzawa tells the story of how, at the age of twenty-five, he secured a photograph of himself with a girl during the first Bakufu mission to America. It was in fact the photographer's daughter; when he showed the prized souvenir to his shipmates they were envious. But it was too late by then for them to get themselves photographed with a white girl using the same trick.[30]

Some of those who went to Europe and America later wrote of their affairs: the surgeon-author Mori Ōgai's 'The Dancer' comes to mind. His flaxen-haired German heroine with her sad blue questioning eyes became for generations of Japanese the ideal type of Western woman. The early Western-style painters, many of whom studied in Paris, were also fascinated by European girls whom they never tired of painting.

Back in Japan, for the majority unable to make the long trip to the West, it was also foreign women who inspired curiosity. Hattori Busshō describes it in his story 'The Western Peep Show', quoted earlier:

In the last show, the Goddess of Beauty lies naked in bed. Her skin is pure white, except for a small black mole under her navel. It is unfortunate that she has one leg lifted, and we cannot admire what lies within. In another scene we regret that only half the body is exposed and we cannot see the behind; in still another we lament that though face to face we cannot kiss the lips. This marvel among marvels, novelty among novelties, is quite capable of startling the eyes of rustics and untutored individuals.

Then as now publishers knew the value of a good book title. A very proper Victorian 'political romance' like Bulwer-Lytton's *Ernest Maltravers*, a best-seller in 1878 in Japan, was sold under the translated title 'Strange Stories from Europe: Pornographic Tales from the Red-Light Districts' (*Oshū kiji, karyū shunwa*).

Today Europe seems to have become fixed in the Japanese mind as an ideal setting for romantic affairs, combining eroticism with culture. Whether this is because of the influence of the

French romantic image, the reputation of Nordic girls or Italian men as 'Latin lovers', I do not know. Sex hotels in Japan are more often than not decorated in what might be termed 'the high French boudoir style'. During one visit to the provinces I was struck by the fact that the main attraction of the live sex show was the performance of the sex act by a Japanese boy with a Swedish girl. After it was over, the girl presented herself for inspection in a manner which had been denied the viewers of Hattori's peep show.

In Chapter 12 we shall see that the Western erotic image of Japan assumed central importance with the popularity of the Chrysanthemum theme. It beclouded a more balanced image of Japan for half a century. The Japanese erotic image of the West on the other hand never played a central role, it merely enlivened the image of the West as a source of high culture and industrial techniques.

The headlong pursuit of Western ways and the desire for Western approval in those far-off days of early Meiji led the government in unexpected directions. One was to sponsor elaborate balls in the specially constructed Rokumeikan, which we shall come across in the incredulous and sneering descriptions of Pierre Loti. To the Westerner, Loti, the Rokumeikan was boring because there was nothing 'Oriental' or exotic about it. The Japanese in Western swallowtails appeared ridiculous to him. Only the Chinese at the ball in their traditional costumes won his admiration because they seemed authentically 'Oriental'.

Seen through Japanese eyes, however, things would have appeared very differently, and indeed this is the theme of Akutagawa Ryunosuke's story 'The Ball'. The heroine, Akiko, recounts how years before as a young girl her father had taken her to a ball at the Rokumeikan where she had been asked to dance by a young French naval officer (Loti). To her the ball was a magical and exotic event because it was just what she imagined a Parisian ball would be like. Only the Chinese officials appeared to her as ridiculous, with their fat bellies and long pig-tails hanging down their backs. When Loti looked at the Japanese women at the ball he saw their clumsy efforts to dance. Akiko on the other hand drew the opposite conclusion from Loti's glances: 'The naval officer was watching her every movement. This simply showed how much interest this foreigner, unaccustomed to Japan, took in her vivacious dancing.'[31]

And the partners in this semi-fictional, but emotionally real, contact sailed on in their lives, both mercifully ignorant of the impressions which each had created in the heart of the other.

7

DISILLUSION

There was a contradiction in the movement for out-and-out Westernization: it was not possible to establish Japan as a Western state simply by adopting Western civilization. Nationalism too was needed, but nationalism implied an indigenous culture and national essence peculiar to Japan, and the rejection of increasingly aggressive Western efforts to control Japan. Under these conditions it became virtually impossible to advocate out-and-out Westernization while remaining a patriot.

The trigger which eventually sparked a revulsion from Westernization was the failure to secure Western respect for Japan's efforts to 'civilize' itself, which came to a political head in the breakdown of efforts to negotiate the revocation of the unequal treaties in 1887. Societies sprang up, dedicated to combating the loss of national identity and to opposing 'Europeanization'. Soon Japan turned back to its own traditions and towards a militant nationalism. In cultural circles the search for the essence of the Japanese tradition began once again, and the spate of translations of Western works declined.

Even without the shock of the failure of treaty revision, the extraordinary speed of the adoption of Western institutions and manners, a speed which sometimes led to indiscriminate borrowing, would probably have produced a revulsion sooner or later.

There were other factors making for disillusion with the West. As more people travelled, there was a growing awareness by the 1880s of a gap between the vision of the West, derived from book reading, and its realities, a lesson which was all too often reinforced by the racialist treatment which many individuals encountered, or felt they had encountered, at the hands of unsympathetic landladies and others during their stay overseas.

The novelist Natsume Sōseki's case from a few years later was no doubt particularly extreme:

The two years spent in London were the most unpleasant two years in my life. Among English gentlemen, I lived miserably like a lost dog in a pack of wolves.[32]

Nakae Chōmin, one of the founders of Japanese socialism, wrote in an 1882 newspaper article on his return from a trip to Europe:

The British in Port Said and the French in Saigon are extremely arrogant, treating the Turks and Indians [sic] almost as dogs and pigs . . . The Europeans, who call themselves civilized people, consistently behave like that.[33]

Individual differences began to be noted: 'Where is the essence of the West in the countries of Europe and America?' asked the aesthete Okakura Tenshin after a trip to Europe in 1887. 'All these countries have different systems; what is right in one country is wrong in the rest; religion, customs, morals – there is no common agreement on any of these. Europe is discussed in a general way, and this sounds splendid; the question remains, where in reality does what is called "Europe" exist!'[34] The question remains valid today.

Tokutomi Sōho, an influential journalist and opinion leader, made an increasingly common objection, already voiced by Itō in his conversation with Baelz: 'These foreigners regard Japan as the world's playground, a museum . . . They pay their admission and enter because there are so many strange, weird things to see . . .'[35]

A few years later Chamberlain remarked that 'the travelled Japanese consider our three most prominent characteristics to be dirt, laziness and superstition.'[36]

The political disappointment of 1887 was soon followed by the major disillusionment of the triple intervention of 1895.

Since the Japanese government had scrupulously followed the

Western model of concluding a war with China by gaining a sphere of interest in that country, all according to the accepted practice of the day, there was severe criticism of the West. The following is a fairly typical later comment (made in the more outspoken thirties) on the triple intervention, 'Japan has perceived that the Western saying, "Honesty is the best policy" is applicable only among individuals. The discovery was made when three international hijackers, Russia, Germany and France, browbeat Japan into relinquishing the legitimate result of her war with China . . . The Manchurian incident may be taken as Japan's formal notice to the powers that she is fed up with the peculiar type of fair play practised by the whites in their association with the non-white races.'[37]

The pattern of Japan playing 'the rules of the game' yet not being accepted fully as a 'member of the club' by the Western powers was to be repeated many times over the next decades.

The turning away from the West in the late 1880s and 1890s and the search for a new national identity, for a specifically Japanese national essence, soon became engulfed in a torrent of jingoism during the Sino-Japanese War. One of the first popular novels depicting a war between Japan and the West was serialized in a Tokyo newspaper in 1895. The high point of the novel, *Asahi Zakura* by Murai Gensai, is the bombardment by a Japanese fleet, which has sailed up the River Thames, of London Bridge.

Out-and-out Westernizers like Fukuzawa or Tokutomi still sought to correct the Western image of Japan as the 'world's playground'. They still wanted to be accepted by the West. But the concomitant of 'measuring up' to the West was 'looking down' on the East. Contempt for the 'Chinks' (*chanchan*, *chankorō* or *tombi*) and other 'Asiatics' now became the vogue. A show of force in Korea or China was the right way of demonstrating to the West that Japan had effectively Westernized and was no longer in the same league as other Oriental countries. 'On the whole,' wrote Fukuzawa in 1899, 'I see the country well on the road of advancement. One of the tangible results was to be seen a few years ago in our victorious war with China, which was the result of perfect cooperation between the government and the people . . . in the heat of the moment I could hardly refrain from rising up in delight.'[38]

Japan's new-found strength began to bear fruit at the turn of the century. It successfully renegotiated the unequal treaties with the Western powers in 1894 (full tariff autonomy followed in 1911). Colonies were also acquired – Taiwan in 1895, and Korea in 1910. China had also been forced to extend most-favoured nation treatment to Japan.

In 1901 Japanese troops fought alongside the allied powers at the siege of Peking. Finally the Japanese resoundingly defeated Russia in the Russo-Japanese War (1904–5). It was the first victory of an Asian country over a Western power in modern times.

The mood in Japan was exultant, but tinged with doubts as to what the West would think. As Mori Ōgai put it:

> Win the war,
> And Japan will be denounced as a Yellow Peril.
> Lose it,
> And she will be branded as a barbaric land.

Although winning the war did arouse fears of Japan in the West, the irony was that Japan gained far more attention and respect from the European powers and America by its defeat of China and even more so by the victories over Russia, than by all its efforts to adopt Western civilized ways. As Okakura Tenshin remarked, 'The average Westerner . . . was wont to regard Japan as barbarous while she indulged in the gentle arts of peace: he calls her civilized since she began to commit wholesale slaughter on Manchurian battlefields.'[39] The official victor of Port Arthur, Nōgi Maresuke, made a triumphal tour in Europe and was decorated by the governments of Prussia, France and Great Britain.

Despite Japan's recognition by the Western powers, discrimination continued, eventually with the disastrous result of encouraging Japan to go down the road which led from the Sino-Japanese War of 1895 to the Manchurian incident in 1931. In California there were the unsuccessful efforts to have Japan included in the 1902 Chinese Exclusion Act, then the President's request in 1906, which the Japanese government accepted, to voluntarily limit emigration to the USA. At Versailles in 1919, Japan's initiative for a clause on racial equality was rebuffed by the USA and Britain. Finally, in 1924 the Oriental Exclusion Act banned all Asian (including Japanese) immigration to the USA. It was repealed in 1952. Many individuals too had suffered personal discrimination of one form or another in the USA or in Europe.

The more Japan shifted to 'Pan-Asianism' (*Ajia ichi*), the more the image of Europe and the USA declined. There were other reasons too. World War I demonstrated that Europe as the home of liberty and enlightenment was a false image. The defeat of Germany also meant the collapse of one of Japan's most respected models during the Meiji period.

Further disillusion with Europe came when, after the war, the Europeans themselves began increasingly to talk of decline. 'Europe is sick, perhaps dying,' said Anatole France, and many Japanese would have agreed, particularly as the corollary of the decline of the West was felt to be the rise of the East under the leadership of Japan. Marxist critiques of Western bourgeois society at this time found a willing ear in Japan. Spengler's *Decline of the West* too was rapidly translated into Japanese and met with a not unappreciative audience. It has sold steadily since the appearance of volume I in 1925 at the rate of about a thousand copies a year and is currently available in six different editions.

In this climate of opinion, and with the development of socialism, people who went to Europe and the USA began to notice unfavourable things, and not only to notice them, but to give more emphasis to them on their return to Japan than they had done in the past. One of the earliest was Kawakami Hajime, whose *Tales of Poverty* (1917) contained graphic descriptions of the slums and suffering in Europe in the years leading up to World War I. It became an instant best-seller. He wrote:

Although England, America, Germany and France and many others are rich countries, their people are very poor. It is surprising that in these civilized countries there are so many people who are poor.[40]

Kawakami was by no means the only young intellectual who went to study in Europe and found unpleasant smells where others had found heady perfumes. Books like Ikemoto Kimio's *Tales of French Villages* (1934) contained graphic descriptions of the squalor and backwardness of French country life, where he discovered to his surprise that baths were virtually unheard of.

In the thirties there was growing dissatisfaction with the West, triggered by the negative images evoked by the trade frictions during the Depression at the start of the decade, and encouraged by the rumours of war at the end of it. This is reflected even in the work of a non-political writer such as Mushanokoji Saneatsu whose novel *Love and Death* (1939) gives an insight into the popular sentiments of those days.

At a farewell party given for the chief protagonist of the novel on the eve of his departure for Paris, a friend says:

I was the first to urge Muraoka to go to Paris. Thousands and ten thousands have gone and will continue to go. But Paris is the cultural centre of the world today. I would like to have him learn from his trip how frivolous the world really is. . . . From the standpoint of knowledge, one would be better off reading a book than going to Europe or Paris. But the awareness that Europe or Paris are frivolous places is something one can get only by going to the West. And that, I maintain, is not at all an insignificant possession. Paris is not the centre of the world; it is wherever we happen to be standing . . . For us the centre of the earth is Tokyo . . . But until we have seen Paris we remain in awe of Paris.

These deliberately anti-Romantic and somewhat chauvinistic words make the same point as Paul Valéry, but the other way round. Valéry's advice was that if you wish to maintain your illusions about the Orient, it is better not to go there. Muraoka's friend is saying, if you want to destroy your illusions about the West, you had better go there.

Generations of Orientalists in Europe have preferred Valéry's advice. Arthur Waley, for example, perhaps the most famous British Orientalist and translator of Chinese and Japanese literature in the twentieth century, never once visited either China or Japan. He preferred to avoid confronting the ideal image he held of them, based on the classic texts, with what he feared would be the humdrum realities of present-day life. He preferred to live with his illusions. In 1964 when I first went to China, I was advised by my professor that if I wished to continue my career as a sinologist, I was wasting my time going there! Advice exactly the opposite of Muraoka's cynical friend.

After arriving in Paris, Muraoka writes home that,

Wherever one goes one sees only Occidentals . . . somehow I have the feeling that we are looked down upon . . . A solitary Japanese among a group of Occidentals is hardly an imposing figure. This is due to a large extent to our not being suited to Western style clothes, but even if we try to make something of the colour of our skin and our physique, we still have very little to boast about. Nevertheless, I am confident that from the standpoint of spiritual power and intelligence we are not in the least inferior. The majority of Europeans love pleasure too much. Few of them have any faith in a future life. For the most part they live idly from day to day.

These thoughts contain many of the most common stereotypes held by Japanese about 'Occidentals' which we have already come across several times. The Japanese may be physically inferior, but they are spiritually superior. Occidentals are self-indulgent and lazy. 'They are', he continues, 'for the most part satisfied with their own culture. They show by their expression that they feel no need to be interested in anything beyond it'.

Muraoka writes much on the paintings, statues and art which he sees in Europe, but he also asserts the equal value of Japanese art. Finally, on the eve of his departure from Europe he sums it all up:

As an Oriental travelling around in Europe I have had to endure a great deal. It's because of the way things are between the East and the West. I believe that we Orientals still have much to learn from the West. But I feel also that there are a great many things about the East that we should try to teach the West . . . Feeling as I do, I have never forgotten my manners or lost my good will toward them, but I have seen no special reason for flattering them. But what a lot of silly tensions I will be relieved of when I get back to Japan! Being aware always that one is a foreigner among foreigners wherever one goes doesn't make for peace of mind.[41]

I fully sympathize with many of the feelings of 'Muraoka', having once spent a year as a minority of one in an alien surrounding. Because you look different you think everybody is watching you. You begin to feel nervous, you suspect that every time a dog barks, he is barking at you and that every laugh is pointed in your direction. You long for the anonymity which only a return to your own people can offer. Sōseki felt this isolation and paranoia so strongly in London that he had a nervous breakdown. Muraoka felt the same in Paris. But such feelings are not always the result of a hostile environment. Muraoka confesses that he could not speak a word of French before going to Paris and made no effort to learn it when he got there, so it was difficult for him to break out of his isolation.

Anybody who has had to live in a totally alien environment will know what the fictional Muraoka is saying in his letters home. Indeed Japanese visitors to Europe or America in the nineteenth century had made similar comments which are still echoed today. Only today the contrast between Japan and the West, between being Japanese and Western is likely to be less strongly felt. And the chauvinistic tone of the thirties is now muted, if not wholly a thing of the past.

The final stage in the rejection of the West was reached during the years when Japan sought to become 'the Light of the Greater East Asia . . . and ultimately the Light of the World'. The commentary on the Imperial Declaration of War which sold more than three million copies continued,

To speak the truth, the various races of East Asia look upon the British and Americans as superior to the Nippon race. They look upon Britain and the United States as more powerful nations than Nippon. Therefore we must show our real strength before all our fellow-races of East Asia. We must show them an object lesson. It is not a lesson in words. It should be a lesson in facts. In other words, before we can expel the Anglo-Saxons and make them remove all their traces from East Asia, we must annihilate them.[42]

During this period when Japanese intellectuals felt they had a mission to throw off Western influence and liberate their fellow Asians, the official image of Germany and Italy was naturally a favourable one. A biography of Mussolini was a best-seller in 1928 and a suitably bowdlerized translation of Hitler's *Mein Kampf* became a best-seller in 1940. Unofficially, the Germans were disliked during the war for their arrogance, and Hitler's views on Japan and the Asians were widely known. Not even the army was particularly pro-German.[43]

The official enemies were, of course, the allied powers in the Pacific theatre, the 'diabolical Americans and British' (*kichiku Bei-Ei*).

There were government-inspired attempts to expel Western influence. But they stood little chance of success. For a start, there was no longer any clear distinction between East and West. Four generations had absorbed Western ways since the early Meiji and a new amalgam had developed which could no longer be separated into such simplistic divisions as 'Japanese' or 'Western'. Second, the Germans, Italians and Vichy French were allies of Japan. Their culture, therefore, could not be rejected out of hand. The censors were left with the impossible task not only of trying to cut out Western culture from Japan, but also of trying to distinguish those elements of it which were Anglo-Saxon. Yet the very basis of the culture, the English language, was an essential tool for governing the Greater East Asia Co-Prosperity Sphere. Despite efforts to limit the teaching of English, it remained on the curriculum. The censors exercised their negative function: there was, for example, a ban on British and US music, especially jazz. It was ineffective because it was unenforceable.[44]

There were two Western best-sellers between 1939 and 1945 apart from Hitler's *Mein Kampf* and Maurois's *Why France Fell*; both were non-political books by Hogben, popularizing mathematics and science, a reminder perhaps that it was European sciences which had breached the tough walls of Tokugawa seclusion. A reminder too that a modern state cannot function without science and technology, those powerful bridges linking East and West.

Many years after the end of the Pacific War, a well-known authority on Europe, Professor Aida Yūji, described how he became disillusioned with the Europeans and discovered the 'limits of European humanism'. At the end of the war, he had worked as a prisoner for two years in Burma and found that the English did not physically maltreat him, but regarded him as sub-human. They treated the Japanese in the same way they treated the Indians – coldly.

Each generation in turn since the Meiji had to learn in its own way the vast distance between its ideal images of the West and what it perceived as Western realities. And at regular intervals, coinciding with nationalism at home and the turning away from the West abroad, the assertion of Japanese self-confidence involved the deflation of the Western image – 'until we have seen Paris we remain in awe of Paris'.

Today more than ever Japanese tourists are flocking to the French capital – and to the USA.

8

EUROPE IS DEAD, AMERICA IS DYING

Defeat in the Pacific War led to Japan's second period of massive assimilation from the West. Only this time it was the USA which was the model, not Europe.

For about ten years, from 1945 to 1955, Japan's institutions were recast in a US mould. As a Harvard professor who visited Tokyo in 1952 wittily put it, the Occupation policy 'was an effort to make of Japan, a new Middle West – not, of course, the Middle West as it is, or in fact ever was, but as it perpetually dreams of being'.[45] An entire generation in Japan turned to the USA as the model for everything from food to fashions, from boy–girl relations to business management.

Bit by bit, economic recovery followed by rapid growth led to the gradual weaning from the US tutelage. The Nixon shocks in the early seventies and the US involvement in the Indo-China War hastened the process. The USA stood highest in Japanese esteem in 1965 according to the polls. By 1973 it was, for a short while, at its lowest since the Pacific War.

The Japanese were just beginning to be aware of their new affluence and that their economy had not only caught up with the West, but in many respects had overtaken the old models of the nineteenth century – Italy, France, England and even Germany. Herman Kahn's *The Emerging Japanese Superstate* (1970) unambiguously heralded Japan's importance. The book sold extremely well there as do most books, such as Vogel's *Japan as Number One* (1979) or Kennedy's *The Rise and Fall of The Great Powers* (1988), which suggest that Japan has finally caught up with the West. Until recently, Japanese intellectuals were not in the habit of praising their own society, which is one reason why foreign works expressing praise and recognition found a larger audience inside Japan than they did outside it.

Changing Japanese views of the world can be traced through the polls and surveys of attitudes towards foreign countries which have been taken since the fifties.

Before the Pacific War, the countries of Western Europe were probably the most popular. After the war they were surpassed by the USA. From about the mid-sixties the pattern changed again with a more diverse range of countries, usually led by Switzerland or the USA, being picked as favourites. In the eighties from time to time there were signs of a swing away from the USA and a greater interest in China and Asia.[46]

A poll which has been taken every five years since 1958 found that the only people which the Japanese have thought of as growing increasingly excellent since the mid-fifties are themselves, the Chinese and the Jews. All the others, including the Americans and the Europeans, were felt to be declining.[47]

The slower recovery in the EC and the USA from the oil shocks in the seventies; the inability of the Americans and Europeans to compete with the Japanese in business; the fact that they appeared to have lost the habit of work; Watergate and Irangate; racial tensions, high crime rates and drug problems in US cities; the feeling that Europeans and Americans were arrogant and self-indulgent; the constant 'Japan bashing'; the conviction that Japan was used as a scapegoat for Western failings, all these contributed to the belief that the USA, not to speak of Europe, was no longer a model to be emulated.

'If we persist in comparing ourselves with England, we run the risk of slipping into a comfortable feeling of self-complacency', wrote an unusually outspoken young Japanese intellectual in 1979. The same writer criticized the 'well-worn cliché' held by Japanese intellectuals 'ever since the Meiji Restoration' that 'Japan is backward and foreign countries are advanced'.

In the new mood of impatience with the West, he also referred to those Japanese intellectuals who act as mediators with the West as 'sellers of imported merchandise'. He quoted approvingly the author of a recent best-selling book about the West as saying, 'in England, it is impossible for the lower classes, and indeed for most middle-class families, to provide their children with a decent supper', but added that 'this is not only true in England, a country that is in the process of collapse and disintegration. In Europe and America generally, people must make do with very little to eat.'[48]

When the Japanese post-war generations were in their teens, the image of the USA (as opposed to US culture) was declining fast, partly because of the scenes of domestic violence there, mingled with the pictures of the war in Vietnam and the US withdrawal which appeared on the TV screens of their childhood. Also, by the end of the income-doubling decade of the sixties, the Japanese had acquired the desired symbols of the US dream, the 'three treasures' (TV, refrigerator and washing machine) and the 'three Cs' (colour TV, camera and car).

Hints of an underlying racial scorn also surfaced, as in 1986, when the prime minister of the day, Mr Nakasone, said that Japan's recent achievements were the result of its homogeneous society, whereas the mental level in the USA was lower because 'there are blacks, Puerto Ricans and Hispanics'.

'Japan bashing' by the USA during the economic frictions of the eighties understandably provoked some strong and also some unexpected reactions in Japan, one of which was a boom in books explaining US hostility as part of a world-wide Jewish conspiracy. Another was the more open expression of the conviction that Americans were racially prejudiced against the Japanese. Why, many began to ask in public, did the USA drop A-bombs on Japan but not on Germany? Why was Japan 'bashed' for its trade surplus, but not Germany?

Despite the gradual disenchantment with the USA from the seventies onwards, US influence still remains paramount on all generations, even though it may now take the form of fascination in the apparent decline of a Great Power. Polls taken in the late eighties reveal that the USA is still usually chosen as the nation with which Japan should maintain the closest relations. It after all is the guarantor of Japan's national security, and in recent years

35 to 40 per cent of Japan's exports and overseas direct investments go there.

Seventy per cent of Japanese studying abroad go to the USA
and 70 per cent of Japanese living overseas live in the Americas
(35 per cent in the USA); most of the record number of Japanese
travelling abroad at the end of the eighties went to the USA, as
did honeymoon couples; at the same time more Americans
visited Japan than from any other country. Most best-sellers
were still US and Japanese books about economic and trade
frictions concentrated almost entirely on the frictions with the
USA.

The USA may be declining, but it is still in many respects
'number one'. The same cannot be said of Europe, whose
countries are regarded as a source of high culture, rather like a
good museum. I first realized this as a research student in the
USA in the sixties, when Japanese friends showed me their
European vacation photographs. Again and again I found myself
confronting photos of the grave of Balzac, Shakespeare's tomb
or Goethe's birthplace. So, much later, when I read memoirs and
travel accounts of Japanese visitors to Europe, I was well prepared for the fact that the first place they went to was the
Panthéon or Westminster Abbey, there to gaze at the busts of
long-dead European philosophers and poets.

'I think that the cause of the decline of West Europe is to be
found in Europe itself,' said a senior official of the Ministry of
International Trade and Industry in a characteristically frank
interview (not intended for foreign consumption). 'They do not
like to think so [laughter] . . . Europe woke up in the morning to
find that the Rising-Sun flag had been raised overnight in the area
which it regards as its own traditional sphere of influence . . . its
own "Greater Europe Co-Prosperity Sphere".' Later in the same
interview he expressed a commonly-held view of Japan's trade
problems with Europe: 'Japan's competitive power is over-
whelmingly great. If we compare it to a golf match, Japan's
handicap is single while that of Europe is 25 or 26.' What
handicap would he have granted the Americans?[49]

Today Europe is a considerable attraction for Japanese tourists and honeymoon couples after the closer and more popular destinations such as Hawaii, the mainland USA, South Korea, Taiwan, Hong Kong, and Australia. And who can be in the least bit surprised? For Europe offers to the Japanese visitor those jewels of the tourist trade – cultural monuments, good shopping and exotic sex; a combination of high culture, *haute couture* and low life – all at reasonable prices. But in other respects such as economic development, knowledge or the will to work, since the seventies only Switzerland, Sweden and Germany have been regarded from time to time as still having something of interest to Japan.

Switzerland has been seen as the home of idealized liberty since the Meiji period. Today it is felt to be a model of neutrality as well as clean, neat and, although small, rich – all qualities held in high regard in Japan. Its popularity also owes much to the mountains. Sweden, too, has made a success of neutrality and is small and rich; in addition, it is esteemed for its women and its welfare state.

Germany has been admired ever since the formidable impression of strength as a newcomer which it made on Japan, following the victory of Prussia over France in 1870. Germany, too, was a model and inspiration for three key professions in the modernization process: the army, medicine and the law, as well as two civilized pastimes: classical music and academic philosophy. Moreover, since the Pacific War, Germany, like Japan, has had to make its way quietly in the world. Its economic success, its deft use of the 'umbrella' of the EC and its ability to handle the demands of Washington are highly regarded in Tokyo.

In admiring all three countries, the Japanese are no doubt unconsciously gratified by identifying qualities which they would wish to associate with themselves. There is, in other words, an element of self-identification, particularly in the case of Germany, whose experiences both as a newcomer in the nineteenth century, and as one of the defeated powers after the Pacific War, have been not dissimilar to Japan's.[50]

When it comes to the European Community, information about the founding fathers is taught in Japanese schools, but general awareness of the EC is slight. Even for those who do know what it is, there remains the difficulty of accurately assessing the balance between the powers of the EC as such and the sovereignty of each member state, a balance which is continually shifting and which inevitably affects the EC's efforts to coordinate at the supranational level the particular interests of each member country.

Since the EC began to develop a more coherent policy towards Japan in the eighties, and especially since it began to get its own house in order with the settlement of budget disputes and the goal of establishing a single unified market by 1992, the Japanese have attached more weight to it.

The EC remains Japan's third most important export market after the USA and the Asian NICs. The only best-seller about Europe published in Japan since 1963 consists of anecdotes relating the quaint customs in Europe and how they affect the Japanese 'business warriors' stationed there. If the book had a serious purpose, it was to assist its readers in understanding the difficulties they might encounter in dealing with the natives.[51]

Japanese images of Europeans are as stereotyped as European images of Japanese. But they are on the whole formed from positive stereotypes. A survey conducted in the mid-eighties showed that the Japanese still associated the qualities of elegance, individualism, sociability and pride with the French. France evokes *èlan*, *joie-de-vivre* and *chic* or modishness (*haikara* in Japanese meaning 'high-collared'); it remains the land of gastronomy, the Eiffel Tower, and *haute couture*. As this poll was conducted, Japanese companies and wealthy individuals had just begun a world-buying spree using the strong yen. It goes without saying that in France they bought an exclusive *coiffeur*, vineyards, châteaux, restaurants, and impressionist paintings. There were fears they would start buying up some of the great names in French fashion and that eventually, for example, Shiseido might replace Chanel. In the nineteenth century the Japanese went to France to study oil painting, and wine and silk making. As a French museum curator said in 1988, 'At that time, the Japanese sought to learn from the best. Now that they are far wealthier, they seem to want to buy the best.'[52]

Various other similar 'national character' stereotypes are applied to the Europeans. The Germans, for example are popularly regarded as prudent, earnest, efficient, diligent, thrifty and orderly people who eat potatoes and sausages and drink beer. Such formulations are more often than not identical to the view about Europeans and Americans held by themselves. I could find nothing specifically Japanese in them. One such witticism is credited to the late Professor Ryū Shintarō, as a young man an ideologist of the Greater East Asia Co-Prosperity Sphere: 'Germans consider then run; Italians run without reflection; the British run while thinking . . .' and he added, in line with the common view of the Japanese as emotional, 'Japanese run, then think'.

The post-war best-sellers list is another useful index, not only of popular interests and reading habits, but also of the sort of things found attractive about Europe and particularly the USA by Japanese readers.

The first striking thing about this list is the large number of translated foreign books or books about foreign countries. There were only twelve years between 1946 and 1989 when there were no such books on the list and in many years there were several. Second, there are far more non-fiction titles on the list than fiction reflecting the strong self-improvement motivation of the Japanese book-buying public. A recent example would be the 1987 best-seller by Ward which is fully in the tradition of Samuel Smiles (the author recommends Bartlett's *Familiar Quotations* (1862) as first on a reading list for his offspring). Next is the perhaps obvious point that foreign books on the Japanese best-seller list, just as they had been in the 1880s have been books which were also best-sellers in the USA and Europe. French and other European books appeared most frequently on the list in the forties and early fifties during the US Occupation. Thereafter they were replaced by US and British international best-sellers.

Those books on the list which were not international best-sellers were either books about Japan or about learning the English language. The appearance of Clavell's *Shōgun* (1975) in the number eight slot in 1980 shows the Japanese interest in their own history or society seen through a foreigner's eyes; in this case the desire to buy the book of the video (the NHK–NBC TV

The West on the Japanese Best-sellers List
(1946–89)

Year	Ranking (out of ten)	Author	Title
1946	5	Sartre	La Nausée
	6	Van de Velde	Le Mariage Parfait
	7	Gide	Intervues Imaginaires
	8	Remarque	Arc de Triomphe
1947	3	Remarque	Arc de Triomphe
	7	Eva Curie	Life of Madame Curie
	9	Van de Velde	Le Mariage Parfait
1948	4	Dostoevsky	Crime and Punishment
	5	Remarque	Arc de Triomphe
1949	2	Mitchell	Gone with the Wind
1950	3	Mitchell	Gone with the Wind
	5	Lawrence	Lady Chatterley's Lover
	6	Mailer	The Naked and the Dead
1952	3	Gain	Japan Diary
	10	Rolland	Jean Christophe, 1
1953	1	Anne Frank	Diary of a Young Girl
	2	Simone de Beauvoir	The Second Sex, 3
	5	Simone de Beauvoir	The Second Sex, 1
	10	Rolland	Jean Christophe, 3
1954	2	Mrs Rosenberg	Love Overtakes Death
1956	7	Viktor Frankl	Ein Psycholog erlebt das Konzentrationslager
1957	9	Lobsang Rampa	The Third Eye
1958	8		World Literature for Young Girls
1959	4	Pasternak	Doctor Zhivago
1961	1	Iwata	How to Strengthen Your English
	2	Oda	Let's Look at Whatever Comes Along
1962	2	Joy Adamson	Born Free
	7	Watanabe	How to Learn Foreign Languages
	8	Joy Adamson	Forever Free
1963	5	Dostoevsky	Crime and Punishment
	7	Joy Adamson	My Elsa
1966	7	Tolstoy	War and Peace
1967	7	De Bono	New Thinking – the Use of Lateral Thinking in the Generation of New Ideas
	10	Drucker	The Age of Discontinuity
1971	1	Ben-Dasan	The Japanese and the Jews
	3	Segal	Love Story
1974	1	Bach	Jonathan Livingstone Seagull
	2	Goto	Prophecies of Nostradamus
	9	Blatty	Exorcist
1975	3	Harold	Sight without Glasses

	5	Solzhenitsyn	Gulag Archipelago
	6	Perliz	The Bermuda Triangle
	8	Taylor	Black Holes: The End of the Universe
1976	10	Fukada	New Conditions in the West
1977	2	Haley	Roots
1978	2	Galbraith	The Age of Uncertainty
1979	5	Vogel	Japan as Number One
	8	McWhirter	The Guinness Book of Records
1980	5	Forsyth	Devil's Alternative
	8	Clavell	Shōgun
1981	7	Goto	Nostradamus, 3
	10	Sagan	Cosmos
1983	9	Frank	Dr Frank's No Aging Diet
1984	7	Forsyth	The Fourth Protocol
1985	3	Iacocca	Iacocca
1986	9	Isomura	Warning from America
1987	2	Ward	Letters of a Businessman to his Son
	8	Morita	Made in Japan
1988	6	Kennedy	The Rise and Fall of the Great Powers
1989	5	Hawking	A Brief History of Time

Source: *Publisher's Annual* (*Shuppan nenkan*), Tokyo, 1989.

mini-series was released in 1980) which had sparked something of a cult in America. It could also be compared with the numerous Japanese long-selling books about Tokugawa Ieyasu, the first Shōgun, which eventually led in 1983 to an NHK series on his life in fifty instalments which was extremely popular, especially among older generations. The extraordinary fascination with Nostradamus as interpreted by Goto is no doubt due to the popularity of fortune-telling and the strong interest in defining Japan's future place in the world which goes hand in hand with a passion for futurology.

The European best-sellers in Japan just after the war continued pre-war trends interrupted by the censor. The titles also reflect the mood of the day. The sense of desolation, isolation and disorientation of Sartre's *La Nausée* as well as Dostoevsky's *Crime and Punishment* made them best-sellers in Europe at this time too. For students in particular there was an obvious element of self-identification. French books are much in evidence, reflecting the old association of France and culture. Sex is also there; it is perhaps not surprising in those years of the post-war baby boom to find a French sex manual (Van de Velde) two years running as a best-seller. And *Lady Chatterley's Lover* or *The Second Sex* also presumably owed their popularity to the erotic image of Europe. Remarque's *Arc de Triomphe*, the only foreign book to appear in the top ten for three years running, is a sentimental story with a timely theme of international love overcoming national hostilities. Remarque, like Romain Rolland, was popular in Japan at this time because of his opposition to war. The film version of *Arc de Triomphe* (1948), starring Ingrid Bergman and Charles Boyer, was released in Japan in the same year which perhaps contributed to its extraordinary success, although in those far-off days it was usually the film which followed the best-seller and not vice versa.

To sum up, Europe's image as a source of high culture was still strong in the post-war years. The erotic image was very much in evidence, but Europe as a source of practical knowledge, so clearly reflected in the translated titles of earlier ages, including best-sellers, is hardly represented at all.

In the sixties and seventies the post-war generation turned to the USA and most best-sellers were now US. These same books were also best-sellers in the USA and Europe. Either they were about US management methods or they reflected the global, homogenized, youth culture which emerged in the sixties. Largely US, coinciding with the spread of hamburger and coke, wash-and-wear pants and jeans, rock, pop and disco-sound, it found its most characteristic and influential expression in movies, television, cassette and video tapes.

Most of the foreign books on the best-sellers list of the last twenty years owed their popularity to the exposure which they gained as films either in the cinema or on television. Thus Tolstoy's panoramic *War and Peace* replaced Dostoevsky's introspective *Crime and Punishment* as a best-seller, not only because it suited the more brash mood of the day, but also because it was a box-office success. It hit the best-sellers list in the same year as the release in Japan of Bondarchuk's spectacular. The film helped sell the book. This applies as well to Haley's *Roots* as to Galbraith's *Age of Uncertainty*, to Segal's *Love Story*, to

Clavell's *Shōgun* or to Sagan's *Cosmos*, all of which gained or consolidated their best-seller status thanks to television. Europe, with its image of a high or élite culture, was usually not in this league.

In line with the view of Europe as a historic source of high culture, European goods are considered especially modish (*haikara*) and they are still referred to by the old phrase, 'goods which come by ship' (*hakurai hin*). The phrase is applied to luxury goods. It was first used of the goods imported by the Dutch and Chinese during the Edo period. Because the Japanese regard Europe as a source of high culture, and by implication a source of expensive luxury goods, roughly 40 per cent of European sales in Japan are characterized by small-volume turnover of consumer goods at exceedingly high prices. It is almost as if European imports were regarded as a sort of expensive garnish to complement the basic fare of Japanese industrial products.

The delight in Western consumer goods as status symbols began somewhat indiscriminately in the Meiji period, as the following satirical comments on a 'beefeater' or Westernizer of those days illustrates:

His hair, not having been cut some hundred days, is long and flowing – in the foreign style. Naturally enough, he uses the scent called Eau de Cologne to give a sheen to his hair. He wears a padded silken kimono beneath which a calico undergarment is visible. By his side is his Western style umbrella covered in Gingham.[53]

The practice continued in the thirties:

It is not at all odd to see a Japanese in the native costume wearing a woolen undershirt made of material brought from Australia and an informal *hakama* made of serge imported from Bradford, covering himself meanwhile with an Inverness made of cloth produced in America. He is also likely to have a wristwatch made in Switzerland, a snakewood cane from the South Seas and a package of Turkish cigarettes accompanied by an American lighter. If it is cold he may be protecting his neck with a scarf bearing the mark of a well-known Parisian haberdasher and his hands with a pair of gloves of Italian make.[54]

Faced with complaints of the unwillingness of Japan to import from Europe, it is common for Japanese politicians and businessmen to counter by offering you a glass of 'Old Parr' Scotch whisky and by pointing to their Savile Row suit (*sebirō*, in Japanese), their Cardin neck tie, their Mont Blanc fountain pen and their Gucci loafers as demonstration of their contributions to closing the trade gap.

9

THE DAWNING OF A NEW AGE IN JAPAN

The dawning of a new age in Japan began in the seventies. It was marked by the search for a new identity at home, balanced by the first tentative budding of a new self-confidence abroad. This dual process was accelerated by a series of external 'shocks' (*shoku*) to which Japan responded with resilience. Eventually it emerged from the mid-eighties onwards in an entirely new and increasingly self-confident role as the world's number-one creditor nation. Throughout this period of 'internationalization' the image of the USA as the model and guide for Japan was eroded.

By the early seventies, the long-term objective of catching up with and surpassing the West had largely been achieved, at least in economic terms. Then, just as this achievement was registering, there was a hiatus; the goal of economic growth itself was questioned and the Japanese began to see themselves as 'economic animals' pursuing 'Gross National Pollution'.

The oil shock of 1973 rapidly put an end to this self-questioning, as Japan, like the rest of the industrialized world, rushed to cope with stagflation at home and declining demand for its exports abroad. It got over these difficulties faster than any other major economy, including the USA. Again, at the time of the second oil shock in 1979–80, it reacted with remarkable resilience. Both the comparatively quick recovery from the first oil shock and the swift adjustment to the second contributed to the new self-confidence. The morale-boosting effects of these recoveries may be compared to the two yen shocks (1971 and 1985), massive revaluations which instead of weakening Japan's competitiveness only served to enhance it.

These were also years when the second period of assimilation from the West had long since ended and the cycle, as so often in the past, had shifted to an internal search to redefine 'Japanese-ness', a turning back to Japanese roots. The search took many forms. There was a boom in books about the Japanese, sparked off in 1971 by a best-seller comparing the Japanese to the Jews – another brilliant, and so it was thought at the time, half-recognized people. The polls began to register signs of a swing back towards such traditional 'Japanese' values as filial piety (oyakōko); gratitude, or repayment of kindness (ongaeshi); living in harmony with nature, and a growing elevation of conformism at the expense of individual freedoms.[55]

By the late eighties, 65 per cent of the Japanese population was born after the Pacific War. The first events which made an impression on the baby-boom generation were the signs of Japan's post-war successes – the Tokyo Olympics, the opening of the 'bullet train', the joining of the OECD (1964), Expo '70, and a flood of high-quality consumer goods, all made in Japan.

The number-one pop song in the summer of 1979, Sada Masashi's 'Your Husband and Master Proclaims' provides a glimpse into the thoughts of the first post-war generation. Its lyrics included such 'traditional' injunctions as, 'before you become my bride, hear this, you will not go to bed before I do, you will not get up after I do; cook nothing but good meals and always look pretty, and keep quiet and follow behind me'. The song stirred up something of a controversy, but the popular press reported a deluge of letters in support of it! A few years in later in 1982 Kenji Suzuki, the author of the number one best-selling book in Japan, Advice on Being Considerate, insisted that a woman's place was in the home as a dutiful mother and loving wife. 'When a husband comes home from work, his wife should prepare clothes for him to change, saying, "Hello, welcome home, you must be very tired".'

In 1983, as we saw in the previous chapter, there was a popular NHK series, in fifty instalments, on the life of the first Shōgun which was preceded and accompanied by numerous long-selling books about the heroes of the unification of Japan. A boom which the business magazines latched on to by researching for their readers the strategic mind sets of the feudal lords as models for the modern manager. A form of flattery which the hard-pressed salarymen found diverting.

There were plenty of other novels, comics and TV series which mirrored the same search for Japanese values other than the pursuit of the good life as defined by consumerism. One was the popular TV series which followed the fictional life of hardships lived by a woman called Ōshin, who came to stand for 'persever-ance in the face of hardship'. Another example is Japan's most widely read comic magazine for teenagers, *Shōnen Jump*, which has a weekly print-run of five million copies. Its success is attributed to its founding formula: Friendship, Effort and Success (against all odds). The 'traditional' Japanese values of Samuel Smiles.

Light years from *Shōnen Jump* and giving a glimpse into the alternative values of those born after the Pacific War, or at any rate the second post-war generation (born in the sixties), is the novel *Somewhat Like Crystal*, which sold over a million copies in 1981. For its author, Tanaka Yasuoka, a 24-year-old university student at the time, the 'crystal' or 'cool' generation is rich, apolitical and drifts with no particular effort or interest from one pleasurable experience to the next. The affluent members of the 'crystal generation' express their individuality by the famous label clothes they wear and the brand-name goods they buy (in a manner not dissimilar to the display of big-name Western paint-ings by the captains of Japanese industry). According to the government's 1986 *White Paper on Youth*, they place importance on being themselves and feel strongly that they are nothing more than ordinary people. Much less ambitious than those born before the war who rebuilt Japan after it, they are even less ambitious than the first post-war generation of baby-boomers. They are called 'new human beings' (*shinjinrui*).

Although the personal-savings rate is down and visible con-sumption is up; although juvenile crime is up and, far worse, juvenile anomie is spreading, I doubt whether the values of the 'crystal generation' are anything more than the expression of a temporary pose in a segment of the newly rich young. Such values are not about to become the mainstream, replacing frugality and hard work. But the number of people with plenty of money and plenty of free time, if they want to take it, has certainly increased rapidly.

The occasional evocation of Japanese roots, the fascination with historical characters such as the first Shōgun, or the various retro-booms which sweep across popular culture, do not represent the beginnings of a shift towards nationalism. For one thing, even if the younger generation should want to make a sharp dividing line between 'traditional' and 'modern' or between 'Japanese' and 'Western' they would find it a difficult task. The huge gap between the villages (seat of traditional Japanese values) and the cities (seat of modern Western values), which formed the social basis of militant nationalism in the thirties, no longer exists today. Eighty-five per cent of the population is urban and 'modern'.[56] Young people today have a more homogenized culture than that of any previous generation and they are accustomed to choosing from many sources, including Japanese tradition, which is itself, just as in other countries, constantly and ahistorically in the process of being redefined.

Externally there have been strong pressures on Japan to reduce its dependence on the USA and stand on its own feet. The post-war period drew to a close in the late sixties and early seventies amid uncertainties in the international, political and economic environment dramatized by the 'Nixon shocks', by the President's surprise visit to China, and by the US withdrawal from Vietnam which seemed to mark the beginning of a larger US pullout from Asia. These were also the years which saw the extension of Soviet power all over the globe including in the Pacific and around Japan, suggesting the termination of a clear US military supremacy.

The most important distinguishing characteristic of the new age is that Japan's role is now at centre stage.

From 1848 to 1914 Great Britain was the leading creditor nation; the United States assumed that role for the next seventy years. In 1985, Japan took over and is today the world's major financial power. It is the largest creditor and the largest net investor in the world. Its financial institutions: the banks, stock markets, brokerage houses, and insurance companies, have become the largest and its GNP per capita has overtaken that of the USA.[57]

History is filled with examples of the periphery overtaking the centre, of the latecomer catching up, what Thorstein Veblen called the 'advantage of coming late'. Rome overtook Greece; Holland overtook Spain; Britain overtook Holland; the USA overtook Britain; Japan overtook China. And now, Japan overtakes the USA? This scenario is not without its proponents in Tokyo but two words of caution are in order.

For the moment Japan's position is not the same as that of either Great Britain or the USA when they were the world's leading creditor nations. Both these were not only the wealthiest, but also the most powerful, countries in political and military terms. They successfully projected their national cultures, including high cultures, as models for the rest of the world. In their day they wrote the scripts which others were eager to act out.

There is a second difference. At that time the world's centre of power was much more concentrated; first in Western Europe, and then across the Atlantic to include the USA. Today the situation has changed completely. We live in a multipolar world economy and a multipolar geopolitical system dominated by two superpowers. Japan has become the largest financial power and one of the three epicentres of the world economy. Its share of world product will be at most 15 per cent in the year 2000, far less than the shares held by both Great Britain and the United States at the height of their power. Its defence budget is the third largest in the world. Elements of Japanese culture have found niches in world culture and its consumer goods and wealth are much admired, but Japan does not yet set the tone for a new world culture.

One advantage which the latecomer at the periphery has over the centre is that it can take over and build on the experience of those at the centre. In the early eighteenth century, Defoe described the genius of the British as being 'better to improve than to invent'. The rise of America in the nineteenth century is filled with such 'adaptations' from Europe euphemistically known as 'Yanquee inventiveness'. Likewise Japan, until recently, was often regarded as better at imitating than innovating. But having caught up with and overtaken the centre, the roles are reversed and the periphery itself becomes a centre. It is no longer possible to turn automatically to others as a model. Japan is now a model for others. This is going to have profound implications for Japan and for the world.

In the nineteenth century, Japan's opening to the West was preceded and accompanied by a turning away from China. In the twentieth century, the same happened to Europe which was relegated to a cultural limbo reserved for models of a previous age – tucked away in an aura of 'high-class' nostalgia. The same process is now under way as the USA begins to be downgraded in Japanese eyes.

How will Japan wish to develop its relations with these previous models? More and more it will take the initiative. As the former foreign minister and economist, Dr Okita Saburō, put it in 1987, 'It is unrealistic for the Euro-American side to try to dictate to Japan any more.'[58]

Much depends with what success Japan will turn its financial power into political clout on the world stage. The biggest uncertainty is the political system which, after forty years of stability, is showing severe signs of strain. The long-ruling Liberal Democratic Party (LDP) was rocked in 1988–9 by the Recruit Cosmos scandal, the worst involving 'money politics' since the Pacific War. Much of the traditional support for the LDP, coming from the farm lobby, the construction industry and the shopkeepers, was temporarily eroded by the measures taken by the Party to dismantle agricultural protection, to open construction tenders to foreign bidding and to simplify the retail distribution system. Aggravation caused by the introduction of a universally unpopular consumption tax and resentment at the high urban land and house prices compounded the LDP's problems, and it suffered a stunning election defeat in the summer of 1989. Within three months there were as many prime ministers; the second in the series was forced to resign in part because of the first ever public criticisms of a prime minister's alleged womanizing. A month later the chief cabinet secretary resigned for the same reason.

The very roots of the old male-dominated, corrupt LDP-style factionalism may have been challenged. But in the elections of Spring 1990 most of the scandal-tainted LDP candidates were safely returned to their seats and the prospects for basic change in the political system faded. As a result, government-led reform of economic structures, as well as Japan's role on the world stage, will have to wait a little longer in the wings.[59]

Future historians will be tempted to draw a dividing line at the death of the Showa emperor in 1989 and the beginning of the Heisei-period. Traditionally, such dynastic changes have been used as convenient demarcation points between historic periods, but fundamental new departures will probably not be taken until the generation whose most important political experience was defeat in the Pacific War has stepped down, either as the result of political scandal or, more likely, in the course of generational change. That will happen towards the turn of the century.

PART III

JAPAN AS SEEN BY THE WEST

10

FIRST IMPRESSIONS

Chipangu is an island towards the East in the high seas, 1,500 miles distant from the Continent; and a very great island it is. The people are white, civilized and well-favoured.

Marco Polo, 1307

China played an important role in the formation of the Western world view. Not so Japan. Or not until much later. In the eighteenth century, the discovery that China had a recorded past more ancient than the biblical chronology led to the fundamental revision of the European concept of history and to the birth of cultural relativism. The pages of Voltaire, Montesquieu, Leibniz and Gibbon are riddled with references to China – but contain virtually nothing on Japan. While the *philosophes* were reshaping the European mind using China as one of their tools, Japan was closed to the outside world, voluntarily shut in upon itself.

In the nineteenth century Europeans and Americans continued their exploration of many of the countries of Asia in search of new markets, new knowledge and new peoples to proselytize. In the process of trading and, in some cases, conquering, settling, administering, and converting these peoples, there developed a practical necessity to learn about them. In this way, interest groups gradually formed which either had direct experience to draw on, or were informed by those who had worked in and studied there. Japan was neither colonized nor converted so there was no such necessity to learn about it.

There is another reason why Europeans and Americans ignored Japan; towards the end of the nineteenth and in the early twentieth century they were convinced that after India, China presented a boundless market for manufactured goods. Japan was felt to be a less promising market because it was already beginning to build up a domestic industry of its own, capable of competing with the West. Major commercial efforts, therefore, were directed towards China rather than Japan.

In the late nineteenth century when the West did finally 'discover' Japan, it was at a period when Europe and the USA were far more powerful than Japan. Westerners, whether business men or missionaries, officials or scholars, felt themselves superior to 'Orientals' or 'Asiatics'. Such prejudices have been slow to change. So, feeling no urgent need to learn about Japan, Europeans and Americans clung to romantic images of 'Chipangu' – an Oriental fantasy land.

Small wonder that they constantly underestimated Japan. When it began catching the attention of the West by the defeat of China in 1895, or by the victories over Russia in 1904 and 1905, the West was completely taken by surprise: having thought Japan fragile as a fan they now found it hard as an ironclad. Reeling from the shock, they quickly decided that they had been cheated, and had been given a false impression. Negative images were evoked, and the ones most readily available were the immemorial images of the Orient. So Japan was seen as a 'Yellow Peril', an image which owed more to past fears of Attila or Genghis Khan or Tamerlane, rather than to any comprehension of the policies of the Meiji oligarchs.

Later, the same pattern was to be repeated and for the same reasons. Western attitudes of superiority persisted with the same inability to learn about or to form accurate images of Japan. Americans were completely taken by surprise by the Japanese attack on Pearl Harbor and the Europeans by the fall of their colonies in Southeast Asia in 1941 and 1942, and again by Japan's rapid economic recovery after the war and successful export drive to the European and US markets starting from the late fifties.

Each time the West was caught by surprise the shock was blamed on the Japanese for being unpredictable; each time that negative reaction was tinged with vague fears of the Orient.

It is to the Orient then that we must turn to begin our inquiry into the formation of European and US images of Japan.

Long before the conquest of the New World, the slave trade or the colonization of Asia and Africa, the Orient was the first meeting place of the West with non-Western peoples, the primary reference for the Other. For millennia it has been an object of wonder and fear in the Occident; its image both powerful and contradictory. It was the source of light and hence wisdom, but also filled with cruelty and torture. Because East is opposite of West, the East was often made the embodiment of values diametrically opposed to those in the West. If the Greeks were democratic and civilized, the Persians were despotic and barbarous; if the Occident was dynamic, then the Orient was stagnant. If the West was materialistic, the East was spiritual.

Later it became common to regard 'Orientals' or 'Asiatics' as inferior, a racist reflex to justify privilege and aggression. The literature is filled with descriptions of 'the Orientals' as subhumans, or animals or ants. In the twentieth century, when industrialism came to Asia, this habit continued and 'Asiatics' were often referred to as machines or robots, divested of human attributes.

The phrases, 'the Orient' and 'Orientals', were applied indiscriminately to many countries and peoples, being gradually extended to cover Persia, Arabia, India, China, Mongolia and, last, Japan. As contacts were made with each new country, past images were simply transferred to them. So China was squeezed into a strait-jacket of images which had begun to grow with Greek perceptions of ancient Persia; Japan is still often palmed off with these cast-off clothes of the European imagination. One consequence of this was that Japan was often confused with China. Sometimes the two were lumped together as a 'Yellow Peril', or when one was praised the other was blamed and vice versa. Whichever way, as we shall see in the following chapters, it has seemed impossible to distinguish between the two and at the same time to form a balanced judgement of both.

It would be natural to suppose that as Europeans and Americans came into direct contact with all the countries of the

Orient, gradually pushing the frontiers of their knowledge further east, and the jumbo-jet tourism and instant communications of our own day had made once-distant countries almost as close as our immediate neighbours, catch-all phrases such as 'Asiatic', 'the Orient' or 'the East' and all the stereotypes associated with them would have faded into disuse. But it has not happened that way. We may live in a world of annihilated distance but it still remains a world of inherited misperceptions. Certainly there is much specialized knowledge available about individual Oriental countries, but the old myths live on as potent as ever, possibly because the geographic extent of 'the Orient' has grown so huge that the meaning of the word has become blurred.[1]

In many ways the images of Japan in the West have been the most extreme embodiment of the myths of the Orient. Japan is in the furthest East, indeed, in the earliest European literature it was actually thought to be the Antipodes. Europeans and Americans never tired of writing that in Japan everything was antipodal, topsy-turvy and back to front; an absurd, Alice-in-Wonderland world, not worth taking seriously. Thus, the fundamental image of Japan in the West was of a country of extreme and paradoxical contrasts. The *locus classicus* of this view was expressed by an Italian Jesuit missionary, Alessandro Valignano, in 1583:

They also have rites and ceremonies so different from those of all the other nations that it seems they deliberately try to be unlike any other people. The things which they do in this respect are beyond imagining and it may truly be said that Japan is a world the reverse of Europe; everything is so different and opposite that they are like us in practically nothing. So great is the difference . . . that it can be neither desired nor understood.[2]

Another Jesuit, Luis Frois, spelled out what some of those contrasts were:

Most people in Europe grow tall and have good figures; the Japanese are mostly smaller than we are in body and stature.

The women in Europe do not go out of the house without their husbands' permission; Japanese women are free to go wherever they please without the husband knowing about it.

With us it is not very common that women can write; the noble ladies of Japan consider it a humiliation not to be able to write.

Our children first learn to read and then to write; Japanese children first begin to write and thereafter to read.

People in Europe love baked and boiled fish; the Japanese much prefer it raw.[3]

Almost exactly three centuries later the first British minister in Tokyo, Sir Rutherford Alcock, could go no further than adopt the same theme, adding a new note of contempt:

Japan is essentially a country of paradoxes and anomalies, where all, even familiar things, put on new faces, and are curiously reversed. Except that they do not walk on their heads instead of their feet, there are few things in which they do not seem, by some occult law, to have been impelled in a perfectly opposite direction and a reversed order. They write from top to bottom, from right to left, in perpendicular instead of horizontal lines, and their books begin where ours end, thus furnishing good examples of the curious perfection this rule of contraries has attained. Their locks, though imitated from Europe, are all made to lock by turning the key from left to right. The course of all sublunary things appears reversed. Their day is for the most part our night, and this principle of antagonism crops up in the most unexpected and bizarre way in all their moral being, customs, and habits . . . and, finally, the utter confusion of sexes in the public bathhouses, making that correct which we in the West deem so shocking and improper, I leave as I find it – a problem to solve.[4]

Twenty-five years later, the Boston astronomer Percival Lowell observed that 'the boyish belief that on the other side of our globe all things are of necessity upside down is startlingly brought back to the man when he first sets foot at Yokohama . . . Intellectually, at least, their attitude sets gravity at defiance. For to the mind's eye their world is one huge, comical antithesis of our own'.[5]

Lowell at least had the excuse that he was writing of a country virtually unknown in the West. But eighty years later, in 1979, a Tokyo-based foreign correspondent could still write: 'An outside observer may find more than a touch of the unreal in the reality that is Japan. What at first appears to be straightforward at a second glance quickly takes on aspects of the absurd'.[6]

The leading western student of the Japanese language in the late nineteenth century and a sympathetic commentator on the country, Basil Hall Chamberlain, wrote an amusing introductory book entitled *Things Japanese* (which is still in print and on sale in Japan). In it he included a special section on 'Topsy-turvydom'. It is largely based on Alcock, but he adds a number of further examples: 'On leaving an inn, you fee not the waiter, but the proprietor . . . They carry babies, not in their arms, but on their backs . . . Politeness prompts them to remove, not their headgear, but their footgear . . . Strangest of all, after a bath the Japanese dry themselves with a damp towel!'[7]

Lafcadio Hearn, the most influential interpreter of Japan to the West from about 1890 to 1920, and a good friend of Chamberlain's, wrote in 1904, having lived fourteen years in the country:

Further acquaintance with this fantastic world will in no wise diminish the sense of strangeness evoked by the first vision of it. You will soon observe that even the physical actions of the people are unfamiliar – that their work is done in ways the opposite of Western ways. Tools are of surprising shapes, and are handled after surprising methods: the blacksmith squats at his anvil . . . ; the carpenter pulls, instead of pushing, his extraordinary plane and saw. Always the left is the right side, and the right side the wrong; and keys must be turned, to open or close a lock, in what we are accustomed to think the wrong direction.[8]

The second half of the nineteenth century was the first period in which Europeans and Americans of all sorts came into sustained contact with Japan. As with people, so with cultures – first impressions are all important. Those few who wrote intelligently about Japan knew each other and shared the same views. They often made the same points, even using the same examples. Constant repetition gave their views a wide currency. So frequently were 'things Japanese' presented as antipodally contrary to those in the West at this time of opening relations that that is how they became embedded in the European and American mind. It is now almost axiomatic that a writer or journalist, or any other pundit on Japan, will begin his remarks by reassuring his audience that Japan is indeed an 'upside-down land' where all is diametrically the opposite of what he is used to back home.

'Most people who go to Japan from Europe or America', pontificated the *Economist* in 1977, 'recognize at once that Japanese society is strikingly different from what they are accustomed to in the West. The explanation of this difference seems to be that Japanese society is organized "vertically", while Western society is organized "horizontally".' Or listen to an academic authority writing in 1983, 'Japan is a complex industrial society . . . based on premises fundamentally different from our own . . . Japan is different'.[9] The jargon is contemporary-scientific, but the basic thought dates back to the nineteenth century and beyond that to the very first Western contacts with Japan in the sixteenth century.

There is nothing unusual in catching the reader's interest by saying that everything in the distant land about to be described is quite different from what he has experienced before. The technique has been used by story-tellers the world over since time immemorial. But it is nothing more than a device – the trouble is that if taken too literally, it fastens the attention on the quaint and the arbitrary, for the point of departure is not the land being described, but those features of it most different from what the writer and his audience are used to at home. The approach, in other words, is subjective; even if some of the examples chosen as contrasts are correct, they may not be significant in terms of the objective realities of the country being described. In surveying an uncharted land, both the lowlands and the highlands have to be taken equally into account, and only then can the similarities and differences with one's own country be traced.

So insistently has the exotic, upside-down image of Japan been repeated, that today, when an American or European visitor arrives in Tokyo or Osaka, try as he will to conceal it, there is often a sense of disappointment: here is no land of Oriental exotica; on the contrary the urban sprawl is all too familiar. In search of the fantasy land which past generations have led him to expect, such a visitor will hurry off to Kyoto and there find with relief that in its Buddhist temples and Zen gardens he has at last been able to find something 'Oriental'. His Japanese hosts understand Western expectations so they will arrange trips to shrines and, in the evenings, dinners with bilingual geishas.

Thanks to these ministrations, the visitor will be able to leave with his expectations intact. On his return, with all the enthusiasm of someone who has made a discovery, he will tell you that Japan is a country of extreme contrasts: between the silence of the Zen rock garden and the bustle of Tokyo's streets; between the bowing, smiling geisha and the sharp-elbowed business commuter; between the neat rice-paddies and the chaotic urban alleys.

Japan was not alone in being painted as a country of antipodal contrasts – at the opposite extreme to the West and filled with extreme contrasts within itself. The same happened to most of the other countries in the Orient as well. Nor was the picture limited to quaint details of everyday life. At one time or another the Orient was felt to contain all that the West most lacked as well as everything it most feared. A mysterious region of wish fulfilment and guilt projection. It is often difficult, therefore, to tell whether an image of Japan has simply been derived from images of the Orient in general rather than from direct contact with Japan itself.

11

EARLY CONTACTS

. . . do not forget these islands where Nature has chosen to show her
greatest wonders. This, that you can only half distinguish where it lies far
out to sea, facing China – it is from China it is to be sought – is Japan,
famous for its fine silver and soon to be famous too through the
spreading of Christianity among its people.

Camoens, The Lusiads, 1572, Canto X, Line 131

Between 1549 and 1639, a small number of Jesuit missionaries,
mainly Portuguese, attempted to convert the Japanese. The
reports of their activities and the country and people they found
introduced the learned reading public of the day in Europe to
Japan. The picture they painted was a favourable one. St Francis
Xavier (1506–52), the founder of the Jesuit mission in Japan,
wrote, 'these people are a delight to my soul'.

The Jesuits recognized that in certain respects the Japanese
were more advanced than the Europeans, for example, in education and in polite manners. 'They are very capable and intelligent', recorded Xavier's successor Valignano, in the mid
sixteenth century, 'and the children are quick to grasp our lessons
and instructions. They learn to read and write our language far
more quickly and easily than children in Europe'.[10]

The missionaries soon found out, however, that the Japanese
regarded themselves as being on the cultural periphery of China.
They accepted this self-image and concluded that the key to the
spiritual conquest of East Asia lay in China rather than in Japan.
Accordingly, after less than two years in the country, Xavier set
out, in 1551, for China.[11]

In 1639, the last of the missionaries were expelled from Japan and the leaders of the country chose a policy of isolation for the next two centuries. The only continuous European contact was the tiny Dutch trading station in Nagasaki. But the Dutch merchants were more interested in account books than writing accounts of Japan. The discoveries of the Jesuits and the occasional visits of Japanese delegations to Europe in the sixteenth century were all but forgotten.

The legacy of these early sporadic contacts was an important one. Educated Europeans and Americans, if they thought about Japan at all, were convinced that it was a rich apanage to China. This view, although based in part on the objective reality of the day, has beclouded the western perception of East Asia and Japan's role in it to the present day.

The early tendency to overestimate China and underestimate Japan was recognized by the small number in the Dutch settlement who actually took an interest in the country to which they were posted. Such men were usually doctors, like Isaac Titsingh (1745–1812), who underlined the desirability of writing on 'a people almost unknown, though fully deserving the attention since a number of years so profusely lavished on the Chinese.'[12] But scholarly doctors such as Kaempfer (1651–1716) or von Siebold (1796–1866), although important in the history of European studies of Japan, were quite marginal in Europe itself and their voices went largely unheard.

The various editions of the *Encyclopaedia Britannica* can serve as a very rough measure of the extent of interest in and knowledge of Japan from the late eighteenth to mid nineteenth century. The first edition (1771) simply contained an abbreviated geographical entry stating, 'Japan, or Islands of Japan are situated between 130° and 144° of E. long. and between 30° and 40° N. lat'. In contrast, the same edition had no less than eight double-column pages on China.

In the second edition of the *Britannica* (1780), the entry on Japan was lengthened. The description is taken largely from Kaempfer's *History of Japan* (1726–8), which remarkable work was compiled on the basis of materials gathered with the aid of his Japanese medical students during his two-year residence in Deshima at the end of the seventeenth century as physician to the

Dutch trading station. The country is described as surrounded by 'such shallow and boisterous seas' that it seems as though 'Providence had designed it to be a kind of little world by itself'. It is a land of earthquakes, with a much revered conical volcano (Mt Fuji). Its people 'embrace, in the most public manner, a voluntary death, either by drowning, hanging or flinging themselves down from a precipice, or by poison, dagger, or any other quick riddance'. The Japanese have a sharply contrasted character: on the one hand they are modest, patient, courteous, hard-working and clean as well as artistic and ingenuous, while on the other hand they are proud, ambitious, cruel and uncharitable as well as passionate and revengeful.

The article did not quote from an earlier work of Kaempfer's written in 1692, in which he had argued that the Japanese did not need the Dutch trade, which was mainly in luxuries, and that it was 'conducive for the good of the Japanese Empire, to keep it shut up, as it now is, and not to suffer its inhabitants, to have any commerce with foreign nations, either at home or abroad'.[13] Later this point of view was frequently held by romantics, who wished to preserve exotic societies in the state in which they found them, untrammelled by the contact with industrialism. But Kaempfer was only stating the plain truth – there just was not very much in his day which the Europeans possessed that the Japanese did not already have. His conclusion, though, cannot have satisfied the growing rumours of Japan's wealth or those jealous of the Dutch monopoly of the trade.

The nineteenth-century search for new markets for Europe's new manufactures is reflected in the seventh edition of the *Britannica* (1842) which drew on a report made during Sir Stamford Raffles's exploratory expedition to Japan in 1812. The article stated that Raffles, while governor of Java, 'was deeply impressed with the importance of opening a commercial intercourse with the Japanese . . . The Japanese islands, containing, according to his estimate, about 25 millions of inhabitants, who require woollens, hardwares, iron manufactures, and glass, besides many other articles, might, he justly conceived, afford a very extensive market for British goods.'

The Raffles report also suggests that the Dutch had

deliberately misrepresented the Japanese as being bigoted and intolerant in order to discourage others from trying to get a share of the market. On the contrary, they were

a nervous, vigorous, people, assimilated by their bodily and mental powers much nearer to Europeans than to Asiatics. The traits of a vigorous intellect are displayed in the greater progress they have made in the sciences and in the arts, which are carried to a much higher degree of perfection among them than among the Chinese, with whom they are frequently confounded but to whom they consider it as a great disgrace to be compared; and the only occasion in which the writer of the report saw a Japanese surprised into passion, and, relinquishing his habitual politeness, lay his hand upon his sword, was on an unguarded comparison being made between the two nations.

The report continued that the Japanese were

eager of novelty, and warm in their attachments, open to strangers, and, bating the restrictions of their political institutions, a people who seemed inclined to throw themselves into the hands of any nation of superior intelligence. They have at the same time a great contempt and disregard of everything below their own standard of morals and habits, as instanced in the case of the Chinese.[14]

It was also recorded in the seventh edition that 'many of the women live with Europeans and others, receiving the wages of prostitution'. In this blunt observation, presumably of conditions in Nagasaki, we get a foreshadowing of the later image of Japan as a land of geisha, a paradise for men.

Although the *Britannica* had gradually extended its articles on Japan, the coverage on China was still much more detailed and balanced. It was not until the end of the nineteenth century that entries on Japan began to reflect more than the summary of missionary reports, tales of shipwrecked sojourners and occasional residents or visitors to the Dutch trading station. Indeed, the actual knowledge of Japan in the West just before Commodore Perry sailed into Edo Bay must still have been practically nil. 'As far as general impressions go', wrote a US contemporary, 'the ordinary floating feeling – we cannot call it knowledge – about Japan, is, that it seems to realize a good deal of the notions conveyed by Swift's Flying Island. We get to think of it as of some Atlantis of the East, a mystery or marvel seldom or very partially revealed to the sons of men'.[15]

If the general knowledge of Japan in mid nineteenth century Europe and America was practically nil, nevertheless the reader will recognize, in the long-forgotten encyclopaedia articles which appeared between 1780 and 1842, many of the stereotypes which were later to become inseparable from the western image of Japan: an isolated, impenetrable world; earthquakes, volcanoes, Mt Fuji; suicides; a clean, hard-working, nervous people anxious to learn, characterized by extreme virtues and extreme vices; a tantalizing market for manufactured goods.

In the second half of the nineteenth century this cluster of images was enlarged to include two further elements. These were the image of Japan as a land of artistic refinement and intriguing geisha.

12

MADAM CHRYSANTHEMUM

In the mid nineteenth century, Japan's period of isolation finally came to an end, as under strong foreign pressure it rapidly began to open to the West. One result was a flow of Japanese woodblock prints, decorative art and fabrics to Europe, and sumptuous displays at world fairs in Paris, Vienna, Philadelphia, London, Brussels and Chicago.

Very soon a craze for Japanese prints and *objets d'art* swept across Europe and America. This sudden boom for *Japonaiserie* (the word was coined by Baudelaire in 1861) is surely not hard to understand. For decades rumours had been circulating about the riches and marvels of Japan, a distant 'double-bolted land' in Herman Melville's phrase, whose products and civilization had for so long been inaccessible to the West. Now for the first time it began to reveal itself in bold prints and refined handicrafts to a Europe whose painting was suffering in the iron grip of academic realism, and whose handicrafts were stifled by the mass-produced kitsch of its new industries.

The Japanese prints were not totally strange. In the eighteenth century Japanese painters and woodblock artists had absorbed some of the techniques of European perspective from the Dutch. There was not the total shock, therefore, of finding something alien, but rather the pleasing sense of discovering something long forgotten but vaguely familiar, not too strange to be incomprehensible, yet sufficiently different to intrigue.

For a while painters such as Degas, Manet, Lautrec, Van Gogh, Monet and Bonnard experimented with Japanese techniques of line and form in two-dimensional patterns. In the evening they would gather in their favourite cabaret, the Divan Japonais, where the waitresses wore kimonos and the walls were hung with fans. Their interest in Japanese prints incidentally has been amply repaid in Japan. The first Japanese students of Western-style painting began arriving in Paris in the 1880s; a hundred years later, Japanese companies began paying record prices for the works of the impressionists who to this day remain the most popular Western painters in Japan.

The echoes of the discovery of Japan were also felt in European ceramics and literature and even as far afield as in film, where a pioneer such as Eisenstein later acknowledged the inspiration he had drawn from Kabuki.[16]

The aesthetic infatuation with Japan was at its strongest in the last quarter of the nineteenth century and it was duly satirized, for example, by the younger Dumas, in his comedy *Francillon* (1887):

HENRI: Annette, may I ask you the recipe of the salad we had this evening? It would appear that it was your own mixture.
ANNETTE: The Japanese?
HENRI: It's Japanese?
ANNETTE: That's what I call it.
HENRI: Why?
ANNETTE: So it has a name: everything is Japanese nowadays.[17]

In London Gilbert and Sullivan's *Mikado* made the same point to packed houses from its opening night in 1885:

> If you want to know who we are,
> We are gentlemen of Japan.
> On many a vase and jar –
> On many a screen and fan,
> We figure in lively paint:
> Our attitude's queer and quaint –
> You're wrong if you think it ain't.[18]

Typically, such infatuations are over almost as quickly as they begin because the novelty of the newly-discovered culture soon wears off. After the honeymoon of mutual discovery comes the humdrum round of day-to-day existence together, and occasional conflict. Indeed, the fashion in the salons and studios in the

West soon switched from the exotic to the primitive, and by the turn of the century it was African art which had become all the rage.

Acquaintance with Japan since the 1850s was not only limited to the welcome imports of prints and *objets d'art* and to the displays at world fairs. Increasingly, travellers and merchants were making their way there, especially after the opening of the Suez Canal in 1869. To these early visitors, Japan seemed like an exotic Eden, untouched by the West, yet highly civilized. One such traveller, the Comte de Beauvoir, was entranced by the sight of men and women bathing together: 'In Japan one lives in full daylight; modesty, or rather immodesty, is not known; it is the innocence of the early paradise, and the costumes of our first parents have nothing which shocks the sentiments of these people who still live in a golden age.'[19]

The Victorian poet Sir Edwin Arnold, during a stay in Japan in 1891, told an audience in Tokyo that Japan

appears to me as close an approach to Lotus-land as I shall ever find. By many a pool of water-lilies in temple grounds and in fairy-like gardens, amid the beautiful rural scenery of Kama-kura or Nikko; under long avenues of cryptomeria; in weird and dreamy Shinto shrines; on the white matting of the teahouses; in the bright bazaars; by your sleeping lakes, and under your stately mountains, I have felt further removed than ever before from the flurry and vulgarity of our European life . . . Yet what I find here more marvellous to me than Fuji-san, lovelier than the embroidered and gilded silks, precious beyond all the daintily carved ivories, more delicate than the cloisonné enamels is . . . that almost divine sweetness of disposition which, I frankly believe, places Japan in these respects higher than any other nation . . . Retain, I beseech you, gentlemen, this national characteristic, which you did not import, and can never, alas, export.[20]

Sir Edwin was of course referring to Japanese women as the highest expression of Japan's aesthetic sensibility. Nor should this be in the least surprising – underlying the aesthetic attraction for Japanese art there was always a strong current of eroticism. Zola decorated the stair of his Paris house with Japanese erotic prints (*shunga*) which he referred to as 'furious fornications'. It is doubtful whether he would have put up French pornography in the same place. The point is that the word 'pornography' in one's own language has a below-the-stairs, furtive feel, while *shunga* sounds exotic. Japan was a land of pure otherness where the ordinary rules did not apply. At least part of the interest of travel in distant places has always been escape from restrictions at home coupled with the anticipation of chance encounters abroad.

For Europeans the Orient as a dream setting for enchanted, if not forbidden, pleasures is at least as old as the garden of Eden. Tales of sweet temptation and wild voluptuousness in the sumptuous courts and harems of the East have always beguiled us, because, by the law of opposites, if the West was Christian and moral, the East was by definition heathen and immoral, a perfect setting for tales of passionate and guiltless romance.

In recent centuries the rich tradition of Oriental exoticism took a new form as colonial conquest and rule provided the opportunity in the form of readily available girls, and encouraged Europeans and Americans to think of the West as active and masculine and the East as passive and feminine.

One outcome was the novel of exotic romance, of '*paresse et caresse*'; the love of a white man and an Oriental woman. Considering that Japan had always been regarded as being in the furthest reaches of the Orient, and that the Japanese appeared to find no contradiction between erotic and religious love, it is perhaps small wonder that one of the first settings of the novel of exotic romance was Japan.

The new genre was the creation of a young French 'man of action', the naval officer and writer, Julien Viaud (1850–1923), better known by his pen-name, Pierre Loti, who based his novel *Madam Chrysanthemum* on a brief visit to Nagasaki in 1885.

Nagasaki had long been the port through which Japanese trade with Europe was centred. Girls were easily available to foreigners, as the Italian adventurer Francesco Carletti had already pointed out in the early 1600s:

As soon as ever these Portuguese arrive and disembark, the pimps who control this traffic in women call on them in the houses in which they are quartered for the time of their stay, and enquire whether they would like to purchase, or acquire in any other method they please, a girl, for the period of their sojourn, or to keep her for so many months, or for a night, or for a day, or for an hour . . . And so it often happens that they will get hold of a pretty little girl of fourteen or fifteen years of age, for three or four scudi . . . with no other responsibility beyond that of sending her back home when done with . . . To sum up, the country is more plentifully supplied than any other with these sort of means of gratifying the passion for sexual indulgence, just as it abounds in every other sort of vice, in which it surpasses every other place in the world.[21]

Since Carletti's day, the few Europeans who stayed at the Dutch trading station in Nagasaki were forbidden to bring their women with them: girls were provided. Occasionally too news must have filtered back to Europe of adventurers who had stayed on in Japan to marry and settle down with a Japanese wife (for example the sixteenth-century English pilot, Will Adams, whose story has been made into no less than six historical novels in the English language, most recent of which being the best-seller *Shōgun*). Thus, by the time Pierre Loti's ship put into Nagasaki harbour for repairs in the summer of 1885, the port's reputation, at least among European and US sailors, was well established. It was Loti's contribution to turn this reputation into a romantic tale which has coloured the Western image of Japan ever since.

Loti's reputation had already been made as the author of romances set in far-away places. The formula was usually the same. A young naval officer for one reason or another has to spend a few weeks or a few months on shore. To while away the time and to 'penetrate the soul' of the strange culture, he has what might be called an '*aventure de plage*'. The girl is usually a teenager and so infatuated with him that when he leaves, she pines away.

Loti's books were reprinted hundreds of times and were translated into all the European languages. His readers' imaginations were no doubt titillated by the dream of romance unfettered by nineteenth-century moral conventions. The setting, too, was an escape from the ugliness of the early industrial age to countries and places when travel was still an adventure. Finally, Loti's style was undemanding. His speciality was the impressionistic sketch of local detail suffused with the sentimental moods of the hero – himself. His mistresses are curiously stereo-typed, treated like pets and discarded as easily on leaving. He has been credited with creating the 'colonial novel' or the 'novel of desertion'.[22]

His most famous book set in Japan, *Madam Chrysanthemum* (1887), followed the usual formula, but with a difference. In an introductory note to the first edition he explained that the three principal characters were 'MYSELF, JAPAN and the EFFECT which this country has on me'. Unlike in his other books, however, Loti made no secret of his dislike for the young lady, Chrysanthemum, with whom he and his inseparable companion Yves lived in that summer of 1885 in Nagasaki.

Paradoxically, in view of the book's later reputation, he also paints the Japanese with many a diminutive as a quaint, ridicu-lous people, living in a country which is only occasionally exotic. Summing it up, he wrote: 'I find it [Japan] little, aged, with worn-out blood and worn-out sap; I feel more fully its ante-diluvian antiquity, its centuries of mummification, which will soon degenerate into hopeless and grotesque buffoonery, as it comes into contact with Western novelties.'[23]

The Japanese are mercilessly caricatured as an inferior yellow people – they are small, fragile, and feminine. They are deca-dent, dangerous and contradictory; full of trickery, superb imitators like comic, aged monkeys.

Loti himself was a tiny, effeminate man, cold-blooded, snob-bish, vain and terrified of old age. It is likely that in writing of the Japanese he projected on to them all those qualities he disliked most in himself. In doing so he made the image of Japan more 'real' for his readers at home, who could now associate the country with many of the familiar negative images of the Orient. His bored, patronizing tone must also have been congenial to the colonial prejudices of the day.

Above all, perhaps unwittingly, he added to the image of Japan as an aesthetic paradise the petite eroticism of the 'mousmé' (from Japanese *musume* meaning daughter, a word which thanks to Loti immediately entered the French language with the sense of 'young lady' or 'pretty prostitute'). And by doing so, he assured the success of *Madam Chrysanthemum* which popularized for the first time the Western fascination with Japanese women.

An English writer of the time fumbled towards the reason for this attraction: 'The Japanese woman is the crown of the charm of Japan. In the noble lady and in her frailest and most unfortunate sister alike there is an indefinable something which is fascinating at first sight and grows only more pleasing on acquaintance . . . the key to the character of the Japanese women lies in the word obedience'.[24]

A few of Loti's more discerning readers in the West took a dislike to *Madam Chrysanthemum*, including Henry James, who wrote soon after its appearance:

The author's taste is for the primitive and the beautiful, the large and free, and the Japanese strike him as ugly and complicated, tiny and conventional. His attitude is more profane than our own prejudice can like it to be; he quite declines to take them seriously . . . I may be altogether mistaken, but we treat ourselves to the conviction that he fails of justice to the wonderful little people who have renewed, for Europe and America, the whole idea of Taste.[25]

Yet, even while criticizing Loti's attitude towards the Japanese, Henry James shares his condescending tone in referring to them as 'wonderful little people'. In doing so he was merely repeating a fundamental conviction of the day, that of the smallness of everything to do with Japan.

Loti was occasionally criticized by his contemporaries, and today most would find his attitude either distasteful or laughable, but in the late nineteenth century Loti's Japan became Europe's Japan. His novels were instant best-sellers; *Madam Chrysanthemum* went through twenty-five impressions in French alone in the first five years after its publication.

His influence on his contemporaries was immense – just as Gauguin left for Tahiti after reading Loti's *Rarahu*, *Madam Chrysanthemum* was one of the two books which decided Lafcadio Hearn to quit Philadelphia and settle in Japan. Van Gogh painted an imaginary portrait of Chrysanthemum, and in 1900 the theme was turned into a smash-hit play by David

Belasco (who based it on a novel by John Luther Long which in turn was partly based on Loti, although by this time the Lieutenant was no longer French but American). When Puccini saw the play in London, he was so impressed that he used it for the basis of his opera *Madame Butterfly* (1904), thereby giving the tale an even wider appeal.[26]

'To tell the truth', wrote a young political publicist named André Chéradam in 1906, 'before the war [that is to say, the Russo-Japanese war of 1904–5], apart from a limited number of specialists and scholars who kept themselves informed by their travels and serious works (seldom read), for us, the rest of the French, what we knew of Japan was that above all it was the country of *Madam Chrysanthemum*'.[27]

If this was true of the French it was also true for everybody else, including the Russians, whose failure to take seriously Japan's intentions for war in 1903–4 may have been due, in part, to the prevailing image of Japan as a land of *mousmés*, full of tricks to be sure, but fragile as a butterfly and certainly unwarlike. As late as 1904, we know that the Russian minister in Washington was still referring scornfully to the Japanese as 'little yellow monkeys'. The phrase is Loti's.

Even after the shock of Japan's victory over Russia, Loti's image of Japan exerted a powerful influence – the book continued to sell well and his imitators were legion. To take but one example from England: a popular novelist and authority on faking photographs, Clive Holland, published a slim volume entitled *My Japanese Wife* in 1895. The book went through sixteen editions in the next twenty years and also appeared with slight alterations under a number of different titles such as *Mousmé*. Holland shamelessly copied Loti, the only difference being that the author-hero, less ruthless than Loti or more hypocritical perhaps, says that he intends to bring his *mousmé*, Hyacinth, whom he has met in a tea shop in Nagasaki, back to England. As in Loti, Japan is described as 'tiny, toy-like and ridiculous'.[28]

French variations on the Chrysanthemum theme such as *Poupée Japonaise*, *Petite Mousmé* or *The Honourable Picnic* abounded; there even developed a colonial sub-genre, set in

Indo-China, with titles such as *Poupée Parfumée* or *Thisen, La Petite Amie Exotique*. The theme was also treated in a first novel by a young British colonial policeman named George Orwell in *Burmese Days*, and inevitably it was taken up by Somerset Maugham in his Malayan short stories.[29]

No doubt the organized movement for women's equality in the West only made the dream of escape to a submissive lover in an exotic land even more attractive. Be this as it may, the genre long outlasted the suffragette movement, as well as the colonial presence in Asia and, after a temporary hiatus brought about by the Pacific War, made a triumphant return with a spate of best-sellers all set in Japan: *Sayonara*, *Tea House of the August Moon*, *You Only Live Twice* or *Shōgun*, all of which contained large doses of the original Loti formula. At a slightly more 'highbrow' level, take Resnais's *Hiroshima Mon Amour* (1959). The plot is little more than the Chrysanthemum theme in modern clothing. The main difference is that the Westerner having a passing affair in Japan is a woman, not a man (a reflection of the enhanced status of Western women or the abject state of Japan after the war?). The heroine, Emanuelle Riva, picks up a Japanese lover in Hiroshima, Okada Eiji who, in the best traditions of Loti's Oriental love-objects, merely acts as a foil to Riva's moods. It is his role to be passionate when she requires it, and for the rest, to listen in sympathetic silence as she dominates the entire film with a monologue about her childhood affair with a German soldier. The film could have been set anywhere, but the director chose to exploit the contemporary horror of atomic war by making Hiroshima the backdrop, and by interspersing the love scenes with shots of A-bomb victims (cribbed from Sekigawa's 1953 film *Hiroshima*).

Only a particularly unpleasant form of French provincialism could have rehashed such a stale image of Japan – a land of extreme contrasts, a sensuous, horrific Oriental country and, as such, an 'exciting' setting for the French heroine's self-discovery.

Another very successful film which makes Japan its setting, *You Only Live Twice*, was based on Ian Fleming's best-selling book of the same title (1964). It contains an amusing pastiche of the Chrysanthemum theme, right from the opening lines, 'the geisha called Trembling Leaf, on her knees beside James Bond, leant forward from the waist and kissed him chastely on the right cheek', to the closing scene, when Bond, on leaving Japan, the exotic Oriental setting of the film, also incidentally deserts the girl who has cared for him and fallen in love with him: 'his life on Kuno, his love of Kissy Suzuki, were . . . of as little account as sparrows' tears'.[30]

The exotic-aesthetic image of Japan in Europe was created by artists, connoisseurs and romantics, many of whom followed Paul Valéry's excellent advice, that 'in order that the word Orient produces its complete and entire effect on someone's spirit, above all it is essential never to have been in the country which it so uncertainly indicates'.[31] Those few of their number who actually did visit the country and willingly stayed on to become 'Japanified', or 'tatamisé', as the French put it, were appalled by the first signs of Japanese industrialization. After all, this was precisely what they were escaping from at home: brick buildings and iron railings, gas lamps and tramways, crinolines and button-boots hardly fitted the stereotype of an exotic Oriental land. So alongside the romantic image of Japan as an aesthetic paradise peopled by obedient mousmés, there also developed a contradictory image, an image mainly of Japanese men, as ridiculous, unaesthetic, untrustworthy imitators of the West.

13

GRAVE OF THE MERCHANT'S HOPES

The negative image of Japanese men was derived from the frustrations of the local Western business community: for those forced to live in Lotus-land, it was Lotus-land no longer. They were confined to the treaty ports and limited in their contacts. An American traveller, Mrs Bacon, explained as follows:

The employment of the merchant being formally the lowest of the respectable callings, one does not find even yet in Japan many great stores or a very high standard of business morality . . . Hence English and American merchants, who only see Japan from the business side, continually speak of the Japanese as dishonest, tricky and altogether unreliable, and greatly prefer to deal with the Chinese, who have much of the business virtue that is characteristic of the English as a nation.[32]

Kipling quoted an English trader he met in a hotel in Kyoto as saying, 'The Jap has no business savvy. God knows I hate the Chinaman . . . but you can do business with him. The Jap's a little huckster who can't see beyond his nose.'

Later in his travels he met a businessman on the train to Yokohama who told him, 'Can't say that I altogether like the Jap way o' doing business . . . Give me a Chinaman to deal with . . . You'll find that opinion in most of the treaty ports.'[33]

One example of the sort of business practice which angered the foreigners will suffice:

If truth must be told, greed leads the Japanese into the most shameless impositions. Half the goods sold as foreign eatables and drinkables are compounded of vile and unwholesome trash, manufactured in Tokyo and elsewhere, put up in bottles and jars with the names and labels of such highly respectable makers as Bass, Martell, Guinness, and Crosse and Blackwell, upon them . . . But to secure themselves in their trade of forgery, these unconscionable villains have establishments at Tokyo, not only for the manufacture of the compounds, but of the labels which give them currency, and some of these are such adroit forgeries as to be completely successful, while others would effectually deceive a purchaser were it not for certain inscrutable vagaries in spelling . . .[34]

However much foreigners disliked Japanese business practices, they did not regard the Japanese as serious commercial rivals. The dominant Treaty Port view is summed up in a comment in the leading English-language newspaper of the day:

Wealthy we do not at all think [Japan] will ever become: the advantages conferred by nature, with the exception of climate, and the love of indolence and pleasure of the people themselves, forbid it. The Japanese are a happy race, and being content with little, are not likely to achieve much.

Japan Herald, 9 April 1881

Another aspect of the new Japan which Europeans and Americans invariably found out of keeping with their images of an unspoiled Oriental paradise was the early craze for Western styles. Clothing styles especially caught the eye. The following quotation is taken from the circular of a Tokyo tailor opening his shop in 1871:

What strange sights we see these days! We see many a man wearing a Prussian cap and French shoes, with a coat of the British navy and the trousers of the US army – a mosaic of different Western countries plaited on a Japanese basis.[35]

A contemporary visitor indicates how incongruous such sights appeared:

It is usually the case, too, that a young Japanese who puts on foreign garments thinks it necessary to adopt other foreign customs, and, not having a very clear idea as to what they are, makes a ridiculous spectacle of himself with the best of intentions. He puts his hat on the back of his head, sticks a cigar in the corner of his mouth, takes a cane in his hand, and thinks that he is the perfect model of an American or English gentleman, when in fact he is a poor imitation of a loafer.[36]

At the other end of the social scale, Japanese in high society wearing European clothes appeared equally bizarre. In 1883 the government had opened a ballroom, the Rokumeikan, for the purpose of entertaining foreigners with cards, billiards, Western music and lavish balls. It was intended to give a cosmopolitan atmosphere to the new capital and thus help convince the Western powers that Japan was 'civilized'. Three years after it was opened, Loti was invited to a society ball at the Rokumeikan, which was, he wrote, 'built in the European style, all fresh, all white, all new and looks, my God, like a casino in one of our watering places and you could truly believe yourself to be anywhere but in Yeddo [Tokyo] . . .' At the dance there were 'innumerable Japanese gentlemen; these ministers, admirals, officers and officials are a little too over-bedecked in gold braid, all dressed up for the ball . . . And how strangely they wear their swallowtails. No doubt their backs were not made to wear this sort of thing; impossible to say for what reason but I find all of them always in some indescribable way very similar to monkeys . . .' And, as for the women, 'they dance quite correctly, my Japanese in French costumes. But one feels that it is something *learnt*; they dance like automatons, without the least personal initiative . . .' As a German observer of the same scene put it somewhat more wittily: 'most of them showed by the expression of their faces that they were making a sacrifice on the altar of civilization'. Loti contrasts the Chinese at the ball with their Japanese hosts:

At ten o'clock, entrance of the Embassy of the Celestial Empire: a dozen superb personages, with mocking eyes, standing a head above this crowd of tiny Japanese. Chinese of the fair race of the North, they have in their bearing, under their dazzling silks, a noble grace. And also they show good taste and dignity in keeping to their national costume, the long magnificently brocaded and embroidered robe.[37]

Of course to a Japanese observer, it would have probably been the Chinese who appeared ridiculous, and the Japanese in their Western clothes would have seemed to be in the height of fashion. This is in fact the theme of Akutagawa Ryunosuke's story, 'The Ball', which was discussed in Chapter 6.

The sight of Japanese adopting Western ways led Europeans to ridicule them as 'pitifully grotesque'. As Hearn put it, 'I fear the future demoralization of Japan is to be effected by Japanese in frock-coats and loud neck-ties.' Many prophesied the end of 'old' Japan and echoed Hearn's lament, 'The opening of the country was very wrong – a crime. Fairyland is already dead.'

Kipling on a visit in 1889, three years after Loti was invited to the ball at the Rokumeikan, foresaw that 'the cultured Japanese of the English pattern will corrupt and defile the tastes of his neighbours till . . . Japan altogether ceases to exist as a separate nation and becomes a button-hole manufacturing apanage of America'.[38]

In another characteristically bitter-sweet comment he wrote:

Japan is a great people. Her masons play with stone, her carpenters with wood, her smiths with iron, and her artists with life, death, and all the eye can take in. Mercifully she has been denied the last touch of firmness in her character which would enable her to play with the whole round world. We possess that – We, the nation of the glass flower-shade, the pink worsted mat, the red and green China puppy dog, and the poisonous Brussels carpet. It is our compensation.[39]

The compensation has long since been denied the British, and the rest of the Europeans, and the Americans too. Japan has shifted from the traditional to the modern – from the tatami to the carpet. In its rush to catch up with the industrialized West it has also displayed a sufficient 'touch of firmness in her character', if not to play with the whole round world, then at least to shake it at times.

The more Japan industrialized, however, the more Westerners clung to the old topsy-turvy image of Japan as a quaint fairyland whose only traces could now be found in a supposedly exotic past. After all, it was far more reassuring to live with this illusion than have to acknowledge the arrival of a new power and competitor on the international scene. Europeans and Americans, therefore, were poorly prepared for the rapid changes which Japan was already undergoing in the late nineteenth century. When they finally woke up to these changes, it was with a profound sense of shock and disappointment; the *mousmé* was charming so long as she was obedient; she rapidly became intolerable when she took on a life of her own.

14

MILITARY AND COLONIAL POWER

The frivolous image of Japan formed by Europeans and Americans in the second half of the nineteenth century was abruptly challenged by the Japanese victory over China in 1895.

A French commentator, De Villenoisy, pointed out that for the British Foreign Office, which had thought China would win the war, 'it was painful to see rising on the furthest borders of Asia a real European state of yellow people without having guessed that its birth was about to take place'. Not without some Gallic satisfaction he noted that the war was 'one of the most important events of modern times' because the emergence of an Asian sea power would inevitably lead to the decline of British influence. He also predicted an eventual rejuvenation of China and 'the awakening of the yellow peoples who would be in competition with Europe'.[40]

A view shared by some of his contemporaries: 'Consider what a Japan-governed China would be', a British writer exhorted the readers of the *St James's Gazette* in 1894,

think what the Chinese are; think of their powers of silent endurance under suffering and cruelty; think of their frugality; think of their patient perseverance; their slow, dogged persistence, their recklessness of life. Fancy this people ruled by a nation of born organisers, who, half-allied to them, would understand their temperament and their habits. The Oriental, with his power of retaining health under conditions under which no European could live, with his savage daring when aroused, with his inborn cunning, lacks only the superior knowledge of civilization to be the equal of the European in warfare as well as in industry.[41]

These warnings, however, did not help to prepare public opinion for the Japanese victories over Russia in 1904 and 1905, which in the words of a contemporary, 'dumbfounded the chancelleries and surprised the people'.[42]

Westerners were simply not in the habit of taking Japan seriously. As *The Times* editorialized in February 1904, just after the sinking of three Russian ships and the Japanese declaration of war:

The story of the last ten days must have fallen upon the Western world with the rapidity of a tropical thunderstorm . . . That is the trouble at the root of the present situation – the past inability of the West to take Japan seriously . . . All this is due to the superficial study of Japan which has characterized Western contact with it. We as a nation alone appear to have formed a shrewder estimate [the Anglo-Japanese alliance had been signed in 1902] . . . But for the rest, they still were pleased to look upon the Japanese through the eyes of the aesthetic penman, and thought of the nation as a people of pretty dolls dressed in flowered silks and dwelling in paper houses of the capacity of matchboxes . . .[43]

Reaction was swift and extreme, particularly in France, which had not only been chiefly responsible for the 'aesthetic penman's' image of Japan, but was also allied to Russia; it was pointed out that Japan's war with Russia was a revival of the struggle between East and West which had started with the Persian Wars of ancient Greece.

Fears of a new yellow peril had been circulating in the West for some time. One of the earliest writers on the subject was the Russian anarchist Mikhail Bakunin, who travelled across Siberia to the Pacific in the late 1860s, and foresaw an alliance of China and Japan, newly armed with Western skills, threatening the West by the end of the nineteenth century. It was following the Japanese victory over China in 1895 that Kaiser Wilhelm II had his notorious nightmare of a yellow peril, the drawing of which he sent to Tsar Nicholas II. But it was only after the defeat of Russia that the image of Japan became equated with the age-old fears of the enemy from the East and the Japanese were seen as a new yellow peril. Japan, it was argued, would throw off its veneer of Westernization and revert to its supposed Mongolian past to lead the Chinese against the West, launching a massive war of

Orientals against Occidentals. A German political commentator, Baron von Falkenegg, expressed his fears as follows:

The European powers should have realized in good time that the cunning, skilled and valiant Japanese people would soon be uttering the slogan 'Asia for the Asians' . . . As soon as the Mongolians were set in a belligerent direction, they knew no retreat, even when the bodies were piled as high as hills. Exactly like the Japanese. Here, as there, we find that uncanny, wild bravery, incomprehensible to the European mind, which sets value of the individual at naught . . . 'Asia for the Asians' has become the slogan in Japan, and is directed at all those Europeans who want to take political and commercial advantages in Asia. But for the Japanese, 'Asia for the Asians' has the obvious implication, 'Japan dominates Asia, and Asia dominates Europe'.[44]

Another writer, René Pinon, having remarked that the war reawakened 'the notion of an external enemy – the yellows', continued:

Whether one likes it or not, the 'yellow peril' has entered already into the imagination of the people, just as represented in the famous drawing of Kaiser Wilhelm II: in a setting of conflagration and carnage, Japanese and Chinese hordes spread out over all Europe, crushing under their feet the ruins of our capital cities and destroying our civilizations, grown anaemic due to the enjoyment of luxuries and corrupted by vanity of spirit.[45]

Such fears also found expression in best-selling novels like Émile Driant's *The Yellow Invasion* (1905) whose main theme was an attack on the West by Chinese brawn led by Japanese brain. In America, against the background of agitation to exclude immigrants from China and Japan, these years also saw the first novels about a future war between Japan and the United States, most famous of which was 'General' Homer Lea's *The Valor of Ignorance* (1909).[46]

Some also thought that the real danger from the East lay in economic competition, as the French economist and editor, Édouard Théry, repeatedly warned:

The Yellow Peril . . . is the violent disrupture of the economic equilibrium at present in force in the great European industrial countries, a disrupture provoked by the rapid industrial and commercial awakening of an immense region with a population of 500 millions of inhabitants . . .[47]

It was felt that the Japanese were in no hurry because 'they will choose the field of action which suits them best, and they will lead the pack and stimulate the organization of the industrial victory of the Far East over the West using our capital, our machines and our methods'.[48]

Even relative moderates like Pinon believed that 'the competition of yellow labour, which although it is not the imminent peril that it is sometimes painted, is none the less far from being imaginary . . . The victory of Japan over Russia will be the start of a new era for the yellow race, which, spurred on by the Japanese, will adopt all the procedures and tools of our civilization, resulting for Europe in economic disturbance which will singularly delay solutions to the great social problems'.[49] There were even those who went so far as to suggest that the solution was to cut off trade with Japan, to boycott Japanese goods and refuse to export to it.

Not everybody thought Japan was a danger. On the contrary, most serious commentators rejected the notion of a yellow invasion as fanciful and some even warned the Japanese of the dangers of Western imperialism. The influential philosopher and prophet of Social Darwinism, Herbert Spencer, for example, had given confidential advice in 1892 (to be passed to the prime minister, Itō Hirobumi) that 'Japanese policy should be that of keeping Americans and Europeans *as much as possible at arm's length*. In presence of the more powerful races your position is one of chronic danger, and you should take every precaution to give as little foothold as possible to foreigners'.[50]

At the time of the Russo-Japanese War, everyone who wanted for one reason or another the defeat of Russia, hoped for the victory of Japan. This was the case in countries such as Finland or Sweden where Russia was viewed as an aggressor.[51] It was also true of the Anglo-Saxon countries where it soon became fashionable to explain Japan's victory in terms of the heroic virtues of the samurai as put forward, for example, in Nitobe Inazo's *Bushido, the Soul of Japan* (1899, 1905), one of the first of a long line of books by Japanese writers instrumental in shaping Western views of their country.

In France, which was allied to Russia, public opinion was against Japan. It was also hostile to Great Britain. A novel such as *The Yellow Invasion* is not only anti-Chinese and Japanese, it is also venomously anti-British. But even in France, socialists took the side of Japan. In a passage much quoted at the time, a character in Anatole France's *Sur la Pierre Blanche* argues for example:

What the Russians are paying for at this very moment in the seas of Japan and in the gorges of Manchuria is not just their avid and brutal policy in the Orient, it is the colonial policy of all the European powers . . . It would not appear to be the case, however, that the yellow peril terrifying European economists is comparable to the white peril hanging over Asia. The Chinese do not send to Paris, Berlin or St Petersburg missionaries to teach Christians *feng-shui* and cause general chaos in European affairs . . . Admiral Togo did not come with a dozen battleships to bombard the roadstead of Brest in order to help Japanese commerce in France . . . The armies of the Asiatic powers have not taken to Tokyo or Peking the paintings of the Louvre or the china of the Elysée.[52]

After the formation of the Anglo-Japanese alliance in 1902, Britons became fond of identifying their new ally as the 'Britain of Asia', and there was considerable sympathy for Japan, the small young country taking on and beating the huge Russian bear. Cartoons of 'Jap the giant killer' were popular. A British novelist, William Plomer, recalled catching sight of a Japanese battleship at a naval review off the Isle of Wight in about 1910.

'Look at the pretty flag, Billy,' somebody had said. 'The rising sun. That great ship belongs to the plucky little Japs who beat the Russians. Yes, they're our friends and perhaps someday you'll go and see their pretty country, where the houses are made of paper and the ladies wear chrysanthemums in their hair.'[53]

The year 1905 was widely accepted as marking the emergence of a new kind of colonial power, an Asian colonial power, and hence the end of unchallenged Western dominance and eventually the end of their colonies in East Asia.[54]

Of the Western reactions to Japan's victories over Russia in 1904 and 1905, some proved to be wide of the mark, but others turned out to be not so far wrong.

Japan's militant nationalists in the thirties did indeed attempt to lead a resurgence of Asian power against the West. They did succeed in driving the Europeans and Americans out of most of their Asian colonies. But what was not foreseen was that Japan would very quickly alienate most of the Asian peoples including the Chinese.

The view that proved most lasting was that Japan would become the leader of peaceful efforts of the Asian countries to modernize. As a contemporary put it,

Her [Japan's] new role may be described as that of the Schoolmaster of Asia. In other words, recent events would indicate that Japan will be the chief influence to modernize China, to awaken Korea, to help Siam, and even incongruous though it seems, to cooperate with Russia in making Eastern Siberia habitable and prosperous.[55]

Also correctly foreseen was that Japan would become an industrial power capable of competing with the West.

The fear that proved completely unfounded was of a racial war of the 'yellows' against the 'whites'.

After World War I, the anxiety that Japan would lead China against the West was not revived, because Japan and China were almost continuously at war with each other, but the image of a Japanese economic peril returned repeatedly. Indeed during the Depression of 1929–32, to many the fears of Japanese competition based on cheap labour seemed to be only too justified. Denunciation of Japan reached a peak in the Western press during these years as Japan alone of the industrial powers continued to expand its markets and to increase its exports. 'Swelling tide of yellow trade', 'unfair competition', 'social dumping', 'a new yellow peril', 'menace of a sharp inrush of Japanese goods', 'manipulation of the yen exchange rate', were some of the typical accusations made, particularly by spokesmen of labour-intensive light industries such as textiles, which were already non-competitive on world markets.

These were also the years when the label 'Made in Japan' on goods such as toys, bicycles, textiles, matches and so on became synonymous with cheap and unreliable.

As Japan industrialized it became fashionable for practically every Western writer to point to the sharp contrasts in Japanese society between 'Western' and 'Eastern' elements. Many Japanese writers, too, referred to 'a dual mode of living – European outside . . . and Japanese at home . . . an amphibian mode of living'.[56] Kipling in his blunt way had applied this to the Japanese themselves when he said, 'The Jap isn't native, and he isn't a Sahib either.'[57] Critics would often not only be disappointed at finding factory chimneys where they had hoped to find an unspoiled 'Oriental' land, but also suggest that the Western elements were only skin deep, a caricature of the West and that underneath the veneer, the Japanese himself was an untrustworthy Oriental. These prejudices have persisted right to this day, even though they are based on a false dichotomy between 'East' and 'West', and even though Japan's modernization process has become sufficiently internalized for it to catch up with Europe and America.

The early thirties were the years when the Japanese military began the conquest of China, drawing unanimous censure from the League of Nations in 1932. Japanese atrocities were condemned in the Western press, particularly after the bombing of Shanghai in 1932 which was among the first scenes of warfare filmed by newsreel cameramen. Next came the rape of Nanking and the aerial bombardment of Canton in 1937:

If the Japan of today has learnt much, she has forgotten much. The levying without cause of 'totalitarian' war on China; the repeated bombings of populous and undefended cities with callous disregard for a hideous toll of innocent civilian lives – these actions are ugly blots on the scroll of chivalry from which the Japan of thirty years ago would have recoiled.[58]

But nobody seriously believed that Japan would ever attack the European and US colonies in Asia – after all, the Japanese were a charming, if occasionally slightly unpredictable, people. During the years 1920–40, there was only one best-seller on a

Japanese theme in Europe. This was Arthur Waley's translation of the *Tale of Genji* which naturally reinforced the old image of Japan as a refined and exotic culture, albeit one capable of producing a major work of literature. About as far from the cockpit of a Zero fighter as Lady Murasaki from a typewriter.

Not only did the Western powers underestimate the strength of their potential Asian enemy, but a probably more important reason for their total unpreparedness was the fatal illusion of their own power in Asia. 'Pride of race, contempt for other races, and an enervating century of security lay at the basis of these illusions', a historian has written on the fall of Hong Kong and Malaya. His remarks could also be applied to the Americans in the Philippines, to the French in Indo-China and to the Dutch in Indonesia. 'Despite all the evidence from the Russo-Japanese war of 1905 onwards', he continues, 'the British still regarded the Asians as inferiors, at once amusing and exasperating, and until 1941 few of them realized how strong Japan had become and how intent on establishing an Asian Empire which it did not propose to share with others.' The Americans were no better prepared – like the Europeans, they thought the Japanese comical. The notion that they could shoot straight or pilot an aeroplane was regarded by most Americans, including General MacArthur in 1941, as simply preposterous.

As the Japanese navy launched its attack on Pearl Harbor and as the Japanese armies descended with the speed of a tropical thunderstorm on the European colonial armies, and annexed or brought under their control all the European territories in the Far East, the old aesthetic image of Japan was temporarily replaced. The fighting was short but harsh, and soon the Japanese were invested with many of the stereotypes applied to previous Western enemies – they were seen as totally different, as savage, childish, cruel, ape-like and mentally deficient.[59]

In an effort to explain the phenomenon of Japan at war, what might be called the 'conspiracy theory' of modern Japanese history gained wide currency.

A popular expression of this theory appeared in Robert Standish's wartime novel *The Three Bamboos*, which links the fortunes of Japan since the mid nineteenth century to the plans of a great *zaibatsu* family to rebuild its own power and, at the same time, 'to make of Nippon the greatest and most powerful nation in the world'; 'to free Asia from the domination of foreigners' and 'to lead Japan to conquer the world'.

Five generations of Furenos, for this is the family name, work single-mindedly and secretly towards these aims. The first generation, young sons of an impoverished samurai family, are sent to Europe and the USA in the 1850s and 1860s 'to suck up knowledge about the West like octopuses'. Next they apply that knowledge to set up a vast industrial and commercial empire based on slave labour at home and quick money and intelligence derived from a pseudo-Buddhist spy network in China engaged in opium cultivation.

The family controls Japanese politicians with its own secret assassination team, 'the little flowers'. After the humiliation of the Triple Intervention of 1895, when Japan was forced to give back many of the concessions it had just won from China, the fictional Furenos decide that the three powers, Russia, Germany and France, must be made to pay for this humiliation. Accordingly preparations are made for war with Russian which duly takes place a decade later. Next, while Germany is at war with England, German trade in Asia, German patents in Japan and German concessions in China and the Pacific are seized. Revenge on France has to wait until 1941 when the Japanese bring under their control the French administration in Indo-China. 'Having beaten the Russians, the white races – all of them, including the English', turn against Japan. The Furenos, who occasionally show their contempt by mixing human excrement with the food served to their Western guests, dominate the small group of influential Japanese industrialists, officials and military who have secretly controlled all important decisions in Japan since the nineteenth century. So when rising tariff walls against 'the flood of cheap Japanese goods' in the thirties forces the Furenos to sell at a loss, it is they who decide that the time has come to launch the last phase of the plan to conquer the world. Appropriately enough, the senior Fureno of the fifth generation is pictured piloting the first dive bomber at Pearl Harbor, which is navigated by his younger brother. The plane crashes.

The reader will readily identify a number of stereotypes in the 'conspiracy theory' of modern Japanese history, magnified to the point of absurdity in novels such as *The Three Bamboos* or in propaganda films such as Frank Capra's *Know Your Enemy – Japan*. One such stereotype which has continued in circulation long after the war is what has come to be called 'Japan Inc.', the notion that behind a façade of democratic institutions and a powerless parliament, top Japanese bureaucratic and business leaders are working (plotting) so closely together that Japan is directed like a monolithic corporation, the mass of whose workers, the ordinary citizens, docilely follow their orders. Behind a veneer of Westernization, in other words, there lurks a modern version of the old stereotype of 'Oriental despotism'.

In Germany during the war years, opportunism dictated that Nazi ideology be played down in the interests of *realpolitik*, and Japan was officially regarded as a fellow victim of the international Jewish conspiracy. Rebutting the view that the alliance with Japan contradicted Germany's racial principles Hitler said, 'The essential is to win, and to that end we are quite ready to make an alliance with the devil himself.'

Already before the war Hitler had expressed, in *Mein Kampf*, his views on Japan in terms as condescending as so much commentary of the day. He wrote, for example, that Japan had only advanced because of Greek spirit and German technique, and reckoned that 'if beginning today all further Aryan influence on Japan should stop, assuming that Europe and the USA should perish, Japan's present rise in science and technology might continue for a short time; but even in a few years the well would dry up; the Japanese special character would gain, but the present culture would freeze and sink back into the slumber from which it was awakened seven decades ago by the wave of Aryan culture'. Hearing of Japan's initial successes in the Pacific War, he remarked, 'It means the loss of a whole continent, and one must regret it, for it's the white race which is the loser.' During the war he referred privately to the Japanese as 'little yellow Aryans' no better than 'half-lacquered monkeys'.[60]

Scenes of brutal and cruel behaviour of the Japanese at war became all too familiar and were later passed on to the next generation in novels such as Norman Mailer's *The Naked and the Dead* or films like *The Bridge over the River Kwai*. The kamikaze pilots at the end of the war reinforced the images of the Japanese as fanatical and inhuman 'Orientals' and, as such, totally uncaring for human life. As a schoolboy in the mid-fifties I can just remember reading popular histories of Japanese war atrocities such as *The Knights of Bushido*; but many businessmen at board level involved in Japanese market decisions today, as well as senior government officials, had direct experience of Japan at war. Their later attitudes towards Japan have inevitably been coloured by these early memories.

In the nineteenth century *Madam Chrysanthemum* had symbolized the exotic image of Japan. To this was now added in the mid twentieth century the completely opposite image of a fanatically warlike, cruel and untrustworthy nation. Book titles such as *Pays de Mousmé! Pays de Guerre!*, *Cannoni e ciliegi in fiore*, or *The Chrysanthemum and the Sword*, sum up the attempt to blend the new perception of Japan with the old aesthetic image.[61]

In doing so Americans and Europeans were grafting on to Japan the age-old myth of the Orient as a mixture of extremes – the exotic and the crooked; the fabulous and the cruel.

15

BUSINESS WARRIORS

Japan's growth as a military power was accompanied by a massive development of its heavy industrial base, but it was only after defeat in the Pacific War and its rapid growth, or 'economic miracle', in the late fifties and sixties that it developed one of the largest economies in the world.

In Europe in the fifties there was already a widespread apprehension, no doubt reflecting memories of the thirties, that Japanese exports would flood European markets.

Such fears seemed only to be confirmed as the Japanese economic miracle, at the speed and with the efficiency of the new 'bullet' train, overtook the rest of the world. Already the process had begun in the fifties: in 1956, Japan replaced the UK as the world's largest producer of ships and in 1957, it became the world's top producer of steel. In the sixties its economy overtook that of Italy, the UK, France and Germany, and in the late seventies, having overtaken the Soviet Union, it became the world's second largest economy after the USA.

Its GNP per capita overtook the UK and Italy in 1979; the Netherlands and Belgium in 1983; France in 1984; Denmark and Germany in 1985; Sweden, Canada, and Norway in 1986 and the USA in 1987, by which time it was the turn of the Americans to feel apprehensive.

The initial shock inspired alarm and admiration, with alarm predominating. The old image of Japan as an economic peril, derived from the fears of a yellow peril, or hordes of cheap labour attacking the industrial bastions of the West, was revived, this time combined with images of Japan at war, images left over from the Pacific War.

A flood of articles in the late sixties warned of the ruthless aggressiveness of the Japanese in their 'military' quest for larger markets:

Should one imagine in the basement of a building in Tokyo, a group of mysterious people with enigmatic smiles, standing before a huge general staff table, placing Japanese flags on the capitals of Europe? . . . *Vision* interviewed the Ministry of International Trade and Industry in Tokyo (MITI) in the Occidental style, without useless circumlocutions: 'Have you somewhere here people who are directing a campaign for the economic conquest of Europe?' The MITI people replied, politely of course, for they are Japanese, that we were stupid.[62]

Time magazine in 1970 compared the Japanese salesmen to the 'warrior trader of the 14th century' and the 'soldier bureaucrat' of World War II. 'The difference is that the latter day *wakō* carries a *soroban* (abacus) instead of a sword and wears blue serge instead of the khaki of General Hideki Tojo's Imperial Army.' To the ambition of conquering world markets 'they bring a machine-like discipline, an ability to focus with fearful energy on the task at hand, an almost Teutonic thoroughness in all pursuits, whether business or pleasure'.[63]

The following year, Ralf Dahrendorf, an EC Commissioner, warned the European Parliament that 'the harsh and sometimes emotional criticism of Japanese economic behaviour will already be invalid in a few years. [But] as with American protection, it may be true of the Japanese combination of isolation and ruthlessly aggressive economic policy that we have a few difficult years before us . . .' A similar thought, phrased somewhat more directly, was attributed to a member of the Nixon Cabinet: 'The Japanese are still fighting the war, only now instead of a shooting war it is an economic war. Their immediate intention is to try to dominate the Pacific and then perhaps the world.'[64]

It would be hard to exaggerate the degree to which this sort of imagery has been automatically applied to Japanese business practices and businessmen. As the Editor-in-Chief of *Le Monde* put it when asked what image he held of the Japanese, 'A powerful, dynamic, hard-working people . . . having come to admit that nothing can any longer be achieved through war, but knowing that economic competition, in a way, can perfectly mean war continued by another means.' To the chief executive officer of Chrysler it was equally clear, 'Right now, we're in the midst of another major war with Japan. This time it's not a shooting war . . . The current conflict is a trade war. But because our government refuses to see this war for what it is, we're well on the road to defeat.' Or in the weighty words of a business school professor writing in 1986, 'Japan's transcendent commitment to economic nationalism has constituted a non-military substitute for its earlier promotion of a Co-Prosperity Sphere embracing most of East Asia.'[65]

Phrases such as 'business warriors fighting outside the country in the trade war' also began to become popular in Japan itself at this time. At first the imagery was drawn from the Pacific War. Later the old connections with 'the way of the warrior' were made inside Japan as well as outside and there was a vogue for the manager as samurai. A less flattering use of this imagery appeared in best-selling US novels such as *The Ninja* (about a criminal *ninja* sent to New York to murder an American industrialist), *The Miko* or *The Samurai Strategy* (a popular novel with an ingenious plot whereby a Japanese financier tries to take over all US high-tech companies and set up a new world power, 'Nipponica'). Many non-fiction works also appeared, often garnished with little Fu Manchu touches such as the following description of one of the actual leaders of 'Japan's new financial empire', the president of Nomura Securities, Yoshida Tabuchi,

known as the 'Mao Zedong of Nomura' – in part because of a slight physical resemblance . . . but more because like Mao, Tabuchi wields power ruthlessly and strategically. If Mao borrowed freely from Sun Tzu's ancient art of war . . . Tabuchi is borrowing some of the same pages to steer Nomura toward leadership of the global financial revolution.

Without stopping to enlighten us as to which pages, the author continues,

Speaking in Japanese with an imperious, electrical whisper, Tabuchi explains Nomura's strategy . . . Seated beneath an original painting by Marc Chagall (in which a red sun is visible), Tabuchi holds himself bolt upright, every sinew taut, ready to pounce. Chain smoking furiously, sometimes shrouding his own visage in a mysterious swirl of smoke rings, he declares: 'We want all customers. We aspire to all nationalities, all borrowers, all issuers, and all investors . . . Now the time has come when the Japanese must fulfill their responsibilities. It is in this area that Nomura finds its reason for being.'[66]

As we have seen, as far as Europe and the USA are concerned, fears of Japanese trade competition began to be linked with Japanese military strength from the time of Japan's first modern war, the defeat of the Qing empire in 1895. A US magazine summed up the linkage in an article written in 1896 in words which have a modern ring, 'Japan has entered upon a commercial war against the great industrial nations of the world with the same energy, earnestness, determination, and foresight, which characterized the war [with China] . . .'[67]

Over the last hundred years such remarks have been repeated every time there has been a business recession in the West and every time Japan has launched an export drive or won a military victory. They show the basic fear that Japan is engaged in a perpetual struggle with the West, either by trade war or by military attack. It is one of the most lasting reactions to Japan and to the Japanese. To appreciate this, one only has to look at the first post-war rash of books warning of the Japanese industrial and commercial threat which were published between 1969 and 1971, with titles such as *The Japanese Challenge*; *Japan: The Planned Aggression*; *The Japanese Threat*; *The Japanese Industrial Challenge*; *Japan: Monster or Model*; *The Japanese Miracle and Peril*; *Stop the Japanese Now.*[68]

The new image of Japan itself which became current in the late sixties and early seventies was a complete reversal of the old aesthetic image. Japan now came to be seen as a country of 'economic animals', a phrase incidentally more widely heard in Japan than in the West, despite General de Gaulle's 1962 remark comparing the Japanese prime minister, Mr Ikeda, to a transistor salesman. The Japanese were felt to be pursuing GNP growth at the expense of everything else, spreading pollution and spawning megalopolises. The admirers of the new Japan readily accepted the officially inspired, tourist-poster image of the 'bullet' train streaking past Mt Fuji, a combination of traditional aesthetics with modern efficiency. But for most a more lasting image was probably the sight of professional pushers cramming commuters into Tokyo's trains.

It was also felt that the polluted monster was directed by a super-efficient interlocking élite of big business (the *zaibatsu* or *keiretsu kigyō*) and government often referred to as 'Japan Inc.'. Nobody stopped to ask themself why, if 'Japan Inc.' really existed and was so efficient, it could have produced such a polluted and apparently joyless result. The notion of 'Japan Inc.' is more easily understood as an echo of the age-old fear of 'Oriental despotism', a phrase first used by the ancient Greeks to describe the Persians. It is a negative image easily evoked at a time of war, and one which satisfies the emotional need to identify a single malefic enemy, rather than face the complex reality of both one's own society, and the country to which such simplistic personifications are applied.

The various other elements of the 'Japan Inc.' image included a population grimly working with low salaries and without vacations and a government pursuing international status and power with a policy of 'malevolent mercantilism': using administrative guidance to encourage export industries at the expense of housing and other social overheads and unfairly protecting the domestic market from foreign competition whatever the cost to the consumer.

The dreary images of an efficient, but polluted, economic monster were occasionally relieved by sudden flashes of fanatical violence or cruelty – the dramatic suicide of Mishima Yukio; helmeted students smashing professors' libraries; Red Army radicals massacring civilians at Lod airport; the grisly activities of the 'cannibal of the Bois de Boulogne' and the 'kindergarten killer', or, in a different vein, Japanese slaughter of dolphins and hunting of whales.[69]

As the recognition of the strength of the Japanese economy became more widespread, especially after Japan achieved the status of the world's number one creditor, the fears of this seemingly invincible and aggressive new financial power grew stronger. The Soviet Union under Gorbachev and China under Deng were perceived as less of a threat than at any time since the Pacific War. Public opinion polls in the USA began to show that many Americans thought the Japanese economy more of a threat than the Soviet military.

These fears and the accusations to which they gave rise during periodic fits of 'Japan bashing' in the USA and Europe are examined in Chapters 22 and 23.

16

MODEL MANAGERS

The initial response to the new Japanese industrial and commercial challenge which emerged in the late sixties and early seventies was largely negative. But a challenge can be accepted as well as rejected; the response may be sympathetic or it may be hostile. Indeed from the beginning, just as in earlier periods, there was a small but growing number of opinion-makers whose response to the new Japan was sympathetic. Their numbers have swelled; today, there is no lack of admirers, but the reasons for their admiration are not always the same.

The first to recognize the achievements of post-war Japan were businessmen and those writing for them. They felt the need to gain an accurate picture of their competitor. Next were all those of an older generation who felt that Japan embodied good old-fashioned qualities, long since lost in Europe and the USA, such as self-reliance, perseverance, thrift, hard work, politeness, discipline, self-control and obedience. For them, reading of the doings of the captains of Japanese industry – Kato Seisi of Toyota, Honda Sōichirō of Honda Motors, Matsushita Konosuke of National Panasonic or Morita Akio of Sony – was to recall a bygone age when it was customary to hang homilies such as 'Try Every Day' on your office wall. They were reminded of what they liked to think were the values and energy of their youth; they may even have caught an echo of the tales of Horatio Alger or Samuel Smiles which had inspired the generation of their own grandparents.

From the late seventies a 'Learn from Japan' boom hit the USA and Europe and soon spread to Southeast Asia where several governments introduced 'Look East' policies. To some, Japan was the very model of a post-industrial society to which all other countries would sooner or later converge, an industrial utopia where everything worked smoothly and none of the afflictions currently troubling the West were to be found. To others, it was a useful stick with which to chastise this or that aspect of their own society.

The boom concentrated on single-factor explanations of the secret of Japan's commercial and industrial success, particularly the art of Japanese enterprise management. A very large number of books, several of them best-sellers, were written, some even based on the curious notion of the business manager as samurai.

One of the earliest publications to recognize the strength of the new Japan, long before the boom, was the *Economist*, which in 1962 began to warn its readers that the Japanese 'could beat us competitively in a much wider field of industry than most people in Britain at present begin to imagine', a warning similar to that made by the Federation of British Industries in 1934: 'It would be unwise to assume that the future export activities of Japan will be limited to cheap goods of low quality'. Even further back, at the beginning of the century, Sir Henry Norman, for example, had made similar and equally unheeded observations.[70] But since the early sixties warnings of the competition to be expected from Japan were for the first time accompanied by the novel advice that Europeans and Americans had something to learn from the Japanese economy. Indeed, the *Economist* articles of 1962 are the first which examined the whole range of economic policy-making in Japan in an effort to draw lessons for another industrialized country. Ten years later in 1975, the *Economist*, taking its cue perhaps from Kahn's *The Emerging Japanese Superstate*, became even more enthusiastic, and widened the field for its readers to learn from Japan to include housing, culture, health care, transport and crime prevention.[71]

Studies and reports began to proliferate arguing that Japan's economic successes were due to everything from neo-Confucian ethics to unique social and organizational structures; from particular economic advantages to astute neo-mercantilist planning.

A popular catch-all explanation which was also often heard in Japan itself was that the Japanese worked harder and saved more.

In the USA, a subcommittee of the House of Representatives, in its second full-scale report on trade with Japan in two years, reached the conclusion, 'It has become increasingly clear to us, and to many businessmen dealing with Japan, that our trade problems result less and less from Japanese import barriers, and more and more from domestic American structure problems of competitiveness and quality. There are clearly lessons to be learnt from Japan.'[72] In the British Parliament, a Japan subcommittee began 'looking at Japanese industry, trying to find out if their methods, particularly in production and development, have lessons for British industry and to assess their success technically in world markets and to discover if we can find the reasons for it, taking into account the very different conditions, background and so on in the two countries'.[73]

In Belgium, the Minister of Economic Affairs called on his countrymen to become 'the Japanese of Europe' in order to get out of their economic difficulties. In France in 1978, a report commissioned by the President on a national strategy for information technology recommended that the French learn from Japan in responding to the new technologies. The report became a best-seller. Two years later, at the 1980 national convention of the French Patronat (Employers' Association), two thousand leading industrialists were urged to abandon West Germany and to turn to Japan as a model for technological innovation. A similar theme was developed by the influential French journalist, Servan-Schreiber, who only fifteen years previously had made his name by warning of the 'US challenge'. Now, in his *The World Challenge* (1980), Japan's rapidly developing new industrial structure, based on the application of information technologies to production, was held up as the wave of the future and as the key to the solution of many current ills.

By the early eighties the 'art of Japanese management' had become a world-wide vogue, and a new myth was born – that of the omnipotence of Japanese management science. One or other feature of enterprise management in one or other segment of

Japanese industry such as on-the-job training, lifetime employment, seniority-based wage systems, total quality control ('QC circles'), enterprise unions, just-in-time inventories or long-term planning were held up as the key to improving management and restoring the competitiveness of European and US business. Ironically it appears to have been forgotten that, as in previous fashions for things Japanese, often the most popular features held up for emulation were precisely those which the Japanese themselves had most recently adapted from the West. The just-in-time inventory system at Toyota, for example, was based on a close study of the Ford assembly line at Baton Rouge, and QC circles were learnt from a US management expert in the fifties.

In describing this or that feature, it was sometimes overlooked that they were not typical of Japanese management and even if they had been, it is doubtful that in themselves they would have been sufficient to explain the Japanese economic success. For example, the large company with over one thousand employees enjoying lifetime employment and a seniority wage system was often taken to be the norm. In fact, only about 25 per cent of the workforce are in such companies or in the government. Half the workforce is in companies with ninety-nine or fewer employees and as of the late eighties, only about 25 per cent were employed in the manufacturing sector.

Closer to home, searching questions began to be asked about Japanese management in the USA and Europe. A number of studies began to show that Japanese manufacturing plants there achieved better quality and obtained higher output levels than locally owned plants. In Britain there was some evidence to show that Japanese electronics factories were twice as productive as British companies and half as much again as US-owned producers operating in the UK. Such studies provided powerful support to those who argued that Japanese industrial successes were not based on mysterious qualities specific to Japanese culture, but on Japanese 'organizational engineering' which was clearly effective in a non-Japanese environment.

By the late eighties, the successes of the Asian NICs, Singapore, Korea, Taiwan and Hong Kong, also undermined many of the single factor or culture specific explanations of Japanese economic success.[74]

Just as the Japanese challenge stimulated a boom in business management, it also led to a re-examination of government structures for handling trade and industry. In the USA there were proposals for an industrial policy, or an export policy, or a Department of International Trade and Industry (a DITI to do battle with the MITI), or consortia, all *à la japonaise*.

In Europe it was frequently suggested that Japan was such an important challenge that it could only be met by uniting to create economies of scale and by adapting similar strategies of technological innovation as those which had helped Japan capture world leadership in one industry after another. Thus it was said that the EC was not keeping pace in the electronics revolution with the USA and Japan because Europe measured technological innovation in terms of jobs lost rather than in terms of the jobs it would create; an attitude typical of a society overtaken by age and making social security its priority. The challenge of Japan was used as a stick to persuade European governments to support concerted EC action in industrial related research projects.

On a larger scale, the move to create a single European market by 1992 was also stimulated by those who believed that it was an essential element of the European response to the challenge presented by Japan and the Asian NICs on the one hand and by the USA on the other.

In industry, although there was some talk of a 'joint defence strategy' against the Japanese, most companies seek partners from whom they can get advanced technology. So many industries in Europe have preferred to join first the Americans and then the Japanese, rather than unite against them. And in the USA, industries such as automobiles, electronics or computers have long since had a strategy of sub-contracting to Japanese or other Asian producers.

From the late eighties, the huge surge in Japanese overseas direct investment has accelerated the trend for joint investments, technology transfer agreements and every form of industrial alliance between Japanese companies and their US and

European opposite numbers. The bulk of these agreements in
hi-tech fields such as robotics, informatics and chemicals were
between Japanese and US companies; in second place came the
agreements between European and US companies; trailing far
behind came the relatively limited number of Europe–Japan
agreements – yet another example of the weakness of the
Europe–Japan side of the US–Europe–Japan triangle.

17

THE MOST PARADOXICAL PEOPLE?

Recent images of Japan were hastily formed following the shock of its emergence as a world economic power, at a period when European economic growth was slowing down and when Americans were having to come to terms with a diminished role in the world economy. The new images were largely derived from older ones, to which they have now been added because today both Americans and Europeans draw upon a fund of stereotypes inherited from the past. The fund is rich enough to hold both positive and negative images which are often contradictory. Such images date from different periods of contact and perception. The public will use whichever one suits the mood of the day.

Few Americans and even fewer Europeans have ever been to Japan or met a Japanese. Older generations will remember the unfavourable images of Japan during the Depression or during the Pacific War. Younger generations are more likely to have had some direct experience with one or another manifestation of Japanese culture, usually impeccably-styled consumer goods rather than traditional arts. For them, names such as Honda, National Panasonic, Nikon, Nissan, Sony, and Toyota are probably more familiar than bonsai, chanoyu, geisha, harakiri, ikebana, kabuki, kámikaze, Noh, and Zen. What they know of Japanese arts they probably picked up from the spate of TV programmes on Japan and Japanese themes.

In 1980, the twelve-hour NBC television mini-series based on Clavell's 1975 best-seller *Shōgun* created a boom with its exotic image of Japan. The BBC–NHK *The Shōgun Inheritance* or the

BBC's *Perspectives on Japan* endeavoured to provide the cultural background to Japan's success and attracted huge audiences.[75] The Japanese martial arts have also had a loyal following for many years and from time to time they surface in fiction (*Ninja*; *The Samurai Strategy*) and are combined with the image of the Japanese as business warriors or samurai salarymen, a popular enough self-image in Japan.

Ever since Kurosawa's *Rashomon* caught the West by surprise at the Venice film festival of 1951, Japanese films, especially samurai films, have had a considerable following. Indeed Kurosawa maintained his popularity for thirty years. In 1981, his *Kagemusha* received rave reviews in Europe and the USA, and a leading Italian fashion designer based his collection for that autumn on 'Japanese' themes inspired by the film – part of a short-lived boom in the eighties for Japanese design, not only in fashion, but also in furniture and interiors.

Japanese literature has been extensively translated but little read. Perhaps the most famous author is Mishima Yukio, but more as the result of the publicity following his sensational suicide than through a wide acquaintane with his writings, even though his later works contain an exoticism which according to some of his critics deliberately intended to appeal to foreigners.

Despite recent vogues for things Japanese and much greater interest in and increased knowledge of Japan in the eighties, there was still widespread ignorance. For example, 60 per cent of those surveyed in France in 1984 by *Le Monde* and the *Asahi Shimbun* were unable to place Japan on a map of the world and a poll conducted in California in 1987 revealed that no more than 50 per cent of the high school children surveyed could locate Japan.[76]

If you ask the man in the street what he associates the Japanese with, depending on his age, he will probably give you a confused picture of cherry blossoms and commuter trains; geisha girls and electronic salesmen; model managers and business warriors. The 'Fuji geisha-san' image has faded, but the picture will still be drawn from the aesthetic image and the crowded and polluted monster image: the erotic and the practical. He will be convinced that the Japanese work too hard, are paid too little and that they compete unfairly in international trade. On the other hand he will admire their management skills and technology.

Western writers and intellectuals who go to Japan, such as Roland Barthes or Paul Theroux, almost without exception can neither read, speak nor write the language, so they remain outsiders. Small wonder that their comments seem superficial and that there is often a tone of ridicule not found in their writing on those countries with whose language or culture they are familiar. The following remark by Paul Theroux is not untypical. Its tone is remarkably similar to the sneering descriptions of Pierre Loti, who suffered from the same linguistic handicap (see Chapter 12), 'All over the country, instruments were commanding the Japanese to act. The Japanese had made these instruments, given them voices and put them in charge. Now, obeying the lights and the sound, the Japanese aspired to them, flexing their little muscles, kicking their little feet, wagging their little heads, like flawed clockwork toys performing for a powerful unforgiving machine that would one day wear them out'.[77]

If there happens to be a wave of fear or dislike of Japan and the Japanese, which usually takes place when there is a recession at home or when there are tensions, such as trade frictions, the differences between Japan and the West are emphasized and the similarities played down. The average man will readily evoke negative images inherited from a previous generation of cruel soldiers, violent suicides and ruthlessly unfair competitors. These associations are drawn from the war image merged with the tricky Oriental image. All the qualities normally attributed to the Japanese will then take on their negative aspects. 'Efficient' becomes 'ruthless' or 'aggressive', 'pragmatic' becomes 'unprincipled', 'group behaviour' becomes 'conformism', 'disciplined' becomes 'regimented' or 'docile', 'willingness to learn' becomes 'slavish imitation', 'paradox' becomes 'contradiction' and so on.

Faced with these sharply contrasted images of Japan, which are now part of our mental landscapes, it is not uncommon to conclude that the Japanese themselves must be unpredictable, if not incomprehensible:

The Japanese are, to the highest degree, both aggressive and unaggressive, both militaristic and aesthetic, both insolent and polite, rigid and adaptable, submissive and resentful of being pushed around, loyal and treacherous, brave and timid, conservative and hospitable to new ways.[78]

Such apparently schizoid behaviour suggests the corollary that, in jumping from one extreme to another, the Japanese must be emotional rather than rational (particularly as reason is felt to be a Western characteristic).

As one of the best informed of the early Japanologists, Professor Chamberlain, put it: 'One is apt to exclaim that Japanese logic is the very antipodes of European logic . . . Were it really so, action would be easy enough: one would simply have to go by the "rule of contraries". But no, that will not do either. The contradiction's only occasional, it only manifests itself sporadically and along certain – or uncertain – lines . . . the result is that the oldest resident . . . may still . . . be pulled up sharp, and forced to exclaim that all his experience does not yet suffice to probe the depths of the mental disposition of this fascinating but enigmatical race'.[79]

This view is not simply that of a nineteenth-century European professor influenced by the prejudices of the day which saw non-Western societies as subservient, like women, and as such 'beyond the pale of reason'. In 1989, a contributor on technology informed the readers of a weekly magazine that 'most Japanese tend to avoid hard and fast logic, preferring to keep things vague'; in 1988, a lifelong US academic expert on Japan, having noted the existence of many different points of view on economic liberalization in Japan, drew the conclusion that 'this illustrates the observation that whatever may be said about Japan, the opposite may also be true'.[80]

Another version of supposed Japanese illogicality is the frequently heard comment that the Japanese language is unfit for clear thought or that the Japanese cannot think philosophically. They are good at hardware, not software; they are application-oriented, creativity-deficient', or, as Hitler put it, 'culture-carrying, not culture-creating'. Those making such observations do not explain how it is that mathematics and technology flourish in Japan.

Today journalists refer as a matter of course to Japan with phrases such as '. . . that most different and exotic country despite its surface modernity . . .', 'made of contradictions', 'the world's newest and least predictable economic superpower', 'things are rarely what they seem'.[81]

Each of the periods in which Westerners formed images of Japan have a number of points in common. They have consistently regarded themselves as teachers and the Japanese as imitators or learners. The first Europeans came as missionaries to teach the heathen, and in the nineteenth and early twentieth centuries they were joined by the Americans as propagators of the secular faith of industrial progress and the political philosophy of the enlightenment to teach the backward. They had a 'mission civilisatrice' as the French put it. That attitude has persisted right to our own day. The following comment made by a well-known expert on Japan as late as 1978 is not untypical: 'When it comes to evaluating the attitude of the Japanese toward any new technology, one could compare them to eager pupils looking up at us, their teachers'.[82]

Because of this sense of superiority Americans and Europeans hardly took Japan seriously and made no effort to find out what was going on there. As a result they held subjective and out-of-date images of Japan.

The missionaries in the sixteenth century expected to find a heathen people, ignorant and primitive. Instead they found the Japanese to be highly civilized. In the nineteenth century, the aesthetic image of Japan was inaccurate, even as it was being formed, and it proved a poor preparation for the emergence of Japan as a military power. This was the case for the Russians in 1904; astonishingly it proved the case again for the Americans and the European colonial powers a whole generation later, who apparently had learnt nothing, so totally did they overestimate their own strength and misread Japanese intentions in the years leading up to Pearl Harbor and to the surrender of Hong Kong, Malaya, Singapore, Burma, the Philippines, Vietnam, Laos, and the Dutch East Indies.

It was in the colonial and imperial period that Europe had its most intense contact with Asia, including Japan. All sorts of prejudices were given full reign and matching images were formed. In the twentieth century, as Europe withdrew from Asia, contacts declined and therefore there were few opportunities to form fresh images, so the attitudes of colonial and imperial superiority towards an Oriental people and the images associated with those attitudes lived on unchallenged. Many of these attitudes and prejudices were also held by Americans whose sense of innate superiority was sustained throughout the post-war years of Pax Americana.

Perhaps this helps explain why, in the seventies, Europeans and Americans were caught by surprise by Japan's rapid economic growth and penetration of world markets. The reaction was based on the thirties' image of Japan as a cheap-labour, Asiatic country operating with an unfair advantage. Little or no attention had been paid to the gradual build-up of capital- and technology-intensive industries in Japan which were the main source of its new competitiveness. Had sufficient account been taken of what was going on in Japan in the fifties and sixties, it is just possible that Westerners might have been persuaded to take a leaf from Japan's book. At the very least there would have been less of a shock when Japan began scoring massive trade surpluses in the seventies and eighties.

Today, despite some improvement, there is still an extraordinary ignorance of Japan which compares most unfavourably with the widespread knowledge of the USA and Europe in Japan. This 'knowledge deficit' is crucial because it places Americans and Europeans at a serious disadvantage in dealing with the Japanese.

PART IV

OPEN MARKETS AND
DOUBLE-BOLTED DOORS

18

EARLY DAYS

The economic and trade frictions which have accompanied the rise of Japan as a world financial and trading power are the most striking expression of the fundamental and ongoing shift in the world balance of economic power which was outlined in Chapter 1. The question of timing is crucial; the problems caused by Japanese exports often exacerbated economic difficulties already being experienced in the USA and the EC, and the problems of access to the Japanese market came before Japan had undertaken the restructuring of its economy towards reliance on domestic, as opposed to export-led, growth. So often relatively minor trade problems became rapidly politicized. The frictions were also compounded by widespread ignorance and prejudice in the USA and the EC about Japan.

They have usually occurred when a decline in Japanese domestic demand leading to strong pressures to export coincided with a downturn of the business cycle in the USA and Europe, especially in labour-intensive industries. Reflecting a previous negative balance on current account, the yen at such times was undervalued, thus giving Japan's exports an added advantage. The knife was given a further twist if, in addition to scoring surpluses in trade with the USA and Europe, the Japanese trade and current accounts moved into the black while its partners were still in the red. It happened during the Depression of 1929–32, and again during the seventies and eighties when massive rises in the price of oil and other raw materials created a sharp new stimulus for Japan to export. Indeed the oil shocks of 1973 and 1979 triggered Japanese export booms which led directly to trade frictions with both Europe and the USA.

These external shocks also encouraged the Japanese to tighten their belts and save; the government adopted stringent fiscal policies and the consequent mismatch with US fiscal policy during the Reagan years led to the sudden reversal of creditor status between Japan and the USA. The massive macro-imbalances of the late eighties in turn became a source of economic friction. There are, of course, many other reasons why there have been trade frictions between Japan and its main trading partners, the USA and Europe.

In the early days when Japan was a newly industrializing country its advantage in industries such as textiles lay in its cheap labour. Competition was primarily price competition. Later, as Japan developed its capital-intensive and knowledge-intensive industries, its comparative advantage was in technology and efficiency, not in cheap labour. So competition was less in price than in quality.

The first reactions to the Japanese challenge in the sixties and seventies were often inadequate, geared more to the previous age when cheap exports from Japan were the problem. Insufficient efforts were made to meet the challenge by restructuring industries and by adopting new technologies. A positive reaction was no doubt made that much more difficult because Japan's export drives, which built up very swiftly, were often concentrated precisely in those European and US industries which were, for one reason or another, already in decline and therefore suffering from high levels of unemployment. Moreover, these industries numbered some of the largest in the entire economy – textiles, steel, shipbuilding, cars, bearings, electronics. The very core of the industrial economy began to seem threatened and political lobbies were quickly aroused. Japan was accused of operating with all kinds of unfair advantage, of keeping its own market closed and of exporting unemployment.

Another reason for the slow restructuring of industries in both Europe and the USA has been the rigidity of labour markets and the practice of employing ethnic minorities and recent immigrants at low wages in yesterday's industries.

Japanese export drives in the seventies and eighties came at a period when the principal economies of the world had become far more tightly interconnected than ever before, but when the expansion of world trade and economic growth had slowed down and the floating exchange-rate system had been less and less effective in contributing to balance-of-payments adjustments. If one country recovered faster from recession than the others, it was all too easy for that country to be seen as recovering at the expense of the others, especially if its recovery was based on export-led growth. To make matters worse, in many European countries, and in the USA, inflation, high levels of unemployment and falling productivity were the norm for much of the seventies and eighties. Under these conditions, timely restructuring of industries and development of strategies to cope with the Japanese challenge were that much harder – particularly as, until recently, Japan was not even perceived as a serious challenge.

Before examining the economic and trade frictions in greater detail, it is perhaps worth taking a quick look at the steps by which Japan turned the tables on Europe and the USA and reversed its trading relationship with the West from one of almost total submission to one of something approaching dominance today.

Trade relations between Japan and the West have been unequal and unbalanced since the first trade treaties in 1866. For a hundred years the balance was tipped in favour of the West, except during the two world wars. During all this time Japan had large deficits with both Europe and the USA. It was only after 1968 that the balance for the first time in history began moving steadily in its favour.

The relations were unequal in the early days in the sense that Japan, although never becoming a colony, did sign unequal treaties which allowed extra-territoriality for the European countries and the USA and denied Japan an independent commercial policy. The government had no tariff autonomy and the duties on all imports were fixed at the uniformly low rate of 5 per cent for almost fifty years from 1866 to 1911. In addition, Japan was obliged to accord most-favoured nation treatment to all foreign powers, without reciprocal treatment towards Japan by them.

The trade itself has also been unequal in that Europe and the USA have been a much more important source of supplies and market for Japan than Japan has been for either of them. This situation only began to change in the eighties when Japan began supplying a larger share of US and EC imports and also became a more important market for both. It remains true however that the USA and the EC are more important markets for Japan than Japan is for either of them (see Annex, Table 7).

From the Meiji Restoration (1868) to World War I, Europe, chiefly Great Britain, was Japan's main supplier of modern goods, from munitions, factories and machines to textiles and cotton goods. In some years upwards of 70 per cent of all Japan's imports came from five European countries (Great Britain, France, Germany, Belgium and Italy). These were also the years when European exporters benefited from especially low tariffs. As a contemporary Japanese observer put it in 1890: 'The evils that Japan has suffered on account of her contact with European people does not so much consist in the overthrow of some of her old industries, by the free and sudden influx of foreign goods, as in her inability, on account of the treaties, to derive a revenue from that importation'.[1]

There was a gradual shift to other suppliers, but it was not until 1915 that the United States exported more to Japan than the European countries (see Table 10). Europe was also Japan's major export market, principally for raw silk, tea and rice until the 1890s, when the USA achieved that position.

In contrast to Europe's importance in Japan's trade during this early period, less than 1 per cent of Europe's imports came from Japan, while at the most Japan absorbed no more than 2.5 per cent of Europe's exports. So the trade relations were typical of those between a developed region and an underdeveloped country, not only in the nature of the goods exchanged, but also in the different degree of importance attached to the trade by each partner. To Japan it was vital; to America and Europe it was marginal. The difference in the size of the bilateral trade in the total trade of each partner goes a long way to help explain the indifference of most Europeans and Americans towards the Japanese market until very recently.

Table 10. Japan's Trade with the EC and the USA, 1873–1965

| | Japan's Exports | | | | Japan's Imports | | | |
| | Share to European countries | | Share to USA | | Share from European countries | | Share from USA | |
	%	Rank	%	Rank	%	Rank	%	Rank
1873	51.9	1	19.5	3	58.5	1	3.6	3
1883	41.8	1	37.1	2	58.0	1	11.2	3
1893	31.7	1	31.5	2	44.9	1	6.9	6
1900	21.0	2	26.5	1	41.1	1	21.8	2
1910	22.5	2	31.3	1	33.4	1	11.8	4
1915	16.1	3	28.8	1	13.0	4	19.3	2
1920	9.8	4	29.0	1	13.1	3	41.6	1
1930	8.0	4	34.4	1	15.3	2	28.6	1
1938	8.7	4	15.8	2	10.3	3	34.4	1
1949	11.1	5	18.1	1	3.0	3	62.2	1
1955	7.6	4	22.3	1	5.5	3	31.2	1
1960	7.8	2	27.2	1	7.0	3	34.6	1
1965	8.8	2	29.3	1	7.0	2	29.0	1

Note: The years 1873 and 1878 are based on Japan's trade with the UK, France, Germany, Italy, Holland and Belgium. From 1883 to 1930 the figures show Japan's trade with these countries as well as Denmark and from 1935 onwards Ireland and Luxemburg are also included.
Source: Ministry of Finance, Tokyo; Exports, FOB; Imports, CIF.

Another reason was that most would have agreed with Adam Smith's optimistic judgement that China was 'perhaps in extent not much inferior to the market of all the different countries of Europe put together'. Nobody felt the same about Japan, particularly as the Japanese were already developing a domestic manufacturing industry (led by textiles) capable of competing with Lancashire or Massachusetts.

Already long before the Meiji Restoration one of the scholars of Dutch learning, Honda Toshiaki (1744–1821), had outlined a basic mercantilist plan for his country:

As part of a national policy, every effort should be made to promote the production in this country of articles that are of as fine manufacture as possible. If such efforts are made, individual industries will be encouraged, and attempts to improve the quality of Japanese products will follow. In that way many articles famed for their excellence will be produced in this country. This will help us gain profit when trading with foreign nations.

He also said, 'Foreign trade is a war in which each party seeks to extract wealth from the other.'[2]

Honda was well ahead of his time. Mercantilism as a doctrine made little impression on his countrymen until the Meiji period, but from then on it was to have great influence on Japanese policy-makers as they sought to win back control of Japan's trade from foreign hands and as they pursued the aim of catching up with the West and 'excelling the nations of the whole world'.[3]

Protectionism as a means of enabling Japan's industries to grow was first extensively aired during the debate over treaty reform in the 1870s and 1880s. It was preceded by an emotional hostility towards foreign goods in the 1860s as recorded by Fukuzawa Yukichi: 'Stores dealing in foreign goods were attacked for no other reason than that they sold foreign commodities which "caused loss" to the country'.[4]

Cromwell and Colbert were praised as 'extraordinary men and the fathers of protection' who had laid the ground for the wealth and prosperity of England and France. It was observed that 'even England initially followed mercantile theories . . . only much later did Adam Smith advocate free trade . . . only when England was prosperous and strong did she move to free trade'. Therefore, looking into the future, 'if we reach the point some years hence where the trade and industry of our people both surpass that of foreigners and where there is no wastage of our human and soil resources, the time will perhaps have come when we too may adopt free trade'.[5]

In 1892 Baron Kentaro wrote to Herbert Spencer asking his advice on Japanese policy towards the foreign powers. Spencer replied and gave his permission for the advice to be passed to the prime minister, on the condition that it not be made public in his lifetime to avoid arousing the animosity of his fellow countrymen. His advice can only have been music to the ears of the Meiji mercantilists:

The Japanese policy should . . . be of keeping Americans and Europeans as much as possible at arm's length . . . It seems to me that the only forms of intercourse which you may with advantage permit are those which are indispensable for the exchange of commodities – importation and exportation of physical and mental products. Apparently you are proposing by revision of the treaty with the powers of Europe and America 'to open the whole Empire to foreigners and foreign capital.' I regret this as a fatal policy. If you wish to see what is likely to happen, study the history of India . . .

There should be, not only a prohibition of foreign persons to hold property in land, but also a refusal to give them leases, and a permission only to reside as annual tenants;

. . . prohibit to foreigners the working of mines owned or worked by the Government.

. . . keep the coasting trade in your own hands and forbid foreigners to engage in it . . .

The distribution of commodities brought to Japan from other places may be properly left to the Japanese themselves, and should be denied to foreigners.[6]

Expatriate businessmen in those far-off nineteenth-century days complained bitterly. Echoes of some of their complaints are still heard even today. The following summary, for example, was contained in a European guide to Japan first published in 1890, which is still in print.

European bankers and merchants in Japan . . . complain it is true, not so much of actual, wilful dishonesty – though of that too, they affirm there is plenty – as of pettiness, constant shilly-shallying, unbusinesslikeness almost passing belief. Japan, the globetrotter's paradise, is also the grave of the merchant's hopes.[7]

Another early complaint, this time from 1892, has also been repeated from that day to this:

In commercial matters the Japanese have exhibited their imitativeness in the most extraordinary degree. Almost everything they have once bought, from beer to bayonets and from straw hats to heavy ordnance, they have since learned to make for themselves. There is hardly a well-known European trademark that you do not find fraudulently imitated in Japan . . .[8]

It was not all complaints however. Observers pointed out some of the reasons for the successes of Japanese business as well as some of the long-range consequences of its industrialization.

Sir Henry Norman, for example, the English traveller, journalist and expert on the Far East, wrote in 1895 that Japan had become a first-class power because of its army and the defeat of China, and he continued:

The second aspect, under which the progress of Japan is of great interest to Western nations, is that of a rival in manufactures. This is a far more serious question, especially to Great Britain, than is yet generally understood. The truth is that our manufactures are actually being driven out of many markets of the East by the Japanese, and that the most competent observers prophesy the rapid development of this process.

Sir Henry went on to quote a Mr Gubbins of the British Legation in Tokyo who had written in a report on industries such as cotton, watch-making and match-making, 'so far as the Eastern market is concerned, no country can any longer compete with Japan'. Sir Henry also quotes another British official, a Mr Hunt stationed in Pusan in Korea, who had reported to London that:

While the great bulk of the piece goods and metals sold in Pusan are of European origin, principally British, the fact should not be overlooked that Japan, by carefully studying arising needs, and supplying articles suitable to the tastes and means of Korea and her Pusan colonists, is able to compete, more successfully each year, with almost all the goods of European manufacture.[9]

Mr Hunt's analysis was simple, but it retains its validity to this day.

In Part III, we saw that Japan's victory over the Qing Empire in 1895 had already touched off a fear of a new 'economic yellow peril'. Some even began speculating that the centre of world power was moving to the Far East. Sir Henry was one of them: 'Under [the Mikado] the dreams of the supremacy of the yellow race in Europe, Asia and even Africa . . . would be no longer mere nightmares. Instead of speculating as to whether England or Germany or Russia is to be the next world's ruler, we might have to learn that Japan was on its way to that position.'[10]

But most people in Europe were hardly aware that the lesson existed. In Britain, which conducted the lion's share of Europe's trade with Japan until overtaken by Germany in 1919, a contemporary complained that:

Japan's material and industrial progress since 1890 has been even more marked than that which she has shown in military and constitutional affairs, though even to this day what she has achieved in this respect meets but with scant recognition among the manufacturers and merchants of Great Britain, who have failed alike to recognize the already great and always growing importance of Japan as a market for their own products or the possibility of her becoming a formidable competitor with them, not only in the Far East, but even in Australia and India.[11]

In the years to come Europeans and Americans were more concerned about Japanese competition in third markets and in their own markets than about their failure to penetrate the Japanese market itself, which had early acquired the reputation of being 'the grave of the merchant's hopes'.

As a result of World War I, Europe was unable to maintain its exports to Japan and the USA became Japan's main supplier. Japan was far from the active theatres of the war and its industries had reached a stage where they were able to take advantage of markets which the European countries and the USA were unable to supply because of war – in Asia or Africa, for example. For the first time in modern history Japan began scoring large trade surpluses and, also for the first time, most of its external trade was now conducted by Japanese companies. After the war, although Europe never regained the central role it had played in Japan's modernization, it continued to be an important trading partner of Japan, but with a much reduced share of the trade.

Bit by bit as Japan developed light industries and began to expand its exports to world markets, the warnings and complaints grew in the USA and Europe. Many of them echoed the remarks already quoted, or observations such as that made by the US historian, Brooks Adams, at the end of the nineteenth century:

Even now factories can be equipped almost as easily in India, Japan and China, as in Lancashire or Massachusetts, and the products of the cheapest labour can be sold more advantageously in European capitals than those of Tyre and Alexandria were in Rome under the Antonines.[12]

For those who did not take quite such a long historical view of the newly industrialized countries of that day, there was also the recent memory of the rise of Germany as an exporter of manufactured goods towards the end of the nineteenth century. At that time too there had been accusations against the Germans, mainly from the British, of low wages and dumping; of state subsidies, of stealing of patents and of fraudulent imitation of trade marks.

Denunciation of Japan's supposedly unfair trading practices reached a peak at the time of the Depression in the early thirties, when Japan alone of the industrial powers was able to increase its exports (two-thirds of which were textiles and raw silk). The most vociferous lobbies calling for the closing of domestic and colonial markets to Japanese exports were labour-intensive light industries, for example, the textiles of Lancashire, Lyons, or Krefeld, which were already non-competitive on world markets and saw themselves dethroned by the Japanese from a hundred-year position of world supremacy. The US market was still firmly closed.

By no means all voices were turned against Japan. A study group in Paris produced a fair-minded report which concluded that the Japanese were not practising dumping and that Japanese industry produced well-made goods at reasonable prices. If Japan had lower wages than in Europe this was because the Japanese were used to a less lavish style of life.[13] In England, the Federation of British Industries (FBI) sent a delegation to Japan in 1934 which reported with equal fair-mindedness that Japanese industry had benefited from the depreciation of the yen, lack of domestic inflation and the absence of an organized movement demanding increased wages. It rejected the notion of 'sweated labour', although noting the very poor conditions in the traditional sector of Japanese industry, which sector it concluded should be held responsible for generating a good deal of the domestic competition which had led to the fierce pressures to export. The vital role of government was noted. The report also drew attention to the high productivity of Japanese industry and warned that 'it would be unwise to assume that the future export activities of Japan will be limited to cheap goods of low quality'.

In its recommendations the FBI rejected protectionist measures whose outcome would be a trade war beneficial to no one and suggested instead 'a means of co-operation between British and Japanese industry'.

. . . There are many different ways in which such co-operation might be realised. It might be by conscious directional control of exports; by means of a division of markets upon a percentage or some other quantitative basis; by some similar agreement on a territorial basis; by mutual action to develop in co-operation some of the more backward markets of the world; by agreements as to the level of export prices; by some rationalization of production according to type and quality; or by joint manufacturing activities.[14]

The report did not enter into further detail on industrial cooperation, recognizing that no general principle could be laid down which would suit all cases. Therefore each industry should decide for itself whether it wished to reach an understanding with its opposite number in Japan.

Because of the economic depression in Europe and the popular outcry against Japan, such reasonable voices went unheeded. It became politically expedient to follow the pack and Japan was the obvious scapegoat. Discriminatory quotas and high tariffs were set whose effect was to gradually close European and colonial markets to Japanese goods. The Japanese reaction was to concentrate on markets closer to home. In 1916, Korea, Formosa and Manchuria took 16 per cent of Japan's exports. By 1937 this had risen to 38 per cent.

These years of rejection by the West and the closing of its markets to Japanese goods saw an ideological 'return to the East' in Japan, whose hallmark was a militant anti-Western Pan-Asianism. Indeed the war in north China was frequently justified as a legitimate search by Japan for new markets to replace those closed to it by Western protectionism.[15]

There was a strong feeling that Japan was being made a scapegoat. In the words of a ministry of war pamphlet of 1934: 'Countries suffering economic stagnation and anxiety concerning the international situation are jealous of the empire's foreign trade expansion and its growing political power'.[16]

It was pointed out that Japan had only been practising what it had been forced to learn from the West, namely free trade. The Japanese, it was claimed, had been able to rationalize their industries with new equipment because of the cooperation of the workers, which cooperation was lacking in the USA and Europe. Moreover, Japanese labour was frugal and worked hard while in the West 'labour aims at working the shortest possible hours, doing the minimum amount of work and getting the highest possible wage'. With some justification a Japanese official writing in a 'non-official' capacity observed in 1934:

Eighty years ago, Japan was compelled to open her door to Europe and America. Small-scale industries of Japan could not stand the competition of Western goods which were produced with superior machinery. Consequently they all ceased to exist. That is history. Japan was then told that free trade was a means whereby the common welfare of mankind was promoted. By discarding industries which did not suit her and by concentrating on those best suited to her, she has now attained that stage where some of her industries are superior to those of the old industrial countries. As soon as she begins competing with them, she is condemned in the name of humanity.[17]

Many of the arguments used on both sides not only had a pedigree stretching back to the turn of the century, but they were also to be repeated in the post-war period and again after the oil shocks in the seventies and eighties.

19

POST-WAR RECOVERY

'In 1951 a group of [Japanese businessmen] held a meeting and decided to ask the government to adopt measures to promote exports and discourage imports to Japan', recalled the engineering genius who founded Honda Motors. He went on, 'If Japanese technology were good and Japanese products were high in quality, then the Japanese would not have to discourage the import of foreign-made goods. Exports of such high-quality products would have to be increased without the help of the government.' And he added, 'It was at that moment . . . that I resolved to discourage imports and promote exports by enhancing technology and developing engines that were the highest in performance in the world.'[18]

Kinugasa's *Gate of Hell* won the grand prize at the Cannes Film Festival and Oscars for best foreign film and costume design. When it opened in New York in 1954, the consul-general of Japan said, 'To me it is entirely conceivable that the export of superior films will greatly help my country in its present unremitting struggle to become self-sufficient, to rely on trade, not aid.'[19]

It takes an effort nowadays to imagine that Japan was an aid recipient until the early sixties, that its representatives regarded its award-winning films as dollar-earning exports and that most of the leaders of its new industries and of the government, although perhaps not Mr Honda, were mercantilists in that they held that an increase in exports or a reduction in imports must be to their country's advantage. Perhaps it helps to recall that the USA itself was no stranger to mercantilism until as recently as the thirties.

A sense of perspective also helps – in 1952 Japan's GNP was smaller than that of Malaya; it was only in 1959 that Japan's exports recovered their highest pre-war level; only in 1965 that it scored a trade surplus; and only in 1966 that it recovered its pre-war share of world exports (5 per cent). Until 1969, more foreigners visited Japan than Japanese travelled abroad.

In 1955 Japan entered the General Agreement on Tariffs and Trade (GATT), but several of the European countries refused to extend most-favoured nation treatment. The problem was that the old fears of Japan flooding European markets with cheap goods, especially textiles, were still very much alive. It was for this reason that several countries not only invoked Article XXXV but also set import restrictions even before Japanese imports had started arriving.

The issue was widely followed in Japan. On a visit there, the executive secretary of the GATT reported encountering a taxi driver in a provincial town who, upon learning that his passenger was a GATT official, immediately exclaimed, 'Ah, that Article XXXV!'

Only when Japan was admitted as a full member of the Organization for Economic Cooperation and Development (OECD) in 1964 did most European countries agree to dis-invoke Article XXXV. Even so, several still insisted on having a safeguard clause included in their trade agreements with Japan entitling them to take unilateral measures to stop Japanese imports in case of 'emergency'. Most of them retained discriminatory import restrictions.

Today the number of discriminatory quantitative restrictions has been reduced, and the remainder will be phased out as part of the preparations for the single European market in 1992. But their existence for nearly forty years was regarded in Japan as psychologically offensive, a stumbling-block to improving EC–Japan relations, and a further reason for Japanese reluctance to make concessions to the Europeans.[20]

In the USA the atmosphere in the fifties was more relaxed. Pax Americana was at its height and Japan was not seen as a threat.

There were fewer memories of Japan flooding US markets because Fortress America had been alive and well in the thirties when the USA's markets were closed to Japanese exports. In 1951, General McArthur informed the US Senate that the Japanese were mentally twelve years old. Three years later, the secretary of state, Mr Dulles, assured a Congressional Committee that Japan lacked the skills to export much of anything to the USA, but might find a few markets in Southeast Asia. While the USA pursued geopolitical influence, Japan pursued exports and no contradiction was seen between the two activities. On the contrary, for strategic reasons the USA was trying to promote the strengthening of the Japanese economy as a bulwark against Chinese and Soviet expansion.

But already by 1956 things had begun to change. In that year the President, Mr Eisenhower, secured from Japan a voluntary export restraint agreement (VERA) on textiles which went into force in 1957. Similar controls were set up to cover the other Asian exporters and then all the other developing countries. The EC and the other importers were obliged to follow suit. The result was the 1962 Long-Term Agreement on Cotton Textiles which a decade later set limits on all developing country exports to the developed market economies under the Multi-Fibre Agreement (MFA) of the GATT. The MFA was periodically extended and continues to this day. Only Japan, as a net exporter of textiles until 1988, never became a signatory.

Protectionism of one form or another has since spread to many other sectors of world trade – steel, food, automobiles, machine tools, electronics, semiconductors. The pattern followed has often been similar to that which led to the regulation of the textile trade. An agreement by Japan to voluntarily limit its exports to the USA was quickly requested by the EC or vice versa. Subsequently such agreements were globalized at the request of Japan's other trade partners. From the mid-eighties the exports of the Asian NICs began to trigger similar reactions.

During the sixties, Japan's world trade was growing at about twice the speed of that of Europe and the USA. The bilateral trade with both was more or less in balance over the decade. It was not very large but it was increasing rapidly. From the end of the decade, Japan began scoring continuously growing trade surpluses with the USA and the EC. Both in the United States and Europe the main concern was to prevent sudden concentrations or influxes of Japanese imports into domestic markets in 'sensitive' sectors such as cotton textiles, sewing machines, ceramics, shoes, umbrellas, and cutlery. These labour-intensive items had also typified Japan's exports in the thirties and were soon to be exported by Japan's successors, the NICs.

At the end of the sixties, Japanese industrial production went up market, and the complaints about its exports shifted to cameras, transistors, TV sets, bearings and steel. There were also criticisms of Japan's rapidly growing share of the world order book for ships.

After textiles, its main export, regulated by a VERA in the sixties and early seventies, was steel. Here again a Japanese agreement to limit its exports to the USA quickly led the EC to request the same: to prevent the US industry enjoying more favourable treatment than its own (which was already limiting its exports to the USA), and to prevent further diversion of Japanese exports. These steel VERAs continued throughout the seventies.

Japan's trade surplus was growing rapidly while the USA scored its first deficit since 1893 and the EC was also in deficit. In 1971 Japan had a higher surplus than ever before. Not for the first time Europeans were taken by surprise and took note of Japan only when they were forced to.

European politicians began to visit Tokyo to register their concern; a wave of protectionist sentiment was touched off and Japan was accused of dumping and subsidizing exports. Ralf Dahrendorf, an EC commissioner, only voiced a widespread view when he pointed out that 'in Japan protectionism is traditional', and he called for the further opening of the Japanese market to EC exports, as a necessary move to stop a chain reaction leading to world-wide protectionism.[21]

Under very strong US pressure including the 'Nixon shock' of suspending the convertibility of the dollar to gold and imposing a

10 per cent import surcharge, coinciding with a yen revaluation, the Japanese authorities in 1971 and 1972 took several measures to reduce exports and to open the Japanese market. These were effective in the short run, but quickly made out of date by the rapid shifts in the world economy in 1973, which rang down the curtain on Act I of the post-war trade frictions with Japan.

20

TRADE FRICTIONS, 1973–84

The breakdown of the international monetary system in the early seventies and the huge increase in the prices of raw materials, highlighted by the dramatic rise in the price of oil after 1973, brought to an end the post-war period. Growth in the industrial countries declined sharply and in many cases became negative. Most experienced massive inflation. The world economy entered its worst recession since the thirties. It was in these years that the novel *Japan Sinks* hit the best-seller list in Tokyo.

The immediate way out for resource-poor trading nations, such as the European countries and Japan, became 'export or perish' and the competition between them became sharper than ever before. The measures taken by the Japanese authorities to open the Japanese market to imports in 1971 and 1972 were not given a high priority. US and European deficits with Japan continued to grow as Japan adjusted to low growth at home by stepping up exports abroad.

It soon became evident that partly through good planning and the 'nurturing' of new industries, partly through large investments in plant and equipment, and partly through luck, Japan in the sixties had better prepared its economy to meet the needs of new export markets in the seventies than had its partners. This was reflected in the more dynamic global export performance of Japan than either the United States or the European Community during the seventies. Over most of the decade Japan had a growing trade surplus with both the USA and the EC for the first time in one hundred years. By 1980, its trade surplus with the EC was slightly higher than with the USA (see Figure 2).

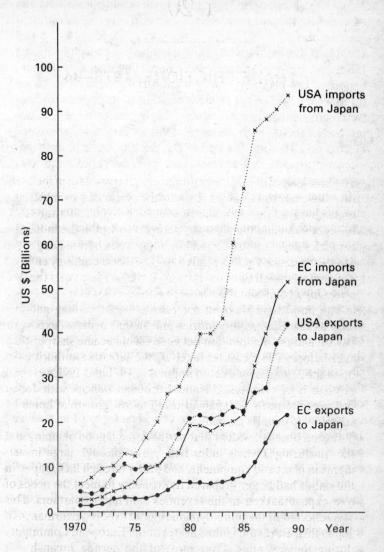

Fig. 2. US and EC Merchandise Trade with Japan, 1970–89

Note: See Annex, Table 6 for figures and sources, and Table 3, Chapter 1 for the trade in invisibles.

Since the Meiji period, Japanese leaders had pursued the aim of 'excelling the nations of the whole world'. By the seventies, at least insofar as merchandise trade was concerned, Japan had caught up. It now had a large and growing trade surplus with the USA and Europe, and instead of importing manufactures and exporting raw materials and light industrial goods as it had done up to about 1955, more than 90 per cent of its exports to them were now manufactures. Increasingly these were capital-intensive goods such as steel, ships, cars and consumer electronics. Then, at the end of the decade, came knowledge-intensive exports such as machinery, pharmaceuticals and tele-communications.[22]

In other words, reflecting the changes in Japanese industrial structure in the fifties and sixties, instead of challenging Europe and the USA in labour-intensive or low value-added industries as it had done in earlier decades, Japan was now competing successfully with some of the US's and Europe's largest and most prestigious industries.

The converse began to be seen in the EC's exports to Japan, where it was increasingly the labour-intensive and luxury consumer goods which alone could find a market, while exports of basic intermediate and capital goods declined. Likewise more than half US exports to Japan are raw materials and food – a situation provoking considerable neo-mercantilist comment. In the words of one US Congressman, 'We now occupy the position of a colony with Japan: we send them raw materials and they send us finished products . . . That's a very clever way of increasing Japanese prosperity at the expense of the United States.' Not only is this shaky economics, it is not even true. While US exports to Japan have always contained a large component of commodities, raw cotton in the early days, agricultural goods today, the largest US export item to Japan is aircraft, both civilian and military, and US exports of invisibles to Japan bring in as much profit as exports of goods.[23]

For most of the seventies, the Americans and Europeans were thrown on the defensive and could only request the Japanese to cooperate by restricting their exports. Voluntary export restraint agreements (VERAs) were negotiated either by government officials or by industries, in which case they were euphemistically referred to as 'understandings'. They covered a very large part of the total of Japanese exports to the USA and Europe – radios, tape-recorders, television tubes, steel and cars all came under one or another kind of 'auto-limitation'. In the shipbuilding sector Japan was persuaded to raise its prices and institute capacity cutbacks. But even after these were implemented it managed to maintain 40 to 50 per cent of the world order book for new ships.

The best that could be done was to seek a breathing space to enable industries to restructure in order to meet more effectively the competition from Japan. The trouble was that too often the breathing space was not used to restructure and improve productivity. The weakening of the textiles industry was followed by shipbuilding, which in turn was followed by steel. In some countries the home electronics and automobile industries had begun to falter already in the mid-seventies. The decline of such key industries in the USA and Europe, many of which employ millions of workers, produced a highly charged atmosphere in which scapegoats were sought. Domestically the blame was laid on the trade unions or on management, or on the welfare state. Abroad, the obvious candidate for scapegoat was the country whose export industries were so successfully cutting a swathe through world markets – Japan.

To head off the protectionist pressures which so easily proliferate in this kind of atmosphere, the EC Commission repeatedly emphasized the necessity of increasing access to the Japanese market for European exporters. US officials adopted a similar approach although the products they stressed, for example beef, oranges or cigarettes, reflected US priorities and were not always the same as those championed by the EC.

One way of achieving increased access to the Japanese market was to lower tariffs, an exercise conducted in the Kennedy and Tokyo rounds of the multilateral trade negotiations in Geneva. Another approach, in consultation with the Japanese authorities, was to remove difficulties encountered on the Japanese market other than those presented by high tariffs.

Such 'non-tariff' barriers (NTBs) usually involved Japanese government regulations covering health, safety, industrial or environmental standards which were considered a real hindrance by US and European exporters, who complained of high costs and long delays. Over the next ten years, talks were held with the Japanese authorities on a long list of NTBs.[24] The results by their nature were not calculated to be dramatic. The trade effects of removing NTBs could never be immediate and they were usually only marginal.

The gradual opening of the Japanese market coincided with the enormous increases of Japan's trade surpluses, which were therefore not the result of a closed domestic market, but the fruit of a successful export drive. When significant increases of European and US exports to Japan came in the late eighties they were made possible by macro-economic shifts in exchange rates and investment – not by the removal of NTBs. But without their removal entry into the market would have been more difficult and perhaps slower.

In 1975, Japan had a small global deficit but a large surplus with the EC, which from 1975 onwards was not selling half as much to Japan as it bought from it. Eventually the storm broke, and this is how it happened. In the early autumn of 1976, it became only too clear in Europe that unemployment would be up again, not least in labour-intensive industries such as steel, shipbuilding and automobiles, all of which were faced by strong competition from Japan. It also became clear that the EC's global trade deficit was going to be as large as it had been in 1974, the year after the oil shock. The global current account was also going deeply into the red. Japan, on the other hand, showed every sign of continuing its strong recovery from the oil shock, as well as moving into the black in its current account and trade balances. These changes had not yet translated through to the exchange rates, so the yen was still relatively cheap, giving Japanese exports a considerable price advantage. Unemployment in Japan was much lower than in the EC, even when the problem of the different basis of Japanese unemployment statistics was taken into account.

Finally, it was observed that the EC would score its largest trade deficit in history with Japan.

Headlines such as 'Is Japan Playing Fair?', 'The Strategy of Invasion' or 'Japan is Back' began appearing in the European and US press. In October, I was quoted in *Newsweek* as saying what my authorities had been saying for several years: 'We view the present imbalance with grave concern. It can't go on much longer.'

The problem became a headline issue for various political reasons. The Hamburg shipyards, for example, were losing business and unemployment was rising rapidly there. Hamburg was the German Chancellor's electoral base. In England, the left wing of the Labour Party and the trade unions were putting pressure on the prime minister, Mr Callaghan, to unilaterally close the British market to imports and to 'save British jobs'. The most rapidly expanding imports into England were from Japan and they were concentrated in highly visible sectors such as cars.

Japanese industry moved rapidly to placate the Europeans by strengthening voluntary export restraint in the five 'problem sectors'; by setting up study groups and by planning to send 'important promotion' missions to Europe. Steps were taken to establish a special centre to help industrially advanced countries to export their finished products to Japan. The government also announced that it would make a number of tariff cuts in advance of the programme agreed in the Tokyo round of multilateral trade negotiations.

Since that autumn of 1976 the EC and Japan went through bouts of trade friction, usually coinciding with spring and autumn, the busy seasons in the international, political and bureaucratic calendar. The rhythm was somewhat complicated by the US and EC negotiators who could not allow the other to steal a march and win concessions from Japan ahead of them. So naturally enough the USA soon followed the EC, coming in with its demands in July 1977, and intensifying the pressure that autumn.

Next, in the long period leading up to the first Tokyo summit of the G-7 industrial countries in June 1979, the USA, starting in the winter of 1978, sought to put further pressure on Japan, which was quickly followed by the EC. So intense did this rivalry become that each time a Japanese negotiator visited Washington, every effort was made to invite him to Brussels and vice versa. As with textiles, Japanese arrangements with the USA immediately affected EC policies towards Japan. The single most important case was that of automobiles, discussed in the next chapter. There were to be many others over the years.

After a cooling-off period following the Tokyo summit, trade frictions with Japan broke out again in 1980. The circumstances were similar to those surrounding the earlier outbreak in 1976. The effects of the second oil shock on the Japanese economy, on the other hand, were to stimulate an export boom which had already been in the making, thanks to weak domestic demand and a large deficit in the Japanese balance of payments in 1979 which had led to a cheap yen. By the spring of 1980 it was clear that this was once again going to be an export-led growth year for Japan which found itself rising to the peak of its current business cycle – as the Europeans and Americans were moving to the trough of theirs.

As so often on previous occasions Japanese exports were concentrated on a limited number of sectors which were already in trouble of one kind or another. The list of such 'sensitive' sectors included not only the old favourites, such as ships, televisions, bearings and cars, but also one or two newcomers, such as machine tools and computers. Another new element was that the most rapid build-up of Japanese exports of cars and television sets was to the German market. This was no coincidence, for by 1980 it was the only major market left in Europe to which access for these goods was still unrestricted.

Calls for protection against Japanese imports intensified and they began to be heard in Germany, traditionally the staunchest backer of free trade in the EC. That spring, the Japanese prime minister, Mr Suzuki, paid official visits to the main EC countries, stressing his country's desire to strengthen its political ties with Europe. He had come to talk politics, not trade. In most capitals he found that his interlocutors had the opposite concern; trade questions were uppermost in their minds. The irony of this situation was not lost on the small number of observers who remembered the visit of a previous Japanese prime minister to Europe (that of Mr Ikeda in 1962). He had then been scornfully dismissed as a 'transistor salesman' by General de Gaulle because of his willingness to discuss such pedestrian matters as trade quotas in contrast to the General's lofty concern with geopolitics.

The danger of the Europeans and Japanese once again talking at cross purposes during Mr Suzuki's visit was avoided by masterly timing: the announcements of Japanese voluntary export restraint agreements (VERAs) on automobile exports preceded or coincided with the prime minister's arrival in each country. A statesmanlike tone prevailed and there was general acknowledgement of the need to place Europe–Japan relations on a sound political basis.

The easing of the bilateral trade frictions was also helped by the antipathy felt by both the Europeans and the Japanese towards US deflationary economic policies and high interest rates which were acting as a brake on economic recovery in Europe and Japan. Indeed these were the concerns mainly voiced at the Ottawa G-7 summit in July 1981, not the problems posed by Japanese exports.

Pressure from the USA on Japan was far stronger. In the Congress, with elections in autumn 1982, there was talk of passing 'reciprocity' trade legislation requiring Japan to import as many cars, for example, as the USA did from Japan. The effects of such mercantilist legislation would have been to bury the post-war multilateral free-trade system. Both Japan and the EC urged the US administration to head off such pressures in the Congress. In addition, the Japanese government moved swiftly to answer US (and European) complaints that the Japanese market was still partially, and unfairly, closed to imports from its main trading partners.

A special Committee for International Economic Measures was set up in the ruling Liberal Democratic Party. The new Committee was able to cut across ministerial rivalries and quickly announced two sets of measures to further ease access to the Japanese market, including advance tariff cuts, the removal of sixty-seven out of a combined EC and US list of ninety-nine non-tariff barriers, and establishing a new Office of Trade Ombudsman (OTO) to handle specific complaints of foreign businessmen. The continuation of Japan's export restraint for another year in key sectors such as cars was also reluctantly agreed. Moves were even started to begin to relax the barriers in the only overtly protected sector of the Japanese market, agriculture.

The market-opening measures taken by the Japanese government in the first half of 1982 did serve to temporarily defuse criticism. The Congress dropped the draft bills calling for strict reciprocity and at the Versailles G-7 summit in June 1982, as at the Ottawa summit the previous year, problems caused by US monetary and fiscal policies were the focus of concern, not Japanese exports.

Results of the market-opening measures were not immediately apparent. Indeed, there was even a decline of European and US exports to Japan in 1982. With the appreciation of the dollar, there was a huge surge of Japanese exports to the USA and as a result the US deficit with Japan grew much more quickly than that of the EC.

Both in the EC and the USA there were calls to limit Japanese exports in specific sectors, including numerically controlled machine tools, colour televisions, VTRs and automobiles. One form or another of restriction was used, including VERAs, quotas, anti-dumping investigations, duties and certain new regulations covering, for example, rules of origin and stricter local content requirements. But the impact of Japan's exports was felt most strongly in the automobile sector.

Draft protectionist bills proliferated in the Congress, culminating in the Omnibus Trade Act of 1988 whose 'Super-301' provision empowered the US trade representative to name 'unfair trading partners' and to retaliate against them if they failed to remove the supposed structural barriers to US exports. The pace quickened the following year when the new administration cited Japan as an unfair trader (along with only two others, Brazil and India) and gave it 18 months to remove barriers on imports of US supercomputers, satellites and lumber or face

100% tariffs (see Chapter 23). Such muscular unilateralism was naturally opposed both by Japan and by the E C.

The immediate effect of the trade frictions, which broke out in the seventies and eighties, was to tigger emotional reactions which reinforced popular hostile images on both sides, thereby making repetition of such emotional outbursts that much more likely. The positive outcome of the frictions was that they stimulated both sides to take each other more seriously. From 1977, in increasing tempo, European heads of state and prime ministers beat a path to Tokyo and trilateralism, which had been rejected as late as 1972, now became the accepted wisdom, although what it implied and how it was to be achieved was not always clear.[25]

A final point remains to be made about the outbreak of trade frictions. It is that the frictions appeared to follow the well-known pattern of *Europe and the USA only waking up to Japan when Japan had become impossible to ignore, and Japan only waking up to an external situation when it had reached the boiling point*. Then both sides reacted to the 'shock' over-emotionally and in a state of panic. Possibly the strength of inherited and outmoded images which each holds of the other, plus the lack of regular and effective communications, make this shock-therapy approach to heightening mutual awareness inevitable, at least until all sides get used to the idea of listening to each other as normal day-to-day interlocutors.

21

THE CASE OF CARS

The automobile industry is the world's largest manufacturing industry and one of its largest employers; it accounts for well over 10 per cent of world exports and a sizeable portion of overseas direct investments. The industry is concentrated in Europe, Japan and the USA which together hold about 75 per cent of total production and 75 per cent of exports. The pattern was the same as in ships, steel, and electronics: the relative weights of the three main players, the USA, Europe and Japan, were completely altered in the space of twenty years by the unexpected and dramatic entry of the third player, the newcomer, Japan. Because of the enormous size of the industry the shock waves were much larger than produced by Japan's entry and eventual dominance of previous industries.

The first step was to build up the strength of the Japanese automobile industry on its own protected market; next, there followed a rapid expansion on world markets. As a result, US and European makers lost market share, then demanded and got protection from their governments. In a third phase, Japanese makers decided that they had no option but to invest in production facilities in their main export markets, the USA and the EC.

During the period of its growth the Japanese automobile industry was nurtured on its domestic market. General MacArthur permitted the production of passenger cars in 1949 and the next step was the setting up of technical ties with European makers. Production grew very rapidly from 165,000 units in 1960 to 3 million in 1970; 7.4 million in 1980, and 10 million in 1990 which represented about a quarter of world production of passenger cars, compared with the EC's 35 per cent and the USA's 22 per cent (plus another 12 per cent produced offshore). Automobiles and components have been a very important export for Japan. In the late eighties they accounted for about 25 per cent of its world exports; one-third of its exports to the USA and one-quarter of its exports to the EC.

Already by 1980, thanks to a timely adaptation of their industry to producing reliable energy-saving cars, and thanks also to the fact that the big three automobile makers in the USA were increasingly subcontracting or manufacturing abroad, the Japanese overtook the USA to become the world's largest producer of automobiles. Another record was broken. Only one car was imported for every forty exported – a ratio which had declined to one to 36 by 1988 (compare the EC with 1.4 cars imported for every one exported, and the USA with 6 imported for every car exported).

While the Japanese industry was gaining its lead in the seventies, the European industry was already in decline. European car exports to the world fell by 30 per cent between 1970 and 1980 largely because they could not compete with Japanese exports. This trend was very striking on the US market.[26]

In the eighties, the Japanese continued to take even larger shares of the major markets. On the US market they tripled the value of their exports while the EC's only doubled. By the late eighties, Japan held 24 per cent of world exports of automobiles and components, the EC 17 per cent (44 per cent if intra-EC exports are included) and the USA 10 per cent. The only external market in which US makers maintained the lead was Latin America, while the EC managed to retain its major supplier role in Africa (see Table 11).

Japan's automobile market was closed in the fifties and sixties. In 1963 only 9,000 foreign passenger cars were imported. Automobile imports were liberalized in the early seventies; NTBs on foreign car imports were eased in the middle of the decade and the tariff set at zero in 1978, but by then the costs of entering the market were so high, and the domestic competition was so strong that most foreign makers did not consider it worth the effort to export cars to Japan. Chrysler and GM had acquired stakes in two of the smaller Japanese makers in 1971; Volvo set up a joint venture with a textile manufacturer in 1974; British Leyland entered an alliance with Honda; and some effort was made to establish marketing systems by Ford, Chrysler, BL, and GM. But the results were minimal.

By 1973 the imports of foreign cars had risen to 37,000 units. Ten years later imports of foreign cars into Japan had declined to 34,000 units. It was only after the revaluation of the yen in 1985 and very considerable investments in sales and maintenance facilities that foreign cars, almost entirely German, began to achieve a significant roothold on the Japanese market.

In quantity terms, although Japanese makers were selling eight or nine times more cars in Europe than the Europeans were selling in Japan, in value terms the difference was not so great because European cars sold on average at a price two or three times that of Japanese cars. Car ownership in Japan is less widespread than in the West: 1 car for ever 4 people compared with 1 for every 3 in Europe and 1 for every 2 in the USA. So the European penetration rate on the Japanese car market by the late eighties was becoming comparable to the Japanese rate in Europe.

The US track record has not been outstanding. In 1980, only 11,000 US cars were registered in Japan compared to 1.8 million Japanese cars registered in the USA. The figures remained low

Table 11. Exports of Automobiles and Components, 1980 and 1989 ($ billion)

Destination Origin	World	Japan	EC	USA	Africa	Asia*	Latin America
1980 Japan	27	–	3	11	2.0	4	1
EC (12)	68	0.4	39	6	7.0	2	2
USA	17	0.2	1	–	0.5	1	3
1989 Japan	65	–	11	31	2.0	6	1
EC (12)**	46	4	88	11	5.0	2	2
USA	31	0.9	2	–	0.2	1	3

Source: GATT, 1990. *Asia refers to all developing countries in Asia except China, Vietnam and Mongolia. **EC exports to the rest of the world.

until Honda (USA) became nearly the biggest US exporter to Japan in 1988 after GM, followed by Mazda (USA) using the Ford label. This helped boost US sales there to over 20,000 units in 1989. Indeed, by 1991 Honda could be the largest exporter of foreign cars to Japan (Hondas from its Iowa plant).

Between 1970 and 1980, the year before import quotas were set in the USA, the Japanese makers increased their market share by leaps and bounds as they did also in the EC. Then, because of the quotas, their share stayed at more or less the same level until they began producing in the USA and the EC at the end of the decade. At which point it started to rise again (see Annex, Table 8).

Japanese wages in the car industry were above the European average by 1980 but about 10 per cent below those of German car workers. The Japanese workers also worked longer hours, were less frequently absent and took fewer paid holidays. Most important of all, investment in advanced technology, reliance on sub-contractors and huge production runs contributed to the higher productivity of the Japanese car industry compared with that of Europe or the USA. As a result, the ex-factory price of Japanese cars was not nearly as high as comparable European and US models.

In Europe from the mid-seventies, and in the USA from the end of the decade, there were calls from both management and the unions to cut back imports of Japanese cars. In Italy direct imports have been limited since 1956 to 1,200 a year by a government quota (originally part of a bilateral deal requested by Japan to protect its own market). Spain and Portugal have similar quotas which are re-negotiated every year. In the UK since 1975 there has been an industry to industry 'understanding' that Japanese makers would not take more than a 10 per cent share of the market (increased to 11 per cent after 1977), and in France, Japanese imports have been limited by government quota to a 3 per cent share of the market since 1977.

At the beginning of the eighties, declining markets in the USA and the EC did not prevent the Japanese from increasing their shares. Demands from the US manufacturers for a cutback of Japanese imports grew in intensity. The Europeans insisted that any agreement reached with the Americans should not lead to a diversion of Japanese exports to the European market.

The US International Trade Commission ruled in November 1980 that Japanese car imports were not causing damage to the US industry, which only had itself to blame for declining market shares because Detroit had failed to switch its production in time to small cars. So the Japanese were reluctant to hold back their exports. When they finally agreed to do so in March 1981 it was only after very strong US political pressure and an undertaking that the US auto industry would use the breathing space to restructure. The initial period of the agreement was for three years, but it is still in force because protectionist measures are easier to install than to remove. Each subsequent year it has been prolonged with slight enlargements of the quota which now stands at 2.3 million units.

Immediately following the agreement with Washington, the EC demanded a similar one. This the Japanese authorities refused, arguing that the EC was not in the same position as the USA because some of the member states already had limitations on imports of Japanese cars. Within days of the signing of the VERA with the USA, the German minister of economics flew to Tokyo and was able to reach an 'understanding' that Japanese car exports to Germany in 1981 would not be more than 10 per cent higher than in 1980. Eventually, in 1986 an export restraint agreement was reached with the EC as a whole. As a result of Japanese VERAs with the USA and the main markets in the EC, the registration of Japanese cars in both markets declined slightly for the first time in a decade, as also did Japan's market share.

In a special study of the costs of restricting imports in the automobile industry the OECD reached the following conclusions:

- The immediate losses to US and European consumers were enormous ($5 billion a year in the USA).
- The short-term benefits to domestic industry and employment were modest at best.
- The long-term effects were negative and included: distortion

of investment patterns; delayed reaction of the domestic companies; and increased import penetration by non-Japanese firms, for example from Korea or Yugoslavia (as had happened in so many other sectors).
- A major plus was the increase of Japanese investment and diffusion of its manufacturing techniques through a wave of joint ventures and other alliances.
- The winners were the firms, especially the Japanese exporting firms, because they were able to take higher profits as they raised their prices and went up market with luxury models such as the Acura, Infiniti or Lexus.[27]

Faced with limitations on their exports the Japanese makers have increased their investment in manufacturing in the USA and Europe. They have also entered into various forms of multinational production or marketing arrangements with most of the US and European makers.

In North America a dozen Japanese automobile plants have opened with an eventual annual capacity of over 2.5 million units. Some three hundred Japanese component makers have also set up shop in the USA. In Europe the six mass car makers (which include Ford and GM) are still in existence but they have been joined by a seventh, the Japanese. Nissan plans to turn out 200,000 units by 1992 and 400,000 by 1999 from its Newcastle plant. Honda was the first to be established in the UK and Toyota, Mazda and Isuzu went there in 1989. Total Japanese production by the late nineties in Europe could be 2 million units.

One result of this shift away from exports to local production is that Japan is far better positioned to compete in global markets than the Europeans and even the Americans, because neither of them has direct manufacturing investments in Japan (although the US makers have equity stakes in several of the Japanese and Korean makers). Another result is that the sting is taken out of the bilateral trade tensions. But in the lead up to the creation of a single unified market in Europe by 1992, there is no lack of Fortress Europe defenders against Japanese investment and imports.

The five protected markets in the EC account for 70 per cent of the total EC automobile market. Ceilings on imports from Japan vary from 3 to 11 per cent. The average is 9.5. These restrictions have been effective. On the seven unprotected markets in the EC, Japan's market share is nearly three times higher. In the EFTA countries it is three times higher and in the USA, twice as high. By 1992, national protectionist agreements will be phased out and the question is what sort of adjustment period will the more protectionist European countries be able to secure. The French and the Italian makers especially have been lobbying intensively. Their major markets are in Europe and they will fight to keep them, all the more so because European makers are at a severe disadvantage with the Japanese in the crucial US market, where they have no major manufacturing investment and where their market share has been eroded by the Japanese.

The length of the 'breathing space' following the removal of national restrictions will be determined by a compromise between the northern countries of the EC who are ready to settle for three years, and the southern countries who are arguing for anything up to twelve years. The decision will be affected by when the European car markers can complete their modernization plans, and set up new alliances, and when and to what extent the goal of a unified European market for automobiles can be achieved. In the words of the chairman of Mercedes Benz, 'I hope that Europe will at least take a first step in 1992. But . . . all in all, I'm afraid we won't have a truly unified European market before the end of the century.' During this period imports from Japan will probably continue to be limited. The Japanese makers are pressing for a quota which would be sightly more than their average market share in 1988 (11 per cent). The European makers want it fixed at slightly less than that.

Whatever the outcome, it may be out of date. Cross-border alliances, mergers and joint ventures, and overseas manufacturing and sales arrangements will soon have made the notion of a self-sufficient national car industry obsolete as has already happened in the electronics industry. In this sense, the Japanese are well positioned to profit from the single European market because of the 'transplants' rolling off their production lines in the

UK and other parts of the European Community. They also have the option of importing transplants from the USA and in a few years maybe also from Eastern Europe. Assuming that the efforts led by the French and Italians to block such imports (mainly those from the UK) will fail, the Japanese will be able to double their share of the European market to 20 per cent by 1995 whatever restraint agreement on direct imports from Japan itself is agreed on.

Thanks to Japanese competition there has been a great improvement in US and European productivity, but it still takes on average thirty-five hours to assemble a vehicle in Europe compared to twenty-six hours in the USA and seventeen in Japan. If Western makers wish to compete successfully with the Japanese and other Asian makers they will have to further improve their productivity, speed up their product development cycle and introduce more stringent quality controls. Many have set about doing this by entering into strategic alliances with former rivals or by inviting the Japanese to do it jointly with them. Others are content to provide the package and labels for cars produced in Japan and Korea and to re-import these 'captives' into their domestic markets.

22

ECONOMIC FRICTIONS, 1985 ONWARDS

After the first oil shock and again after the second, Japan adopted policies of fiscal austerity thus encouraging export-led growth and the accumulation of huge surpluses, which in the early eighties were stimulated by the mirror-opposite policies adopted by the Reagan administration – tax cuts, spending hikes, high interest rates and a strong dollar. The results of this policy mismatch eventually led to the emergence of Japan as the world's leading creditor nation and the USA as its biggest debtor. One side effect of this change was that the US deficit with Japan increased much more quickly than that of the EC. In 1980, the EC's deficit had been larger than that of the USA ($12.8 billion as opposed to $12.1 billion). By 1989, the US deficit with Japan was just over $50 billion whereas the EC's stood at $29 billion.

The USA was also running massive deficits with its other trading partners and in its own budget. So the deficit with Japan, although the largest of the US bilateral deficits in most of these years, was neither the key nor the only factor. No amount of market-opening measures or stimulation of the Japanese economy would have been sufficient to bring down the US bilateral deficit with Japan, let alone the US global deficits. The solution, it seemed to America's trading partners, lay in a fundamental change of course in US fiscal policy. A view shared even by the President's budget director, David Stockman, who later summarized the 'fiscal folly' of the Reagan years as follows, 'By 1984 [the White House] had become a dreamland. It was holding the American economy hostage to a reckless, unstable fiscal policy based on the politics of high spending and the doctrine of low taxes. Yet rather than acknowledge that the resulting massive build-up of public debt would eventually generate serious economic troubles, the White House proclaimed a roaring economic success.' It also argued that the burden of adjustment should be mainly shouldered by the surplus countries, notably Japan and Germany.[28]

The discussions at the G-7 summits from 1981 onwards focused on these issues. But the finance ministers of the seven had been unable to come up with a coordinated strategy to put to the heads of government. These in turn found it difficult to tell the US President to spend less when much of that spending was on imports from their countries or went to the costs of the US security umbrella. Figure 3 shows the rapid growth of the deficit in the US current and trade accounts after 1981 and conversely the massive increases of the Japanese surpluses. The EC on both accounts had a less dramatic record although the German surpluses were as impressive as the Japanese.

In the early eighties as the dollar grew stronger and stronger the view became widespread in the USA that the yen was undervalued, thus giving Japanese exports an enormous, and to many, an unfair, advantage. If only the Japanese capital markets were liberalized, it was felt the yen would appreciate against the dollar thus helping to make US exports more competitive. But following the Yen–Dollar pact of 1984, which laid out the steps to deregulate the Japanese markets, the yen actually depreciated. Meanwhile, as a result of the enormous global imbalances, exchange rates oscillated wildly and the calls for protection in the USA and the anti-Japanese mood there reached new and alarming heights. A quick fix was needed. So in June 1985, exploratory talks between the USA and Japan on how to correct the trade imbalance focused on what was felt to be the politically least costly solution, currency realignment.[29]

Eventually these talks were expanded to include the other G-5 countries (Germany, the UK and France) whose central bank governors and finance ministers met in September at the Plaza Hotel in New York and announced a joint effort to reduce the global imbalances by cutting the value of the dollar. Within a year the yen rose 29 per cent against the dollar. The ECU

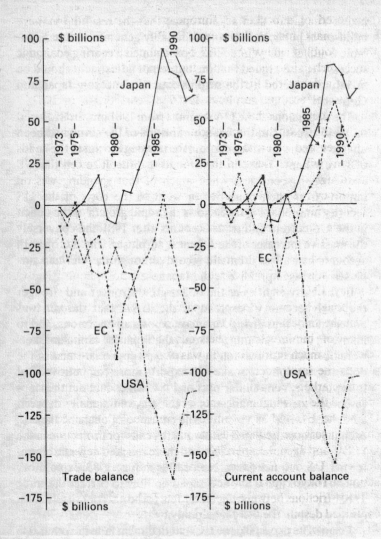

Fig. 3. Global Trade and Current Account Balances of Japan, the EC
and the USA, 1973–90

Note: See Annex, Table 5 for figures.

(composed of a basket of European currencies led by the Deutschmark) rose by 22 per cent. By 1988, the yen's value had almost doubled against the 1985 dollar and Japan was well and truly launched into the age of the high yen (*endaka*).

After a delay, the first annual decline of the Japanese trade and current account surpluses for five years began in 1987. Japanese companies had adjusted so successfully to the higher yen that the decline was only slight. Until the USA brings down its budget and external deficits, the surpluses of Japan and Germany will continue and the US deficit with Japan will also remain high.

Currency realignment alone cannot hope to solve global imbalances unless it is accompanied by a greater degree of macroeconomic policy coordination than in the event has proved possible. The imperfections of the single factor approach were underscored two years after the Plaza accord when world stock markets, starting in Wall Street, went into a tail spin on Black Monday, 19 October 1987.

Although the main focus was on using currency realignment to adjust the imbalances, and the main arguments were over the degree of burden-sharing between the deficit and surplus countries, much more attention was also paid to access and fair play in the service sector, for example in banking, insurance, capital markets, communications and public procurement. This reflected the growing importance of the service industries in the USA, the EC and Japan and of their share in external trade (trade in services now represents just over 50 per cent of total US, EC and Japanese merchandise trade). It also reflected the desire of US and European businessmen to gain a slice of the action in Tokyo capital markets.

Trade frictions between Japan and its principal trade partners continued despite the fact that already by the mid-eighties, 30 to 40 per cent of its exports to the EC and to the USA were covered by voluntary export restraint agreements (VERAs), and its direct investments in the USA and Europe had helped take the sting out of many of the old bones of contention – most notably, as we saw in the previous chapter, cars. So trade frictions caused by Japanese exports were typically over new products not yet under restraint, such as photocopy machines, microwave ovens, semi-conductors and products, such as systems software or high-definition television (HDTV), where the question of which company or group was going to set world standards had not yet been settled. Complaints about the closed nature of Japanese markets centred on new products such as supercomputers, mobile car telephones or satellites. These shifts of emphasis reflected changes in the international division of labour and the perception in the USA, Europe and Japan that economic strength in the future depends on developing tomorrow's information-technology industries as well as restructuring smokestack industries using the new technologies.

As Japan took the lead in certain high-technology industries and production processes, a strong feeling developed in the USA that it had acquired too much technology for too little in return. Attitudes towards selling or sharing technology with the Japanese became more guarded and 'technology frictions' have now become as common as trade frictions. Hitachi executives were caught stealing IBM secrets in a much publicized sting operation in California in 1985. Fujitsu was refused permission to acquire Fairchild Semiconductor (a pioneer US computer company which had fallen into the hands of a French conglomerate). Most damaging of all was the Toshiba Machine scandal in 1987 which arose from its sales (together with Norwegian and French companies) to the Russians of technology for the production of super-quiet propellers for nuclear submarines.

From time to time the technology and trade frictions spilled over into bilateral defence issues as in the bitter arguments early in the Bush administration when the 'technonationalists' in Congress and the commerce department, profiting from the stalled nomination of the defence secretary, challenged plans to co-develop the prototype for a new Japanese fighter plane, the FSX. They argued that Japan would get too much from the deal: access to US military technology and help in developing its commercial aircraft industry. As on many previous occasions, they insisted that the onus was on Japan to take steps to reduce its trade surplus with the USA and that one way of doing this was to buy US military hardware off the shelf. Two new elements in the debate were the extreme reluctance in Japan to accept this pressure and the Pentagon's conviction that it needed access to Japanese technology as part of any deal.

Eventually a compromise emerged, but the bitter taste left by the dispute encouraged all those in Japan who sought to reduce their country's dependence on the USA for weapons technology by developing their own arms industry.

A major reason for the Pentagon's respect for Japanese technology was the discovery in the early eighties that it was dependent on Japan for 40 per cent of its requirements for microchips.

In 1973, the USA was the world's leading manufacturer of 64K ram chips with six main makers. By 1983, the Japanese makers had taken 70 per cent of the world market and there were only two US companies left. In 1986, NEC overtook IBM as the world's largest producer of microchips. The administration felt the need to step in to negotiate a bilateral deal with the Japanese to try to keep prices to a level at which US makers could stay in a temporarily depressed market (US–Japan Agreement on Semiconductors, 1986). At this the EC protested and indeed eventually won its case in the GATT against US–Japanese price-fixing in third markets. But in the short space of a few years, the EC had taken a leaf from the US book and concluded early in 1990 a floor-price deal with the Japanese manufacturers on high-end microchips. As on so many other occasions, the end loser was the end user as well as manufacturers of computers who were forced to pay higher prices. Japanese makers made even larger profits. As a result they were able to consolidate their domination of the world semiconductor market, including that for one-megabit chips, while simultaneously challenging Intel and Motorola in the production of high-speed 32-bit microprocessors.

Traditional trade frictions caused by exports from labour-intensive industries such as shoes, leatherware, textiles and garments and household electronics continued. But the exporters putting on the pressure were the newly industrialized countries, mainly of East Asia, whose industrial structure and export-led growth policies closely followed those of Japan in the fifties and sixties.

The differences over macro-economic policy and over the management of the interface between domestic and international policy were the consequences of four long-term trends. The first arose from the changing conditions in the world economy – widely different levels in savings and investment, in the USA on the one hand and in Japan, Germany, Taiwan and Korea on the other, led to massive swings in the exchange rates and huge trade and current account imbalances. Amid these uncertainties it became clear that Japan was now a dominant, if not the pre-dominant, financial power in the world.

It had long been said that when Washington sneezed, Tokyo caught a cold. But now, in the new age starting from 1985, when Japan emerged as the world's leading creditor nation and the USA its leading debtor, both the Americans and the Japanese found it extremely hard to adjust to the new situation. As a young Japanese economist put it, 'The Americans do not even realise that they have lost the war. Perhaps they would get the message if we offered to write off their debt.'

The second was the continued growth of interdependence between national economies as world exports of both goods and services accounted for an ever larger share of total world product. More than ever before decisions taken for domestic political reasons had an immediate international impact and there was neither the experience nor often the political will to handle that impact.

The third was the weakening of the post-war institutions for managing the world economy and the declining ability of any one of the three main players, the USA, Japan or Europe, to provide alternatives or even to agree on how best to coordinate their separate efforts. Instead each pursued its own advantage usually in the form of bilateral deals.

The fourth reason why the frictions with Japan focused on new areas after 1985 has something to do with the working habits of the officials, and the occasional politician, responsible for setting the agenda for discussions with Japan. As in the previous rounds of trade frictions, the form was usually the same. Mounting Japanese surpluses in trade and current accounts, both global and bilateral, encouraged businessmen and lobbies in the USA and Europe to seek protection from Japanese competition in their sector. For twenty years trade officials had responded by insisting that the onus was on Japan to reduce its surpluses. And they were not reticent in telling the Japanese how this should be achieved. By the eighties, step by step, pretty much everything had been tried – Japanese exports had been restrained, the market had been opened, the yen had been talked up, but still the surpluses kept mounting.

So the agenda for the 'Japan problem' in the eighties, by a natural progression, began to focus on those issues which had not yet been tried. It became the accepted wisdom that the principal reason for Japan's enormous surpluses was its decision to pursue belt-tightening policies and therefore the best solution would be to rely on domestic- rather than export-led growth; to persuade Japan to consume more and to produce less for export. In a sense this was pushing against a half-open door.

Already in the seventies there was recognition inside Japan of the need to adjust the industrial structure to integrate the external trade of the country more into the international division of labour, allowing a higher ratio of manufactured goods imports where comparative advantage lay outside Japan. This move was encouraged by the shift of emphasis in the economy from manufacturing industry to long-overdue efforts to improve the quality of life – housing, drainage, roads, hospitals, parks and the like. As a former vice-minister of MITI summed up the efforts of ten years, not without a hint of exaggeration,

Japanese companies tended, until very recently, to concentrate primarily on expanding their sales and their export ratios, and the Japanese government on raising the GNP and the export ratio . . . while the Japanese government and Japanese companies were pushing to increase exports, they were not in the least interested in expanding imports. Now it is imperative that the Japanese economy be restructured . . . Japan has to lower its dependence on exports (especially . . . to the United States) and sharply increase the importance of domestic demand and imports . . . For starters, the market regulations and other forms of protection afforded less competitive industries should be sharply curtailed or eliminated. This is not a politically palatable prescription for many people – especially in agriculture.[30]

The need for a greater degree of market opening, including of capital markets, gradually became the consensus during the eighties under the catch-all phrase of internationalization (*kokusaika*) of the Japanese economy. One blue-ribbon advisory panel after another reinforced the message. After the Action Programme of 1985 (designed to increase access to the Japanese market over a three-year period) came the two Maekawa reports (1986 and 1987), which in turn were followed by the Gaishi report of 1988 and many others. The basic message of all of them, as well as many of the government *White Papers*, was that Japan had reached a turning point, requiring, in the words of Maekawa (1986), nothing less than 'a historical transformation of Japan's traditional policies on economic management and the nation's lifestyle'.

The five-year plan for 1988 to 1992 (*Economic Management Within a Global Context*) foresees the promotion and consolidation of domestic-led growth and anticipates the changes that this will entail under three heads: first, improvement of individual lifestyles by making more land available for private housing, reducing work hours and lowering consumer prices by simplifying the distribution system, and dismantling the protection for agriculture; second, development of regional economic centres; and third, rectification of external imbalances and increase of contributions to development aid and to the costs of the Western alliance.

All these ideas have been under constant discussion in Japan since the mid-seventies and there has been some progress in putting them into practice. They touch on key values and institutions in Japanese society including attitudes towards work and leisure, therefore they will not be turned into reality overnight. Take the question of shortening the work week. Already in 1986 the first Maekawa report had recommended a general shift to a five-day week (at that time 72 per cent of Japanese industrial workers were on a six-day week). The government also announced that it would seek the first revision of the Labour Standards Law since its passage in 1947, namely a reduction of statutory working hours from forty-eight to forty per week by 1993. But it will take more than a change in the law to change a social custom. Many people like to stay long hours in the office as a sign of loyalty or out of a feeling of camaraderie. Others do so under the strong pressures in Japanese society to conform and to compete, pressures which are not likely to disappear for as long as there is an acute shortage of labour.[31]

There are, however, new elements which are already helping to speed the process of transforming Japanese society and economy along the lines set out in the reports just quoted. Perhaps the most important is the emergence of Japan as a rich creditor nation. Chapters 25 and 26 take a closer look at these changes and examine their implications for Japan's neighbours in Asia and for the USA and Europe.

23

CHARGES AND COUNTER-CHARGES

As the industrial system spread from one country to the next in the nineteenth and early twentieth centuries, those previously established were forced to adjust, whether they liked it or not, to the new arrivals. Likewise the rise of Japan has been accompanied by continuous frictions whose immediate effect was to stir up negative emotions. The frictions had one positive result in that they forced all those involved to begin the difficult task of readjusting their perceptions of themselves and of each other.

The first round of post-war trade frictions with Japan, from the fifties through to the early seventies, was mainly over Japanese exports to Europe and the USA. Efforts were focused on preventing, by one form of protection or another, 'sudden influxes' of Japanese goods which it was claimed were over-concentrated and had expanded too quickly, in the Japanese phrase, like a 'torrential downpour'.

In the second round of frictions, during the seventies and early eighties, as Japan's bilateral trade and current account surplus increased every year, the question began to be asked: whether our markets were more open to Japanese imports than the Japanese markets, including capital markets, were open to ours. In other words, did Japan enjoy an unfair advantage?

In the third round of frictions, starting from the mid-eighties, accusations and counter-accusations about the conduct of each other's macro-economic policy and about structural impediments to imports; criticism of Japan's domestic institutions, as well as arguments over service trade and technology increasingly moved to centre stage. The rapid build-up of Japan's overseas direct investments, especially in the USA, touched off the type of fear and resentment which US investment provoked in Europe in the early sixties.

Running as a US leitmotif of criticism through the first two phases of friction, from the seventies into the eighties, and extending into the third, was the contention that Japan was enjoying a 'free ride' in that its defence and development aid contributions were too small.

As the frictions intensified, the view, first heard in the sixteenth century, that Japan was totally different from the West, in economic structure as well as in cultural values, re-emerged.

In each period the problems and arguments of the previous one were carried over. Concern over Japan's exports in particular sectors continues to this day, although the main worries are now shifting to the effects of Japan's direct investments as its companies turn themselves from exporters into multinationals.

The perception that the Japanese market is not fully open is still held as an article of faith by many who are therefore also convinced that the Japanese have operated and still deliberately operate with an unfair advantage.

Whatever the demands placed upon them, the Japanese believe that the Americans and Europeans, because of prejudice or jealousy, have been using Japan as a scapegoat for economic and social failings in their own countries. They frequently ask why criticisms levelled at them are not directed at other surplus countries such as Germany. They also feel that all the various problems would be solved if only US and European businessmen would make greater efforts on the Japanese and world markets. The question of efforts is taken up in the next chapter.

To start with Japanese exports – the Japanese were requested to restrain them. They had complied until, by the late eighties, about 30 to 40 per cent of their exports to the USA and the EC were controlled by one or another form of VERA (voluntary export restraint agreement), an unprecedented practice in world trade, as indeed were the numerous import-promotion missions sent to buy goods in the USA and Europe in an effort to reduce the trade surplus.

Next is the question of whether or not the Japanese market is open to Western imports. Despite the Japanese government's market-opening measures (which began in the sixties) and notwithstanding the increase of Japanese imports since 1985, many still believe that it remains closed. In a refined form of the fashionable pastime of 'Japan bashing' even the eminent management pundit, Professor Drucker, for example, wrote in 1987, 'Despite all the threats of trade sanctions in the West, there is still mostly only talk of opening Japan to imports.'

With the insight of one whose industry had enjoyed seven years of 'frozen' imports from Japan, Mr Iacocca of Chrysler agreed when he said in 1988, 'To me, the solution to the trade problem is simple. We have to freeze our deficit with Japan, and tell the Japanese that the limit will get 20 per cent smaller next year, and 20 per cent smaller the year after that. Take my word for it the Japanese like to work toward objectives. It's time we gave them one. They can sell us less or buy more – we don't care. The choice is theirs.'[32]

The arguments that Japan is still partially closed to imports are often ill-informed and out of date, but some are legitimate and based on recent experience of the Japanese market.

First, two key points. It was correctly argued that economic liberalization (i.e. deregulation) and the easing of foreign investment and other controls came much later in Japan than similar moves in Europe. In the USA, the market was essentially open to Japanese and European exports in the post-war period although, as detailed in Chapter 19, restrictions gradually began to multiply from the late fifties onwards. So it was correctly argued that Japanese traders had the advantage of earlier access to the US and European markets than US and European exporters to the Japanese market. For example, if there were many more dealers handling Japanese automobiles in the USA than there were dealers handling US cars in Japan, this was partly because the Japanese automobile makers had been able to spend many years investing in and building up dealer networks in the USA. But while they were doing so, foreign investments in Japan were restricted, and the Japanese auto industry, during the period of its growth, was protected from outside competition. By the time the imports of cars were liberalized, the domestic industry was sufficiently strong to maintain its control of the market against any newcomers. The twin policies of promoting exports and building up import substitution industries were the central objectives of all Japanese governments in the fifties and sixties. The fruits of these policies were harvested in the seventies and eighties.

Second, the slowness with which Japan had begun to liberalize its market in the late sixties, and the fact that it only continued to do so in the seventies and eighties, under strong US and European pressure, suggested to many that the Japanese were reluctant to really open their market, that it was, in short, still partially closed.

This mistrust is a good example of the poor communications between the two sides. Japanese readers will perhaps acknowledge that the pattern of waiting until strong external pressure has built up, and an internal consensus has formed, before taking action, does often suggest extreme reluctance to take the action in the first place. The view that the Japanese market was not fully opened to imports naturally also received apparent confirmation from the time when Japan began to score huge trade surpluses with the USA and Europe, which continued to mount year after year for more than two decades.

The complaints about high tariffs protecting Japanese domestic industries became less common after the successful completion of the Kennedy round of tariff cuts, and even more so as the Tokyo round drew to a conclusion.

All sorts of arguments were adduced to support the view that, despite *de jure* liberalization, the Japanese market was *de facto* still partially closed. The argument shifted to non-tariff barriers (NTBs) or government regulations and business practices which inhibited, or were claimed to inhibit, not only the export of goods and services but also attempts to buy into the Japanese market. Some examples were mentioned in Chapter 20.

Real and imaginary trade barriers exist in every market, and there is no doubt of the problems they can cause in Japan. They probably act more as a discouragement to enter the market, however, than as a real cost factor. The trouble was there were many who used trade barriers as an excuse for European and US failures to penetrate the Japanese market. When the removal of NTBs failed to lead to significant increases of US and EC exports to Japan, the argument took a new turn. The EC went to the GATT in 1982 to put the case that Japan had little propensity to import manufactured goods because of 'structural obstacles hampering access to the market'.

Chief among the 'structural obstacles' singled out was the Japanese distribution system. A view confirmed by the president of a new-style retail chain, who was quoted in 1988 as saying that the distribution system remained a major impediment to imports and a contributor to Japan's high cost of living. (Indeed, a MITI survey conducted in 1989 showed that high-class foreign goods sold at three to six times more than in the countries which produced them.) 'Mom and Pop' stores still account for 57 per cent of sales compared to the USA where they only hold 3 per cent. Small shopkeepers in Japan, like small farmers, are politically influential. 'Laws and cartels apart, Japan's maze-like distribution system has been the country's most efficient obstacle to the passage of foreign goods', but reforms have been introduced and gradually the system is changing.[33]

It was also said that the large Japanese trading companies maintained a near oligopoly of imports and favoured the large industrial and banking groups (*keiretsu kigyō*) to which they belonged. Thus the French prime minister, in a discussion in December 1980 with leading Japanese businessmen, while acknowledging the 'insufficiencies' of French industry, was reported to have recalled that the Japanese market was difficult to approach because of non-tariff barriers and a 'screen' of trading companies which prevented the establishment of after-sales networks.[34] It is still widely held that Japanese companies (especially public corporations) follow a patriotic instinct to buy Japanese even if it means paying higher prices.

We saw in Chapter 15 that it was commonly said the Japanese government and business acted in 'collusion' (the 'Japan Inc.' image) to keep imports out when necessary, or to subsidize export industries. It was frequently claimed by foreign businessmen that, whatever the goodwill expressed at the upper levels of

Japanese officialdom, at the operational levels, in the customs or in the regulatory agencies, for example, there was a dilatoriness and lack of enthusiasm towards imports reflecting an older, more protective phase of Japanese industrial and commercial policy. Nor was it felt to be a coincidence that foreign shares of the Japanese market in major industries such as ships, steel, automobiles, tobacco or banking were in the region of only 1 or 2 per cent. Only after fifteen years of pressure did they begin to rise in the mid-eighties (cigarettes, 12 per cent; automobiles, 5 per cent; but banking, 2 per cent and ships and steel, less than 1 per cent).

In 1978, Japan undertook 'to take all appropriate steps to increase imports of manufactures . . . and that the share of these imports in Japan's total imports would increase steadily and return within a reasonable period of years to a more normal level under current international economic circumstances'. The trouble was economic circumstances soon changed – oil prices shot up in 1979–80 and as a result the relative share of manufactured imports in Japan's total imports actually declined. It was only in the late eighties that the combination of a strong yen and low oil prices saw the volume, as distinct from the dollar value, of manufactured imports begin to rise substantially.[35]

As early as 1971, the attempt was made to solve the bilateral deficit problem by devaluing the dollar and forcing the yen up. Currency realignment was used again in 1978 and in 1985 but it did not achieve the desired results, partly because the increased price of Japanese exports was more than offset by the lower cost of imported energy and raw materials upon which so much of Japanese industry depends, and partly because Japanese products were increasingly finding markets on the basis of their reliability, quality and design rather than on their low price. Finally, when the yen appreciated, higher productivity growth and lower inflation in Japan meant that at any given exchange rate it experienced a growing advantage in international competition.[36]

When the depreciation of the dollar failed to bring about a reduction in the deficit, this intensified protectionist rhetoric in the USA and in Europe. There were even those who felt that the yen exchange rate was being unfairly manipulated in such a way as to keep its value artificially low.

The fact that steps toward reforming and liberalizing Japanese capital markets and foreign exchange transactions were extremely slow in coming, only encouraged such suspicions. Moreover the track record of foreign banks in Japan bore witness to the tight control exercised by the authorities. In other capital markets European and US banks had proved themselves fully competitive. In Japan, their share of banking activity is still rather small, although their numbers, if not their profits, have grown enormously in recent years.

Many of these arguments were taken up again in 1989 when the USA launched its structural impediments initiative with Japan, including the difficulties of penetrating the distribution system and many of the problems of buying into rather than just exporting to the Japanese market.

To cynics, the fundamental point was that the Japanese did not behave sufficiently like the Americans in that they still saved too much, produced too much and consumed too little.

But this time the talks broke out of the normal pattern of the USA or the EC demanding that Japan introduce policy changes to bring it more in line with the West. Now the Japanese felt confident enough to argue that structural impediments in the USA were equally important causes of the bilateral trade imbalance. They cited the low savings rate, the short time horizons of US companies, their inadequate investments and low productivity, and the poor education and training of the workforce.

There was more than the usual theatrical element in trade negotiations; each playing to its own domestic audience ('finding meat to toss to the animals,' as one US negotiator put it), while neither can have had any realistic expectation that the government of the other could possibly introduce the dozens of changes requested of it, and certainly not within the eighteen months required by the US Trade Act.

Japanese government has consistently and correctly argued that the rapid growth of the twin US deficits in the eighties was caused by high spending, low savings and fiscal profligacy. However, it too must take some responsibility: it kept its own interest rates low, encouraged export-led growth and resisted taking expansionary measures until the late eighties.

Eventually, under increasing pressure from the US administration led by the President himself, the Japanese government felt the need to provide some 'meat' for the Congress. So in Spring 1990, just before the deadline set, it announced concessions on sales of US super-computers, satellites and lumber. More significantly, perhaps, both sides renewed committments to fundamental reforms and policies (many of which had been on their domestic agendas for years). In the case of the USA, these included strengthening procedures to meet balanced budget targets by 1993, studying ways to lower the cost to US corporations of raising capital, enhancing education programmes and increasing spending on basic Research. The Japanese for their part agreed a number of steps towards de-regulation and domestic-led growth which if they ever reach the statute books and are put into practice would not only lead to increased competitiveness of Japanese industry but could also contribute to improved living standards for the consumer. The steps included tougher penalties for antitrust violations, a relaxation of the law on the establishment of large stores, a change in tax laws to halt surging land prices, and an increase in public works spending.

The question of Japan's share off the costs of its defence within the alliance and its contributions to development aid are discussed in Chapter 25. Here it is sufficient to note that the response to strong US pressures to bear a larger share of the defence burden was often that Japan could not do as much as it hoped because of budgetary difficulties. Hardly a very convincing argument, it seemed, when Americans (and Europeans) were not without their own budgetary difficulties and were daily reminded that Japan's economy was outperforming theirs by far. The other field where Japan's contribution was held to be incongruously small in comparison with the size of its economy was the extent of its official development assistance (ODA). Here again, many of the other advanced industrial democracies have been more generous, despite the fact that their economies have not been doing so well as Japan's. And here too the Japanese programmes, while growing very rapidly from their inception in 1965, were often perceived as primarily designed to further Japanese commercial interests rather than to benefit their recipients.

In the thirties, the Japanese were accused of 'social dumping' because their wages were much lower than in Europe and the USA. Today this is no longer the case, but the Japanese are still commonly regarded as exceptional in that their values towards life and work and leisure are felt to be different from those in Europe and in the United States. They work harder, take fewer holidays and spend far less time complaining about their lot. Or so it seems from the outside.

They also put up with cramped housing, crowded roads, and few public amenities such as urban parks or sports facilities. Investments are concentrated in industry and all energies appear to go into competing with rival Japanese companies to capture ever larger shares of world markets in a growing number of key industries. Japan, it is often claimed, has therefore an 'unfair' competitive advantage with its more luxurious trading partners, who spend more on improving living standards than on improving the competitiveness of their industries. Japan is, in other words, in fundamental ways different from Europe and the USA. As an anthropological expert on Japan phrased it, 'Japan is a complex industrial society . . . based on premises fundamentally different from our own . . . there are alternative ways in which a mass society can be constructed. Japan is different.'[37] The chairman of Germany's most powerful trade union, I. G. Metall, spelled out one common conclusion: not the need to catch up with the Japanese, but the danger of being dragged down to their level – 'To work like the Japanese,' he said, 'with their labour conditions and social practices, would be to revert to the stone age.'

To many, trade disputes were symbolic of a larger struggle between old and new economic forces, between declining powers and dynamic newcomers, a struggle which involved a clash of fundamentally different values. As one writer on the US–

Japan 'car wars' put it, 'To some, it was more than just a growing imbalance in auto sales and a mounting trade deficit. They feared it might reflect an imbalance of values between the two societies, one poor but careful with its resources, the other rich and blessed and increasingly careless with vast resources – the conflict, in sum, between the culture of adversity and the culture of affluence . . . Japan was better prepared for the coming century. The American century was no more.'[38]

One variation on the theme, the 'revisionist' view, was that 'the Japanese are different in that they are not rational consumers in the sense of classical economists. They will sacrifice their interests as consumers for the nation as a whole. They will buy on the basis of who is selling and not of what is sold. They would rather pay more for something than less for it. Corollary: only force will work in dealing with Japan, not the market'. As Professor Drucker put it, 'The West will no longer tolerate Japan's adversarial trading methods of recent decades – a wall around the home market to protect social structures and traditions, plus a determined push beyond it for world dominance for selected Japanese industries.'

Leaving aside whether 'the West' is any longer in a position to impose its will on Japan, it is disappointing to find Drucker basing his 'revisionist' analysis on the age-old, false dichotomy between the West as rational and the East as irrational: 'The western pattern of an autonomous, value-free economy in which economic rationality is the ultimate criterion, is alien to Confucian society. Therefore he concludes, 'Reciprocity may make possible close economic relationships between culturally distinct societies.' In other words, to paraphrase the revisionist view on trade policy, we liberals should abandon our free trade principles when dealing with Japan, because they are neo-mercantilists playing a different ball game which gives them an unfair advantage. Therefore we have no option but to introduce 'fair', 'managed', 'organized', 'planned' or 'results-oriented' trade [or whatever other euphemism is used to refer to protectionist measures].

Today, all governments pursue economic nationalism and intervene in every branch of the economy. In Europe and

America, industrial labour lobbies have often successfully persuaded governments to introduce protectionist policies; in Japan and many of its followers, it is the producer lobbies which have been more influential. To lable the one liberal and the other neo-mercantilist is merely to introduce the type of misleading contrast which has typified so much of the discussion on Japan.[39]

One of the most persistent of the illogicalities in the debate is that which connects the increase of Japanese global or bilateral surpluses with the perception that the Japanese market is closed. It was repeatedly said or implied that if the Japanese market was fully opened, the American or European deficit with Japan would be reduced and the Japan trade problem would be solved. This is not necessarily a logical outcome at all. We have seen that the opening of the Japanese market did not lead to a boom in European or US exports, which were often insufficiently competitive and inadequately launched and followed up, to secure many breakthroughs similar to those made by the Japanese on European and US markets. Moreover, even if exports to Japan increased, fears of market disruption in sensitive sectors in Europe and the USA would remain. The problems caused by Japanese exports, in other words, would still continue.

As a recent study by an American economist put it, 'all too often, US politicians, government officials, and private-sector spokesmen have confused the issues between Japan and the USA by attaching too much importance to the bilateral trade imbalance and by connecting the imbalances to Japan's trade barriers . . . Trade imbalances are not a reflection of trade policies and of trade distortions, but of savings and investment behaviour unrelated to trade policies . . . If the problem is the size of global and bilateral trade or current account imbalances, then the solution is to alter the macroeconomic policies that have produced the problem. If the concern is with Japan's import barriers, pressure should be applied for their removal, without the expectation that removal will bring any major change in the imbalances. Each of these solutions is important and desirable on its own merits.'[40]

Typical of the inability to agree on the terms of the dispute was the failure to agree on what constitutes an 'open market'. If the degree of a market's openness is measured by the formal structure of tariffs and quotas, then by the conclusion of the Tokyo round of multilateral trade negotiations, Japan's market was as 'open' as that of the EC or of the USA. If non-tariff barriers such as the setting and administration of industrial standards, or customs procedures are taken into account, then again it would be difficult to decide whether the Japanese market was less open than the European countries or the USA. Indeed, the argument about Japan's market in the last resort often came down to the accusation that it was a *marché enigmatique* (in the words of the French President), impenetrable for cultural reasons, closed by 'non-specific' barriers such as national attitudes towards foreign trade. In this view even the Japanese language was considered a 'non-specific' barrier. The language problem is real enough, but whose fault is that? As the OECD 1989 country survey on Japan remarked with dry humour, 'The imbalance between the number of Japanese learning foreign languages and foreigners learning Japanese implies that this problem is asymmetric.'

Again and again Western businessmen and officials who put forward such arguments seemed to be saying that it was self-evident that our markets were fully open and the Japanese was not, because our imports from Japan were so much larger than our exports to Japan. Considering that Japan is a much smaller market than either the EC or the USA, whether measured by population, GNP or volume of external trade, there is no reason to expect that Japan's imports from these markets should be of the same order in absolute terms as Japan's exports to them.

The notion too that an increase of domestic demand in Japan would lead to more imports from the USA and Europe is another example of a false linkage. What often happened was that imports of raw materials or manufactured goods from Japan's neighbours increased – not necessarily imports from the USA and Europe (see Table 6 in Chapter 2).

In a similar fashion, when the Japanese government was persuaded to open public sector contracts to foreign bidders, few came forward. Instead, as the US commerce secretary complained, with just a hint of exaggeration, 'We opened up the [Japanese] market to the Koreans, which is what we do all the time.'[41]

One glaring example of the inability to define the terms of the dispute was the failure to agree on a common set of statistics or even on how to measure trade flows. Each side used its own figures which were often at variance with the other's.[42]

Nor is it enough to look at the statistics of merchandise trade between nation states as collected by their customs authorities. In many sectors of manufacturing, such as automobiles and electronics, up to half the total of world trade is conducted as a two-way exchange between parent companies and their overseas affiliates. Twenty per cent of US imports from Japan are either imports by US companies from their subsidiaries in Japan (as in the case of Hewlett-Packard's LaserJet printer) or are components and products made under contract in Japan expressly for US companies. An even larger percentage of US imports from Japan is imported by Japanese affiliates in the USA from their parent companies. Japanese multinationals have some distance to catch up in this respect, but about 15 per cent of all the manufactures already imported into Japan are from their own overseas subsidiaries.

US, Japanese and European companies now manufacture and sub-contract increasingly in each other's markets, so a complete picture of US sales in Japan, for example, would have to take account not only of direct exports from the USA to Japan, but also of goods assembled or manufactured by US subsidiaries there.

As one Canadian economist put it, 'the American [and European] practice of looking at the final balance of trade and then demanding that the other nation do something to reduce the surplus is a political gesture aimed at domestic constituencies suffering from competition. It has nothing to do with the realities of international trade . . . The so-called enormous trade imbalances reflect the impossibility of analyzing trade by means of the traditional categories . . . if the calculations are based on the production of US versus Japanese companies, the balance is about equal' [because the US has some very successful manufacturing investment in Japan].[43]

Another false causal connection was often made between Japanese exports in a given sector and high unemployment in that sector in the USA or Europe, leading to the accusation that Japan was 'exporting unemployment'. As a French minister complained in 1981, 'Every Japanese car imported equals five French workers out of a job.' The minister did not explain why imports of cars from other countries did not have a similar effect. Nor did he estimate the number of jobs gained from inward investment from Japan. Perhaps he believed that imports of goods from a given country should be exactly balanced by exports of the same type of goods to that country (the so-called 'reciprocity' argument). Or perhaps he was trying to justify the French government's limitation of imports of Japanese cars to 3 per cent of the market.

No doubt the lumping together of separate issues and the assumption of linkages which are more apparent than real arises from political rhetoric and common misunderstandings about economics and international trade. It also reflects the weakness of bureaucratic procedure. each specialized agency and geographic desk draws up a list of the particular problems for which it is responsible. When the time comes for a negotiation with Japan the separate files are gathered together. But the chief negotiator may not be in a strong enough position within his own administration to co-ordinate all the discrete problems or to resist the various political pressures connected with them. Therefore, without firm priorities even minor issues can come to play a major role in such negotiations and major issues may be left for another day to another agency.

The danger of false linkages such as those given above is clear. Not only do they obscure the root causes of the problem but they also invite popular frustration and resentment when the achievement of one step fails to lead to the next. This contributes to the fear and distrust of Japan which breaks out from time to time in the USA and Europe and can be seen in inflammatory headlines in the press or the smashing of Japanese goods in front of the TV cameras.

24

COMPARATIVE EFFORTS

The possibility that the European and US deficit with Japan was at least in part the result of a lack of competitiveness was for many years, perhaps understandably, not given prominence in the presentation of their case. But this point is of course now fully recognized both in the USA and Europe, especially after the Japanese management boom described in Chapter 16. In 1988, for example, the US commerce secretary, Mr Verity, hardly caused a ripple when he said that the US imbalance with Japan was not solely the result of restrictive Japanese trade barriers. 'If we are to bring our trade accounts with Japan (and the world) back into balance, we must first stop spinning our wheels in the mud of protectionist trade legislation. Instead we need to roll up our sleeves and address the major causes of the trade deficit – exchange rates, federal budget deficits, declining product quality, deteriorating human resources, and inexperience in foreign markets.'[44]

Some of those who had reached a broadly similar view, ten to fifteen years before, have already been quoted in Chapter 16. In making the point in a 1977 article in *Le Monde*, I concluded that 'today the EC has a choice: either make a better job of restructuring its industries or resign itself to losing markets to more competitive trading partners. To continue to complain of the bilateral deficit with Japan as the result of Japanese protectionism only serves to obscure the problem, not to resolve it.' In other words the shortcoming was first and foremost with our own industries, not with commercial policies or Japanese trade barriers.[45] The article was based on a detailed study of Japan's changing export structure and its rapid switch from labour-intensive industries, such as textiles, to capital and knowledge-intensive industries, such as automobiles and electronics. This study, which circulated among government departments in Europe and was eventually published in Paris, reached three conclusions.

First, the EC's failure on the Japanese market in industries such as cars, ships and electronics was paralleled by its declining share in these industries on the US market. The failure then was the result of a decline in the EC's competitiveness in these industries rather than the result of unfavourable conditions keeping its exports out of the Japanese market.

Second, although it was probably possible for the EC to reduce the sharpest tensions in its trade relations with Japan in the short term by various measures such as VERAs, in the long run, the EC would not be able to compete with Japan, on its own markets, on the Japanese market, or on third markets, unless it regained its competitiveness by restructuring its industries.

Third, if the EC wished to avoid being caught between the greater competitiveness of the newly industrialized countries (in labour-intensive industries) and the USA and Japan (in knowledge-intensive industries) then it would have to restructure its industries, especially knowledge-intensive industries, before it was too late.[46]

The same elementary point concerning competitiveness was made a year later in a report of the EC Commission analysing the causes of EC–Japan trade frictions. Although it was a confidential internal document, it leaked to the press in the spring of 1979. The report became notorious in Japan because two phrases, about Japanese living conditions ('What Westerners would regard as little more than rabbit hutches') and working habits ('workaholics'), were quoted out of context and became the focus, initially, of a somewhat emotional reaction. What the report actually said was, 'the basic consideration is the relative economic strength and competitiveness of Japan'. It then paid tribute to the 'hard work, discipline, corporate loyalties, and management skills of a crowded, highly competitive island people'. It went on to say that in Europe 'the Protestant work ethic has been substantially eroded by egalitarianism, social compassion, environmentalism, state intervention and a widespread belief that working hard and making money are antisocial'.

The preamble of the report put its finger on the reasons for the Japanese surplus with Europe – not unfair Japanese trading practices or non-tariff barriers keeping European exports out of Japan, but the lack of competitiveness of certain European industries compared with their Japanese counterparts. Such plain speaking in an official document, even an internal paper such as this one, is rare in bureaucracies, which sometimes find it more expedient to address the margin of a problem, rather than the essential core, which is either too embarrassing or too unpleasant to reveal. On this occasion the message in the preamble was a novel and a bitter one for Europeans to swallow. To make sure the paper was read in Europe, blunt language was used.

The week in which the report was leaked to the press I found myself in Tokyo in the unusual position of being summoned to the foreign ministry to receive an official complaint, as well as receiving criticism from our own ambassadors. The Europeans were annoyed that the EC Commission spoke so frankly about Europe, and the Japanese appeared totally to miss the point of the paper, and feeling that they had been insulted, concentrated solely on the term 'rabbit hutch'. It was a busy week. Many complained that such crude language should not have found its way into a policy paper. To these the best I could reply was that the paper was an internal document not intended for public consumption. Second, I reminded them of the practices of the estimable Walter Bullinger, the foreign minister in Harold Nicolson's novel *Public Faces*, who 'tried to give his minutes that personal note which differentiated the pronouncements of Cabinet Ministers from the suggestions of civil servants. A homely turn of phrase here and there; the avoidance generally of technical or professional expressions; the introduction even of a few topical catchwords, of a few examples even of current slang.'

The phrase 'rabbit hutch' as a description of Japanese housing immediately became a catchword in Japan in a manner very similar to the sudden spread of the expression 'economic animals' in the early seventies. Only weeks after it had appeared in the press, it was used as a slogan in the spring labour offensive to argue for better living conditions. Later in 1979, a leading newspaper listed the phrase as among the 'Best Ten Catchwords' of the seventies and the top catchword of 1979. To some it was seen as an argument justifying European protectionism on the old grounds that the Japanese had an unfair competitive advantage because they worked too hard, spent too little on social overheads and saved too much. To others the phrase was taken as an indication of European racial prejudice by its implication that the Japanese were sub-human.

But the majority did not draw such extreme conclusions as a nationwide poll by the *Asahi Shimbun* indicated. While nearly two thirds of those polled felt there was some truth in the phrases, nearly half did not like having this pointed out by a foreigner. Few stopped to ask themselves whether the average Japanese living space was in fact smaller than in Europe (it is, but only marginally).[47]

Three basic Japanese views about all the various complaints and pressures coming both from the USA and Europe over the last twenty years have remained unchanged. Whether the demand was that they should open their market or reduce their surplus, or reflate their economy, Japanese officials consistently argued that complaints about bilateral trade balances were irrelevant. Second, along with the general Japanese public they were convinced that the Americans and Europeans, because of prejudice or jealousy, were using Japan as a scapegoat for economic and social failings in their own countries. Finally, they felt the problem would be solved if only American and European businessmen would make greater *efforts* either to penetrate the Japanese market or to compete with Japanese companies on third markets.

The line taken by US and European negotiators for many years was that unless the Japanese opened their markets, restricted their exports, and reduced the bilateral surplus, they would be unable to prevent protectionist lobbies (in the Congress or in European industry) imposing a far worse solution to the 'Japan problem' than that proposed by the negotiators. The weakness of this line is obvious; it puts the negotiator in a middleman position with no control over the outcome in his own country. In response, the Japanese side would repeat over and over again that it was wrong to look at bilateral balances. We lived in a multilateral world. What you lost on the roundabouts you gained on the swings. Japan was in a vulnerable position because its dependence on imported energy was much greater than that of either the USA or even Europe, therefore it needed surpluses with Europe and the USA to make up for its huge deficits with the Middle East. Its negotiators also pointed out that the current balance (which includes 'invisible' payments such as transport, insurance and tourism) was a fairer yardstick for judging the bilateral economic relation than the trade balance because Japan usually has deficits in the 'invisible' account with both the USA and the EC.

To these lessons in elementary economics, US and European negotiators would counter by drawing attention to the trend for their trade deficits with Japan to grow, against a background of stagflation and slow economic recovery, much slower than in Japan. Unemployment was a political problem and, while it made sense from an economist's point of view to include invisible payments, even if both sides could agree on the statistics (which they have not yet been able to do), to jobless shipyard or steel workers, for example, often concentrated in single electoral districts, this was hardly a very convincing argument. In other words, the problem was fundamentally a political one.

The Japanese view that the trade frictions were caused by the lack of discipline and inability to work hard in Europe and the USA is in line with the reflex which credits the other person with the opposite qualities of one's own. The Japanese self-image is of a frugal, hardworking and disciplined people. If the Americans and Europeans had difficulties on the Japanese market, then it must be because they lacked those very qualities which enabled Japan to build up its industries and its exports. So Americans and Europeans must be extravagant, lazy and undisciplined. Needless to say, this view found all the more ready acceptance in that it is one of the most basic Japanese perceptions of Westerners dating back at least to the nineteenth century.

Japanese visitors to Europe in the Meiji period a hundred years ago noted that the Europeans were so lazy that their post offices were closed on Sundays. Later, during the Depression, it was pointed out that in Japan labour was frugal and worked hard, while in the West, 'labour aims at working the shortest possible hours, doing the minimum amount of work and getting the highest possible wage'.[48]

Forty-five years later in 1977, a senior official in MITI was putting forward exactly the same argument as the main reason for Europe's deficit with Japan:

A comparison between the labour force of Europe and that of Japan shows clearly that European workers lack discipline . . . The decline of Britain, in my opinion, is basically attributable to the fact that discipline has waned . . . Workers (in Europe) are like undisciplined troops. They stop marching and go to bed . . . Europeans today lack spirit . . . Europe is seriously lacking the will to develop the Japanese market.[49]

There is no doubt some truth in such statements. They do not explain everything though – why, for example, Germany, with its more disciplined workforce than Britain's, usually has a larger deficit with Japan than Britain does.

Nor was the weakness of certain European and US industries such as textiles or steel in the 1970s and 1980s caused by the laziness of workers in those industries. Japan too had depressed industries, particularly in the basic materials industries such as aluminium smelting, as well as in textiles, and I never heard it argued in Japan that the workers in those industries were especially lazy. Obviously, the reasons for the weakness of a particular industry may lie in structural conditions which go beyond the working habits of a particular people (for example, lower wages in developing countries, or high costs of imported raw materials or a decline in world demand). To ascribe the structural weakness of some industries in the EC or the USA to the laziness of their workers is to draw a simplistic veil over a complex problem shared by all developed countries, including Japan.

Now that there are highly competitive newly industrialized

countries around Japan, it too begins to experience difficulties in keeping up with the newcomers. In other industries, the problem is not the lack of discipline of the workers as compared with their Japanese counterparts, although these may often contribute to the core of the problem, but also the relatively low productivity in many European and US industries.

Turning now to the different question of 'efforts', or lack of them, in exporting to a foreign market – how can such efforts be judged? Two reasonable indications are, how many businessmen take the trouble to go to the market they wish to sell in, and how much head offices are prepared to invest in a particular country.

Take the first indicator. Many tens of thousands of Japanese businessmen and bankers are stationed in the USA and the member countries of the EC. By comparison, until the late seventies, there were only a handful of western businessmen in Japan – indeed, there were more Christian missionaries from the USA and Europe. By the eighties all this was changing. About ten times more three-year business visas were being issued than three-year visas for missionaries. Another major change is the significant number of foreigners being hired by Japanese companies. The total number of US and European businessmen stationed in Japan or on short visits is still far less than the numbers of Japanese businessmen going the other way.[50]

A second indicator of 'efforts' on a given market is the amount of direct investment put into that market (see Table 3 in Chapter 1). US cumulative direct investments in Japan by the end of the eighties only amounted to just over 5 per cent of total US investments abroad. By comparison, 40 per cent of US investment went to the EC.

The direct investments of all the EC countries in Japan have greatly increased over the last ten years, but they are still less than 2 per cent of their investments in the United States and they lag far behind the $17 billion invested in Japan by US companies.

On the other hand, by 1989, cumulative Japanese direct investments in the EC stood at $29 billion, ten times more than the EC invested in Japan. Per capita, the ratio is 25 to 1 in Japan's favour. And Japan's investments in the EC have been increasing much faster than the EC's investments in Japan. The same applies to Japanese direct investments in the USA which, by 1989, totalled $72 billion. Per capita, the ratio is 8 to 1 in Japan's favour, a ratio all the more extraordinary in that in 1979 it had been 1 to 1.

The 'investment gap' has certainly been affected by the liberalization of the Japanese market coming later than that of the European countries and the USA. 'If an outsider wishes to invest in the world's third largest economy, he finds access limited for a host of reasons: heavy regulation, high taxation, extensive state ownership or outright domination in key industries and anemic securities markets with few new entrants and only halting acceptance of innovation.'[51] These comments were not made about Japan but about Germany, although many of them apply as well to Japan. Private business practices such as long-term relationships with specific suppliers, often cemented with cross-shareholdings, make it more difficult for a foreign investor to come in through merger or acquisition than in the USA or the UK. The degree of cohesion within the giant industrial and banking groups (the *keiretsu*) has sometimes been exaggerated; nevertheless, they remain a far more cohesive force to be reckoned with than any group of companies in the West. The Japanese market has been traditionally much more self-sufficient than the European or even the American, and its industries are extremely competitive; therefore it is not an easy market to buy into.

But the relatively small number of US and European businessmen in Japan, and the low level of US or EC investments there, are also further indications of the high priority they have placed on each other's markets and, by comparison, the low priority still placed on Japan's. Japanese strength in selling to the European and American markets, on the other hand, is one result of what we found in Parts II and III. In short, the Japanese have taken enormously more interest in Europe and the USA than the Europeans and Americans have done in Japan.

These arguments and counter-arguments began to be heard in the nineteenth century. They grew in intensity as Japan increased its share of the world economy. They were heard most clamorously when Europe and the USA were in recession or as Americans began to feel themselves in decline. Behind the arguments there stands a simple truth – Japan is the first Asian country to have gradually reversed its economic and trading relationship with both Europe and the USA by developing a fully competitive industry, not only light industry, but also heavy and knowledge-intensive industry backed by powerful financial institutions. In doing so it has changed the balance of world economic power by creating a huge new centre of wealth and of opportunity in the Asia Pacific region.

PART V

CONCLUSIONS

25

LESS FRICTION

Adjustment to the rise of Japan as an economic giant has generated a lot of friction. Much of this has been the result of sharply increased competition, although some of it has been caused by short-sighted policies and false assumptions. In any event, the previously established players, Europe and the USA, have been forced to change their view of themselves and of Japan – a process by no means completed.

An essential part of the adjustment has been the reallocation of roles and of costs in the Western alliance. An equally essential part has been the shift of responsibilities for managing the world economy. In both spheres the process is still under way. After considering some of the changes, a number of suggestions are made to reduce economic friction either by joint action or singly by one or other of the players.

Global security

The USA, Europe and Japan are members of the same alliance. Their security is interlinked. As the heads of state and government of the G-7 declared at the Williamsburg summit in 1983, 'the security of our countries is indivisible and must be approached on a global basis'. They share the same political values and face many of the same economic problems. It is in their common interest to ensure an open trading system even if they compete strongly within that system.

After the post-war economic recovery in Europe and Japan, the USA has tried to persuade its allies to take on more of the costs and responsibilities of their own defence. The pressure on Japan has been particularly strong because Japan's defence budget has been lowest in proportion to GNP of any member of the alliance although, in absolute terms, the costs of Japan's armed forces are high.

The common perception of Japan, as an aggressive and successful merchant protected by a bankrupt cowboy, is not very flattering to American self-esteem. In polite language Japan was frequently accused of enjoying a 'free ride' at the expense of the American tax payer.

Although an economic giant, Japan has been extremely reluctant to become a military power. And for good reason. Article IX of the Japanese constitution which was written during the US occupation in 1947 states in part, 'land, sea and air forces, as well as other war potential, will never be maintained. The right of belligerency of the state will not be recognized.' Under pressure from the USA during the Korean War, the Japanese established a 75,000-man national police reserve, which developed into a 250,000-man Self-Defence Force, but Article IX has consistently been interpreted as prohibiting the dispatch of troops overseas. A ban is also observed on exports of armaments. Successive prime ministers have adhered to three non-nuclear principles: Japan will not manufacture nuclear weapons, will not maintain such weapons on its territory, and will not permit them to be introduced into its territory. In 1976, the Japanese government decided that defence expenditures in each fiscal year should not exceed 1 per cent of GNP. In 1981, the Japanese agreed with the Americans that in addition to defending their own islands, they would protect the sea lanes to within 1,000 nautical miles. In 1986, a politically important barrier was broken when defence spending reached 1.004 per cent of GNP (rising to an estimated 1.006 per cent by 1989).

Despite its 'war renouncing' constitution, Japan does spend a lot on defence. It is the third largest spender in absolute terms (after the USA and the USSR) and its forces are the seventh largest in the world. The 50,000-plus US troops in Japan have rent-free accommodation and Japan pays well over half their costs. Large sums are paid for arms and equipment most of which

Japan buys from the USA or makes under licence from US companies.

Before increasing military expenditure, both Japan and its allies should be clear as to the nature and extent of its defence role. For a start, what are the defence requirements facing Japan? Are they the same as the other members of the alliance? As an island, Japan needs a smaller infantry than Germany or France, but by the same token, its naval and air force requirements may be larger. How can Japan's defence capability be improved? Should it pursue a 'miniskirt' strategy under the US nuclear umbrella of leaving its extremities exposed and protecting only its vital parts? Should it maintain a 'midi' approach and seek to cover its economic lifelines, the oil routes in Southeast Asia, by increasing naval and air strength? Or should it take a 'maxi' policy and build its own nuclear shield? For the moment no clear consensus has emerged, although the second is the current position, and the third is unacceptable.

Even a cautious extension of the second option is highly controversial as Japan's fumbled reactions to the Gulf war demonstrated. The USA, Europe and Japan depend heavily on regular supplies of oil from the region, so they have an enormous stake in contributing to stability there. Yet when Iraq invaded Kuwait and the USA and the rest of the international community quickly responded, Japan was only able to decide its cash contribution after the war had already ended.

As Japan increases its defence capability, its arms manufacturers will probably succeed in gradually having the current rules forbidding arms exports relaxed. Manufacturers of military hardware in Europe and the USA may then find themselves with rapidly declining overseas markets. The Americans in particular will stand to lose a lot on the Japanese market itself which, since the Pacific War, has been an important captive market for them. Much pressure will therefore continue to be exerted to 'buy US' or to share hi-tech as Japan girds itself for a slightly broader defence role. The controversy over the FSX fighter plane mentioned in Chapter 22 is, in this sense, a pointer to things to come.

Although direct security cooperation between Europe and Japan is far less important to both than the defence ties linking each with the USA, there are surely areas where Europe and Japan could benefit by increasing such cooperation. The incentives are not hard to find. The 'Soviet threat' (*Soren no kyōi*) is based on a Japanese perception of Russian expansion dating back to the eighteenth century, when Russian warships began cruising Japanese waters long before the arrival of Commodore Perry. Today the USSR is the only power with which Japan has a serious territorial dispute (over the Northern Territories).

The Soviet Union is still considered the main threat to both Europe and Japan, so it matters greatly to Japan what happens in the European theatre. Likewise, Europeans recognize that instability in the Asia-Pacific region could readily affect the distribution of Soviet forces. Responses to Soviet military interventions and initiatives in other parts of the world also require coordination, as do economic relations with the Soviet Union and aid to Eastern Europe.

US and European sales of military equipment and technology to China could eventually have more immediate repercussions in Japan than in either the USA or Europe (if only by stimulating a greater Soviet presence in East Asia), so the speed and extent of the build-up of China's military power is another important trilateral question.

Given their shared interests and recognizing the necessity of a comprehensive global approach to national and regional security, the USA, Europe and Japan have little to lose and much to gain by instituting, as a first step, regular trilateral consultations leading to coordination on security matters.[1]

Managing the world economy

Now that the economic weight of the USA in the world has declined relative to Europe and Japan, it is no longer possible for it to take the lead in managing the world economy as it did in the post-war years. In Europe there is no single voice or institution which can speak with authority on the main issues in its relations with either Japan or the USA, spanning both economic and political matters. And in Japan, which has only recently emerged as a world centre of wealth, there is still reluctance to take a larger share of the burdens of managing the world economy. Under these conditions, the tendency has been for the USA to speak first with Japan (the G-2 approach) and then to seek agreement with the Europeans. So long as the Europeans are unable to coordinate their policies and to speak with one voice, this practice will continue.

But the economic importance of the three partners in the trilateral system is now roughly comparable. So not much can be achieved towards managing the world economy by any two of the partners without the full involvement and support of the third. One example would be the gradually evolving new world monetary system which will have to be based on a three-way balance between the US dollar, the Deutschmark (in the EMS), and the yen. Neither the dollar, nor the dollar plus one of the other two main currencies is sufficient to act as a world reserve currency. All three will have to share the burden. The efforts to coordinate monetary policies will continue to involve the G-5 central bankers and the G-7 finance ministers from the USA, Japan and Europe.

An example of the dangers of bilateralism are the many voluntary export restraint agreements (VERAs) mentioned in Chapters 19 and 20, which usually began as an understanding between Japan and the USA and ended by triggering trilateral and then global protectionism in one sector after another.

In the world economy, just as in international politics, the solving of specific issues one by one as they come up is difficult enough. What is much more difficult is when problems overlap and when responsibility for one issue does not necessarily cover another. Only through much better coordination in economic policy-making between the trilateral partners will it be possible to find solutions to interconnected issues (for example, the correction of macro-imbalances; the maintenance of a world trading system which allows growth in exports between countries whose production functions and political economies are different; the necessary conditions for such a system's continued functioning – stability in financial and exchange markets and adequate safeguards and rules of conduct to guarantee fair play on all sides).

Most would agree on the first points on the agenda: the United States to reduce its budget and external deficits by consuming less and producing more; the European Community to complete its internal deregulation exercise leading to a single market without erecting external barriers; and Japan to continue to rely on domestic-led growth. In the trading relations with Japan the first and most obvious joint step to be taken to avoid fruitless arguments is to agree on the terms of the dispute – what is being argued about, what is being requested and what is being denied. This may seem an excessively naïve proposal but, as we saw in Chapters 23 and 24, too often these basic questions were not resolved, leaving both sides talking at cross-purposes with each other, and the door wide open to those who sought to politicize the disputes.

A rapidly expanding field for joint action is industrial and technological cooperation. Already American and European companies have set up all kinds of joint venture with their Japanese counterparts in industries such as steel, cars or electronics. In some cases leaving the manufacturing entirely to Japanese (or other East Asian) companies and keeping only the marketing for themselves. Industrial research and joint development projects, and access to each other's laboratories and research results could also prove extremely useful to both sides. It is an area in which the Americans have the edge over the Europeans because of their security links with Japan and because they have more high technology to offer.

All three partners should continue to bring industrial and safety standards, including testing and approval procedures in the USA, Japan and in Europe, into line with the best international practice. Such standards should be introduced with adequate prior notification and mutual consultation and with regard for possible effects on international trade. Norms certified by officially accepted agencies should be recognized without requiring that they be repeated in the importing country. Problems will occur in new technologies which are being developed in competition and so fast that no accepted standards have yet been agreed on. Systems software and high-definition television (HDTV) are cases in point.

Western Actions

We turn now to the actions which each side could take to prevent the outbreak of economic and trade frictions, and start with the Europeans and Americans. A clearer recognition of the causes of the trade problems with Japan is required. During the French–Italian 'wine war' of the mid seventies, in which French producers complained of a flood of Italian imports, the president of the EC Commission, F.-X. Ortoli, received a French delegation, whose leader with admirable clarity remarked, 'We are faced with two difficulties with Italian wine, namely its quality and its price. It is too good and it is too cheap.' The same used to be true of most of Japan's exports to the USA and Europe except that they are no longer cheap. If they sell well it is for the simple reason that they are popular with consumers, who appreciate not only their high quality and reliability, but also the excellent delivery schedules and after-sales service.

While I was stationed in Tokyo a US colleague once made much the same point when she wryly remarked how amusing it was to observe trade negotiators coming all the way to Tokyo to complain bitterly of deficits with Japan. And then to see the same negotiators snapping up Japanese cameras, pearls, CD players and anything else they could carry, before returning home.

The first thing to acknowledge then is that Japan's trade surpluses with the USA and Europe were made possible by the high quality and strong competitiveness of its exports.

In the nineteenth century, Japan reacted to the Western industrial challenge first by shutting its doors and hoping the Westerners would go away. When it was only too clear that they would not, the Japanese embarked on an all-out and carefully planned programme to learn what it was that made the West so powerful and successful. They recognized their weakness and decided to catch up.

Today the tables are turned and the USA and Europe are

faced with an industrial challenge from Japan and its neighbours in East Asia. When this finally became clear in the seventies, the initial reaction was negative. Then the pendulum swung to the opposite extreme and, as we saw in Chapter 16, there was a boom among Western businessmen for things Japanese, from consumer goods to designer clothes to techniques of enterprise management. Now there are sounds of panic in the air once again.

Competitiveness on a given market today is the result of investment decisions and marketing strategies taken yesterday. The relatively poor performance of US and European exports to Japan, compared with Japan's exports to the USA and Europe in the eighties, was the result of decisions taken or not taken in the seventies. But the same pattern need not be repeated in the nineties and the first decade of the next century if the right decisions are taken now.

The Japanese are for the moment no longer pursuing policies of export-led growth, but in the age of *endaka* and low oil prices, they relied on domestic demand to stimulte growth. Imports of manufactured goods increased after much faster than total imports from 1986 to 1990 (by 23 per cent a year on average as compared to 13 per cent for total imports). In some sectors, such as cars, import pentration ratios will soon be comparable to those achieved by Japanese makers on the European market.

Tokyo has long since announced the details of its industrial restructuring programme which entails on the one hand, making mature industries such as steel newly competitive, and on the other, a continued switch from energy and labour-intensive industries to service industries such as banking, leasing and insurance, and also into technology, and knowledge-intensive industries such as: aircraft, biotechnology and genetics, new materials (kevlar, carbon fibre and carbon fabric), computers, both hardware and software, semiconductors, industrial robots, medical equipment, numerically controlled machine tools, office automation, optics, pharmaceuticals, satellites, telecommunications, and consumer durables such as performance cars, videotape recorders and high-definition TV (HDTV).

The only way to export successfully to a strongly competitive market is to get into the market early on . The Japanese market is not competitive in every sector. But already the Japanese authorities are preparing the ground by encouraging research and by strengthening their industries of tomorrow. Unless the Americans and Europeans can start to meet this challenge by

(i) restructuring their own industries by applying high-tech to smokestack and by developing the growth sectors of tomorrow;

(ii) investing in the Japanese market to lay down the infrastructure to manufacture or to market,

they will find that the Japanese will take the lead in a select handful of the new industries in their own market, and then in the world market, just as they did in garments, cutlery, cameras, steel, ships, cars, robots, numerically-controlled machine tools, home electronics, semiconductors and office automation in the sixties, seventies and eighties.

The main impetus to act will have to come from the private sector because, as Japan shifts the cutting edge of its exports to knowledge-intensive and service industries, and as its companies become multinationals producing in local markets rather than exporters, the political impact of its exports will be diminished. Traditional trade frictions in the coming years, therefore, will no longer be mainly with Japan, but between the developed countries and the newly competitive exporters of the developing world. On the other hand, disputes over grey areas not yet covered by international agreements, such as services and software, especially where these are related to military applications, will probably increase.

Several additional steps could be taken to prevent a repetition of past failures:

1. Encouragement of more practical knowledge of Japan, including Japanese industrial and investment plans. Much more thorough training of officials and diplomats who deal with Japan (a point discussed in the next chapter).

2. Encouragement of more direct investment in Japan, including

joint ventures and company takeovers, particularly for distribution, after-sales service and other infrastructures for the sale of US and European goods. Where volume was sufficiently high to justify it, more investment in manufacturing industries in Japan is required. Also, more manufacturing investments in low labour-cost countries such as Malaysia or Thailand, with the intention of exporting to the Japanese market.

3. More promotional activities, especially of high-volume sales items to the Japanese market (it is, after all, not an isolated market in Asia but the second largest national market after the USA and it stands at the hub of the third largest regional concentration of wealth in the world). Less talk of the closed nature of the Japanese market and more emphasis on US and European success stories there.

Even if these steps were to be taken, they could not succeed without certain moves on the Japanese side.

Japanese Actions

Most of Japan's trading partners have a deficit in their manufactured-goods trade with it. Is everybody else out of step, or is it possible there is something on the Japanese side which has prevented access to its markets equivalent to that enjoyed by Japanese companies in the USA and Europe? If the EC and the USA were the only trading partners of Japan having a weak showing on the Japanese market, it might be reasonable to conclude that this was the result of their lack of competitiveness and general decline of interest in distant and difficult markets. Indeed this is precisely what Japanese spokesmen have argued. The argument would be more convincing if it was not for the fact that the Japanese import structure differs in one crucial respect from that of its main trading partners.

A country's domestic demand is met either by its own production or by imports. In an open economy, entrepreneurs and consumers choose between home-produced and foreign products on the basis of price and quality. In both the USA and the EC imports of manufactured goods in 1970 satisfied about 7 per cent of domestic demand. By 1985 this figure had risen to 13 per cent. In Japan, on the other hand, imports of manufactures have taken the lowest share of domestic demand of all the OECD countries, remaining stable at 5 per cent from 1970 to 1985. After the yen strengthened in the mid-eighties and government policies switched to domestic-led growth, Japan's imports of manufactures increased, but they had risen to between only 6 and 7 per cent of domestic demand by 1989. So not only is Japan's dependence on manufactured imports the lowest of all the major trading countries, but the import penetration ratio remained stable for nearly twenty years. And those were the years which saw the announcement of dozens of 'market-opening' measures intended to significantly increase imports of manufactures. They were also the years which saw Japan's export performance (exports as a percentage of domestic demand) steadily improve although it still remains lower than nearly all other OECD countries.[2]

On the basis of these and other indicators many have concluded that access to Japan's market must have been far more hampered by various impediments than those of its main competitors. Before jumping to a conclusion, several points should be taken into account. Not every country has the same natural and human resources. Japan, for example, is more dependent on imports of foodstuffs and raw materials, especially energy, than either the EC or the USA, because its domestic supplies are limited.[3] Unlike most European countries, Japan has not in the past been surrounded by equally advanced neighbours, enabling close horizontal integration and the growth of cross-investments and of an extensive intra industry trade in manufactured goods. This encouraged a more autarkic development of Japan's economy than that of most European countries or even the United States. Given these differences in resource endowment, location and comparative advantage, it would be astonishing if Japan's trade structure was anything but different from its principal trade partners.

In addition, the main aim of government economic planners in

Japan in the post-war period was to reduce imports of manufactured goods and to build up a competitive manufacturing industry. Another aim was to maintain rapid economic growth. Both policies were enormously successful; among their results was an industrial structure heavily weighted towards manufacturing industries, including several world export leaders, and an ever increasing demand for raw materials to supply those industries. The other side of the coin was a level of manufactured imports far below that of Japan's main competitors in both relative and absolute terms. Opportunities on European and US markets were therefore much greater for Japanese exporters than for European and US exporters to the Japanese market. The Japanese were not slow to make the most of the opportunities which offered. The result has been huge surpluses in its trade with both the EC and the USA and most of its other trading partners as well. Another result has been the very small shares achieved on the Japanese market until recently by foreign exporters – either by the advanced industrial countries or by the NICs.

The third set of reasons why Japan has had such a low level of imports of manufactures is because the government pursued fiscal austerity after the two oil shocks, even after continued savings surpluses in the private sector. The result was slow growth of imports and a rapid expansion of exports leading to massive external imbalances. It was only after Japan entered the age of *endaka* in 1985 that the government began to switch to domestic-led growth policies and the import penetration ratio began to rise.

The political support for this shift will no doubt come from post-war generations more used to the comforts of life than their elders. As the five-year plan introduced in 1988 put it, 'The economic progress that has been achieved has not always redounded to the benefit of the individual Japanese, and there is a disparity between the nation's economic strength and the individual's perceived quality of life, as seen, for example, in the spartan housing, the long hours of work, and the high cost of living.'[4] Japan will have the oldest population pyramid in the world by 2025; one in ten will be over seventy-five-years old and one in five will be over sixty-five. By 2050, there will be no less than a million centenarians. So there will be more spending on health and social welfare as the structure of the population tilts further towards older age groups.

De-emphasis on heavy industry, especially energy-intensive industries, coupled with slower rates of growth, will lead to a falling share of imports of raw materials. Growing investment earnings from abroad also imply an increase in domestic income that will go into both consumption and savings. Rising consumption ought to cause more demand for manufactured products, which could either divert goods from exports or lead to greater corporate investment to expand production or to more imports.[5]

As one of the first results of the transformation of the Japanese economy from export-led growth to domestic-led growth, exporters of manufactures from the Asian NICs are now doing better on the Japanese market. This is welcome because Japan still imports far less from these countries than does the USA.[6]

In the sixties, the Americans jumped the hurdle of nascent European protectionism by switching from exports to direct investment in manufacturing in Europe. By the end of the decade they were deriving more revenue from their investments there than from their exports. At first there was a certain amount of resentment and friction (*le défi américain*) but soon US companies in Europe were providing a bridgehead for popularizing US management methods, and the US way of life in general. The initial fears were forgotten.

Japanese multinationals have invested abroad since the fifties and more so since the seventies (mainly in Asia). But the world build-up of Japanese overseas direct investment only began in the age of *endaka* from the mid-eighties on.

More Japanese direct investment in manufacturing in the USA and Europe has already played an important role in preventing trade frictions, especially where it provides employment on a scale sufficient to take the sting out of the main accusation against Japanese exports, namely that they increase unemployment. Most Japanese factories have created an excellent impression of Japanese management methods, and they have on the whole received a positive press. They help modernize local industries where a transfer of technology takes place and they can also improve the effectiveness of local management. They have had a less positive reception when the operation is simply to assemble components imported from Japan. Such 'screwdriver' plants in the EC have been the object of antidumping penalties since 1987. Employment policies in Japanese factories have been criticized for paying too little attention to minorities or women. Japanese purchases of glamorous nuggets of Americana, for example, CBC Records, Columbia Pictures or a large stake in Rockefeller Center in New York, have sparked negative and emotional reactions.

Over the coming years, Japanese companies will without doubt buy up many more desirable American and European properties, and they will invest more in manufacturing (overseas production still only accounts for 5 per cent of total Japanese production and is expected to grow to 20 per cent by the end of the century). So there may be more friction and hostility but, as with US investment in Europe in the sixties, it should die down as the novelty wears off and the advantages of Japanese capital become better known.[7]

Apart from these structural changes in the Japanese economy and in the pattern of its imports – changes which have already begun but will take many more years to achieve – a number of practical steps could greatly assist US and European exporters to the Japanese market. These include:

1. A policy review of such obviously protected sectors as agriculture, and as a starter, the removal of the remaining twenty-two import quotas (to be reduced to thirteen by 1991) and the liberalization of the rice trade on the assumption that the best way to achieve food security is to allow the development of a competitive agriculture.[8]
2. Continued efforts to simplify and open up the distribution system.
3. Foreign companies to have equivalent opportunities for takeovers as Japanese companies enjoy in the USA and

Europe (implying *inter alia* regulations to prevent impenetrable cross-shareholdings between companies and strict enforcement of regulations governing the prohibition of cartels).

4. Foreign banks to have the same operating conditions as Japanese banks; continued efforts to deregulate capital markets, and to liberalize the insurance sector.

5. Continued efforts to bring testing and approval procedures in line with the best international practice.

6. On the export side, Japanese companies should avoid 'torrential downpours' of exports in particular sectors or particular markets. The government could try to encourage a greater diversification of exports to spread their impact.

7. Pricing policies of exporting companies can also do much to help reduce trade frictions. Prices should be adjusted taking into account price levels in export markets and not, for example, adjusted as an immediate reflex to foreign-exchange fluctuations.

The Japanese find themselves in a similar position to the Americans at the beginning of this century as expressed in the 1905 inaugural speech of Theodore Roosevelt, 'We have become a great nation, forced by the fact of its greatness into relations with the other nations of the earth, and we must behave as befits a people with such responsibilities.'

Japan already plays a crucial role in managing the international economy through such behind-the-scenes groups of central bankers and finance ministers as the G-5 and G-7. At the G-7 economic summits in 1987 and 1988 in Venice and Ottawa, the Japanese prime minister for the first time put forward more initiatives than the other participants. The Bank of Japan for some years has played a key role in efforts to stabilize international currency fluctuations, even if this means keeping the yen high and the dollar low. One way in which Japan will shortly take a more public role in managing the world economy and contributing to the developing countries is by increasing its capital share in financial institutions such as the International Monetary Fund. Despite some resistance from the other members of the G-5 who currently make the running in the IMF, this will eventually bring more of the top posts and increased voting rights including the power of veto, hitherto held only by the USA.

Another way in which Japan is already showing its leadership is in acting as one of the main intermediaries between rich and poor nations. Between 1978 and 1989 Japan's aid nearly quintupled. In 1989, it became the world's largest aid donor. Appropriations in 1990 stood at over $10 billion. Japan now provides one-fifth of all aid to developing countries. Since the late seventies, large amounts have been given to countries of strategic importance to the Western alliance such as Pakistan, Thailand, Egypt, Yugoslavia and Turkey. Starting in 1990, Poland and Hungary also began to receive Japanese aid and loans.[9]

The government has been cautiously stepping up its contributions and, in some cases, sending civilian personnel for United Nations peacekeeping operations, not only in Asia but also in the Middle East, Africa and Latin America.

Unlike the USA, and Britain before that, Japan is in the unusual position of having immense wealth without military power. Its contributions therefore will depend upon judicious use of its wealth – in defending the free-trading system, in finding solutions to the problem of developing-country debt, in playing a more active role on humanitarian issues, such as the plight of refugees, or in discovering ways to combine altruism with commercial gain through its aid and loan programmes, or in pioneering new technologies and the creation of a knowledge-based society. If it can be innovative in areas such as these without projecting military power abroad it will provide a unique model for others to follow.

26

BETTER COMMUNICATIONS

Il est plus facile à un Asiatique de s'instruire des moeurs des Français dans un an, qu'il ne l'est à un Français de s'instruire des moeurs Asiatiques dans quatre, parce que les uns se livrent autant que les autres se communiquent peu.

Montesquieu, *Lettres Persanes*, 1721

As with individuals, so with countries – if you wish to be understood, you must be clear in your own mind what role you are playing, what image you wish to project and what message you wish to convey. In Part III we saw that Japan's image has often been distorted and inaccurate in the West. This is certainly the result of ignorance. But it also derives from the Japanese inability to project a clear and unambiguous message abroad. This inability is exacerbated today by the uncertainty as to what role the country could or should be playing on the world stage. Japan's image in the West is fragmented and arbitrary. This is cause for concern, because Japan's actions will be interpreted in the light of these fragmented images. It may well be that the images and stereotypes of Japan are no more inaccurate than those of other countries, but given the new and influential role of Japan in the world, the consequences of such 'misunderstandings' are far greater.

If you wish to influence what other people think about you, you must find out what is already in their minds, what images they hold, what expectations they cherish. How does the other see the world and how do his perceptions of your actions differ from your own? In answering such questions, the net should be cast wide, because images nestle in every nook and cranny of the collective mind. Some of the main lines of inquiry were suggested in Parts II and III. The next step is to examine the flow of communications between Japan and the West. Is a clear message being sent? Is the message being distorted by incompetent intermediaries? What role can public relations play in improving communications?

To start with the first question.

Sending a Clear Message

It is often said that Americans and Europeans, having formulated their thoughts, are better at conveying them to others, as well as better at presenting their culture to outsiders, than are the Japanese. I suspect that this is as much a question of power as of ability. The rest of the world listened to the Europeans in the nineteenth century and to the Americans in the twentieth. They did so because the Europeans and Americans had power and prestige, which made their cultures that much more attractive. On the other hand, there were many reasons which led the Japanese both individually and as a nation to adopt an unassuming role in their dealings with Westerners. In the first place they were latecomers to the industrial system, and having learnt it, they were defeated in the Pacific War. Now that they have recovered and become the world's top financial power, this situation is beginning to change and they are more assertive, even arrogant.

Nevertheless, at meetings between a Westerner and a Japanese, or at international fora in which they both take part, the Westerner will still often do most of the talking, usually in his own language, and afterwards say, 'Well, I think he understood what I was trying to tell him.' At which, if you ask him what he thought the Japanese was trying to say, you will be met by incomprehension and the defensive retort, 'He did not seem to have very much to say at all.'

Europeans and even more so Americans believe that frankness is the measure of honesty; you should say what you mean and mean what you say, whether or not this entails revealing 'private faces in public places'. But the Japanese are not like that. They attach great importance to social roles. It may be a prestigious one such as company president, or it may be as humble as gasoline station attendant, but the commitment brought to the role and the sense of achievement in fulfilling it are of the same intensity. You define yourself by the emblazoning on your shield, by the title on your business card, therefore you dress your part, whether for work or play; much more than in the West, your satisfaction in life derives from maintaining correct appearances (*tatemae*) while leaving unsaid private motives (*honne*). So, your sincerity is judged by the degree to which your behaviour matches the expectations attached to your role. Not, as in the West, by the degree to which your behaviour matches your personal feelings.

In addition, the Japanese, it is probably true, also believe more strongly than most other people that the important things, such as 'innermost sincerity' (*magokoro*), should not, indeed cannot, be expressed verbally. It is therefore the measure of a good relationship that both sides can sense each other's feelings without their having to be articulated. So non-verbal, intuitive communication is taken as a sign of solidarity, of real understanding.

The distinction between statements suitable to the occasion, the public façade (*tatemae*) and one's real intentions (*honne*), left unspoken, has led to the common complaint made about the Japanese, 'They never say what they mean.' And the value attached to 'visceral understanding' (*haragei*) hardly makes for easy communication with foreigners. Indeed it has been a principal source of misunderstanding.[10]

The virtue of reticence in the individual in Japan has its equivalent in public life; blowing one's trumpet is frowned upon – it is more effective to 'kill one's enemy with silence' (*mokusatsu*), that is to shame him by refusing to acknowledge him, than it is to drown him with a flood of words. Rhetoric is not a form of art which flourishes in the schools and public halls of Japan. Takeshita Noboru, the former prime minister, was speaking for many when he said, 'My words are clear but often my meaning is not.' People who articulate too clearly, especially those younger or more clever than oneself, are quickly labelled 'reason freaks' (*rikutsuppoi*) and frowned upon.

The strong sense that Japan is isolated and unique is matched by the feeling that its culture is not universal and that even if the Japanese should try to explain it, foreigners would not possibly be able to understand. In the same way, the Japanese feel that their language is uniquely difficult for foreigners to learn. Objectively this is an unwarranted assertion, but nevertheless one which appears to be confirmed by the extremely small numbers who make the effort to master Japanese. The Japanese themselves have a bad reputation as foreign language speakers. The reason usually given is that Japan was so long isolated from the rest of the world. Equally important reasons are the bias against verbal communication and an education system which stresses learning the grammar of foreign languages over acquiring the ability to speak them.

No doubt language difficulties are one of the major sources of misunderstandings between the Japanese and other peoples. The reserve of many Japanese abroad is the result of an inability to handle the necessary foreign language with sufficient skill to risk breaking out of a safe silence. And even if he knows the foreign language well, he may not wish to offer too many opinions or be too flexible for fear of upsetting a consensus position already decided back home in Japan.

Above all, the memories of the jingoistic bombast of the militarists during the Pacific War, followed by crushing defeat, reinforced a whole generation in their preference for silence and a low profile in international affairs, a preference which, after all, appears to have been validated by the spectacular success of Japan's economic growth since the war, the attainment of which was a national objective, a means of breaking out of the isolation imposed by defeat. It implied no explicit ideology and was eagerly accepted. Why, then, discard a winning formula? To many, especially of the older generations, although Japan may have become a rich country, it is also felt to be powerless because the indispensable sources of its wealth – oil and raw materials – have to be almost entirely imported from an unstable world. The feeling that Japan is isolated and fragile contributes to a certain hesitancy on the world stage.

Whatever the reasons, many Japanese still see themselves not only as militarily weak, but also as culturally backward; as learners, rather than teachers. Hundreds of thousands more Japanese students go abroad than foreign students go to Japan. Tens of thousands more foreign books are translated into Japanese than Japanese books are translated into foreign languages.

The zest for foreign knowledge and culture has been one of the strengths of modern Japan. But surely the time has now come, as was suggested at the end of Part II, to reassess this old priority and for the Japanese to ask themselves whether they have something more to contribute to the world than consumer durables. In the words of Saji Keizo, introducing a symposium appropriately entitled *Japan Speaks*, 'Although Japan has become a major economic power in the world today, she has yet to express her unique cultural heritage in universal terms . . . If Japan is to find a viable role in the world community and contribute to the true progress of that community, she must discover anew, from an international perspective, the essence of her own culture and national character. Japan must also develop the means and ability to express this essence.'[11] At the very least the costs of being misunderstood by other countries have now become so high that a major effort to project a clearer message would appear to be only prudent.

In an age when 'money talks' as never before and its pursuit has become a universal goal, the Japanese are well placed to win friends and influence people.

There are signs too that many Japanese are more open to the idea of Japan playing a more active role in international affairs. Japan has long since been the world's third main centre of technology innovation and, in an increasing number of fields, it is now second to none. As it translates its wealth into political influence it will gain more prestige and more and more people will be eager to look into every aspect of its culture.

Public Relations

All governments and most government agencies conduct public relations both at home and abroad, as do private corporations. The Japanese government began in the early Meiji period by establishing the Rokumeikan which was intended to present a modern image of Japan to foreigners. Then, in 1898, the Foreign Ministry began collecting in a systematic way comments about Japan in foreign newspapers and journals. During the Russo-Japanese War this activity continued, and it formed the basis of an all-out effort to correct the yellow-peril image of Japan in the West. Newspapers were bribed, editors were offered decorations, journalists were taken on junkets and friends of Japan were encouraged to express their views; a special press agency to disseminate news about Japan was set up in Germany and roving officials were seconded from their regular duties to go to Europe and the USA to argue, refute and propagandize.

Such public relations activities continued, on and off, in the years which followed. In the thirties, for example, a deliberate effort was made to justify Japanese actions in China through radio broadcasts, pamphlets, specially commissioned books, goodwill missions overseas and conducted tours of Japan for foreign visitors. Particular efforts were made to bring school teachers to Japan because it was assumed that a favourable impression created on them would have ripple effects on the next generation. In 1936, Domei news agency began full-time dissemination of Japanese propaganda. In terms of the Japanese–US relationship, 'more time, attention and funds were probably devoted to cultural exchanges in the years preceding Pearl Harbor than in any previous period'.[12]

Possibly the single most effective piece of public relations after the war (apart from the Tokyo Olympics) was the decision in the sixties to present an image of Japan as a northern country both technologically advanced and of great scenic beauty. The resultant photograph of the 'bullet' train flashing sleekly past a snow-capped Mt Fuji became well known abroad and no doubt helped convey the additional message which its sponsors intended, namely that Japan was not to be confused with a tropical Asian country and also that the image of 'Fuji geisha-san' should be discarded.

Judging from the data collected in Part III on the Western image of Japan, these PR activities were not too successful. Westerners were not at all impressed by the Rokumeikan – what won their attention were the government's activities in building a modern state and army. Again, during the Russo-Japanese War, Japan's propagandists probably did no more than provide arguments for those already disposed to take its side. In the thirties, Japanese efforts to persuade the West that its activities in China were benevolent fell on deaf ears. If cultural exchanges before Pearl Harbor served to reassure Americans that the aesthetic image fitted Japan and therefore helped close their eyes to preparations for war, then it was a brilliant propaganda success. It is more likely, however, that such people-to-people exchanges had little or no influence on government decision-makers. Even the enormous circulation of the photo of the bullet train streaking past Mt Fuji was apparently insufficiently effective to mitigate the polluted monster image of Japan.

Official public relations can at best provide effective arguments to those already disposed to listen and to take a sympathetic view. It can sugar the pill for those who have decided to take the pill, but it cannot persuade them to take it in the first place. The most effective official PR is that which limits itself to explaining and providing further information about government aims and activities in as objective a way as possible. It should provide a steady flow of information – on failures as well as on successes – and should establish a reputation for integrity.

In most periods, positive images of Japan have usually been present in the USA and Europe, even when negative images have been predominant. Naturally official PR should seek to confirm the positive images and to correct the negative ones. But PR can only succeed if there is a story to be told. The trouble is today that Japan is a country in search of a role; it will only be able to find its voice when it has decided its role.

The advantages gained by Japan in adopting a low profile in the post-war years were no doubt great. But we have now entered a new period of history in which the dangers of fuzziness may be equally great.

Because I believe the Americans and Europeans need no encouragement to talk about themselves and explain their positions to others, I have limited my comments to an area in which I have had some direct experience: the EC's presentation of its case.

Not only are EC decisions very often of a technical nature, but they are also based on complex compromises as the result of the high number of interested parties involved – the bureaucracies, politicians and parliaments of twelve countries; the half-dozen institutions of the Community itself; the courts, the industries, the unions and the media – all of twelve countries. Even insiders find it hard to know what is going on and why. Decision-making in all our countries today is complex enough and the language of government is not that of poets and philosophers. That said, the uncertain nature of the EC – something more than a customs union but less than the United States of Europe – and the uncertainty as to what role it is playing can make its policies and their expression exceptionally opaque.

To make matters worse, because of its special nature, the Community of twelve too often speaks with a confusion of tongues. This has frequently happened in its relations with Japan. For example, in May 1981, the EC Council of Ministers called for a united strategy towards Japan and empowered the Commission to seek a self-restraint agreement on exports of Japanese cars to the EC analogous to the agreement reached by the USA with Japan. Within weeks of the decision, however, Germany and the Benelux had come to bilateral agreements with Tokyo, thus undermining the Community approach.[13] Given this sort of confusion and fumbling, can anyone blame third countries for finding it hard to distinguish who speaks for the EC?

Lastly, the PR of the EC faces the difficult task of explaining policies which to the outsider appear too often as negative or ineffective. It is no easy matter, for example, to explain why it is that the EC's efforts to keep foreign imports out of Europe appear to receive so much more attention than efforts to promote its own exports to foreign countries.

Whenever the EC begins to set its own house in order and move towards attainable goals, it immediately becomes more easy to present to others because it naturally attracts interest and attention. The establishment of the single unified market by 1992 is a case in point.

There is no hope of a policy or an objective being understood, or of improving relations with a foreign country, unless a clear message is sent. As a minimum, therefore, the EC should ensure that three things are done, once a policy decision has been taken which has external implications:

1. Spell out clearly to the affected country what the policy is and the reasons why it was adopted.
2. Put the explanation in plain language, not in jargon.
3. Speak with one voice.

The Scholars

Turning now to the transmission of messages between Japan and the West and the interpretation of each to the other by professional mediators such as academic specialists, journalists or diplomats and officials: are they doing their job well? The initial response, based on the copious evidence of blurred communication cited in previous chapters, must be clearly that they are not. To anyone familiar with the large amount of high-quality research on Japan conducted in US universities and think-tanks, this must seem a harsh judgement. But there is a gap between the findings of academics and their diffusion to a broader public.

And in Europe Japanology is far behind that in the USA. There is over-specialization in the hands of language experts who justify their own role as intermediaries by emphasizing the differences between Japan and other countries. There is also an over-emphasis on past culture at the expense of the present, because it is more esoteric and hence better suited to academic investigation. This is related to the bias of many of the early enthusiasts of things Japanese, whose romantic search for the exotic led them to highlight what were often untypical and marginal features. This criticism applies as well to journalists and diplomats all of whom, to the extent that they share the same guild mentality of cultural intermediaries, over-emphasize the differences between cultures, and focus their attention on the supposedly unique and unusual features of the culture they are writing about. And like all specialists, they fall too easily into the habit of talking exclusively to members of their own circle, neglecting to address themselves to other specialists, let alone to the public at large.

Academic experts on Japan pursue their field with hardly a glance at related disciplines. This 'tunnel approach' is found in both the West and Japan in the fierce loyalty to one country or culture. European Japanologists are usually ignorant of other countries around Japan, and Japanese experts on Germany, for example, will ignore France, and a specialist on Italian culture will rarely know Germany.

As a heritage of Pax Americana perhaps, US scholars often discuss other countries primarily in terms of their bilateral relations with the USA. This is particularly true of US writing on Japan. Studies of Japan 'in the international context' turn out to be studies of US–Japanese relations. This single-country focus is particularly regrettable in today's world of global markets and interdependence of national economies and decision-making. Another disadvantage of the single-country approach is that it often leads to the uncritical acceptance of a country's own self-image.

One source of concern pointed out by US specialists on Japan is the very high proportion of US–Japanese studies and technological research which is now being funded by the Japanese.

When it comes to the students, the contrast is striking: there are many more Japanese studying in the USA or Europe than vice versa, and the Western students in Japan mainly study the arts, whereas Japanese students in the West mostly study science and technology. Each, in other words, pursues the old image of the other.

The following four proposals are put forward to improve the educational contribution to mutual understanding between the West and Japan:

1. A more effective way to encourage knowledge of modern Japan in US and European universities would be not to give grants to the traditional centres of Japanology (except in the limited sense of language schools) but rather to encourage knowledge of Japan in general undergraduate courses. The aim would be to make knowledge of Japan part of the normal education of young people, not an exotic option – a first step towards closing the enormous gap between the knowledge of Japan held by specialists and the ignorance of Japan among the general public. At the graduate or faculty level, funds should be made available to economists, doctors, lawyers, chemists, engineers and any others who expressed a serious interest in finding out about the Japanese experience in their special fields.

2. As part of the attempt to get more students to go to Japan, more travel scholarships and grants could be made available. Government and business should be encouraged to contribute funds as much as the universities. Establishing a Japanese equivalent of the Fulbright awards, especially for young scientists to train in universities and companies, would have great impact.

3. In Japan it is regrettable that there is not an opening of the university system, including the élite state universities, whose doors still remain largely closed to foreign staff. Although they were partially opened in 1982 and international research exchange was eased by a 1986 law, the fact remains that the apprentice-like system by which professors slowly climb their way up the academic ladder makes it difficult for outsiders to enter the system.

4. In most countries it is recognized that fluency in foreign languages, especially English, is vital for communicating with the rest of the world, so provision is usually made in the education system for early exposure to speaking a foreign language or two. In Japan, on the other hand, fluency in speaking English is positively discouraged by the many examinations on written English and its grammar which students are forced to take in order to get in to the right schools and universities. The result is that most students can

get no serious exposure to foreign languages until after they graduate from university and by then it is usually too late to acquire fluency. Those who for one reason or another do go abroad and become fluent in foreign languages can often find themselves penalized in the job market when they return to Japan. The recent introduction of a special university entrance examination for children returning from abroad is a step in the right direction.

If Japan wishes to play a full role and to develop an effective voice in today's world culture, it must reform its educational system in such a way as to encourage fluency in foreign languages at an early age and to give much greater recognition to young people to achieve such a vital skill.

The Journalists

Information about the USA and Europe is fed back to Japan accurately and in considerable detail. On the other hand, information about Japan in the USA and Europe concentrates mainly on the economy. There is much less interest in internal politics or social trends. Such reporting as there is appears only sporadically and is usually found tucked away in the business section of newspapers.

Japanese newspaper coverage of the USA and Europe is usually accurate but lacking a sense of flair. Japanese foreign correspondents appear to prefer official briefings rather than to go out and investigate a story. As a consequence the coverage is a bit wooden and, although detailed, sometimes misses the point. In contrast the same reporters are often much better informed when it comes to covering the overseas visits of Japanese politicians.

The number of accredited foreign correspondents in Tokyo from all over the world has doubled since the seventies. At any given moment there are also several hundred journalists visiting on special assignments.

There has been a marked improvement in the coverage of Japan in the quality Western press over the last ten years. Newspapers such as the *Economist*, the *Financial Times*, the *Far*

Eastern Economic Review, the *Los Angeles Times*, the *New York Times*, the *Asian Wall Street Journal*, the *Neue Zürcher Zeitung*, *Die Welt* and *Le Monde* have developed a consistent record of first-class reporting on Japan which increasingly covers the arts and social trends as well as the economy.

With notable exceptions, the foreign correspondents are usually unable to speak or read Japanese, so it is perhaps hardly surprising that the bulk of the reporting out of Tokyo rarely gives the impression of being based on direct contacts or interviews. A common practice is for correspondents to rely on local staff who act as intermediaries. Even the best of the bilingual correspondents, however, can still face a discouraging lack of interest in stories filed from Tokyo. Much of what they send home either never appears or is relegated to a corner of their newspaper. Most major Western TV channels have produced predictably similar mini-series on Japan.

Perhaps the single most effective way of improving the level of reporting on Japan would be to put an end to the practice of excluding foreign correspondents in Tokyo from the Japanese journalist 'clubs' attached to ministries, politicians and political parties. A move in this direction was taken in 1979 when the foreign ministry club was opened to foreign correspondents, and most other ministries have now followed, but many of the private sector clubs remain closed.

Diplomats and Officials

Both academic specialists and journalists can be judged by their output. The same cannot be said of diplomats whose reporting and activities are shrouded in secrecy. This was not always the case. In the old days, many of the best Western experts on Japan were diplomats. They would be trained to fluency in the language and then posted and reposted to the country for long periods. As one of the last and greatest of the scholar-diplomats, Sir George Sansom, put it, they were not 'faced with quintuple bits of nonsense, piles of misleading statistics and even the awful likelihood that somebody may distort the studies by giving a call on the trans-oceanic telephone'.[14]

Today the scholar-diplomat has long since ceased to exist; diplomats are too busy, not only with the flood of internal communications, but also with the endless stream of visitors who jet into town.

In the old days, the embassy was often the only source of information and knowledge about a country which the home government could rely on. It was a vital and independent link between sovereign states. The ambassador for months or years on end was the senior and only representative of his country on whose behalf he had to negotiate on a wide variety of issues. Today all that has changed with the proliferation of many different channels of communication and opportunities for direct meetings.

The growth of interdependence between states has created a new-style multilateral or alternative diplomacy concentrating on economic issues, not conducted by diplomats handling political relations, but by peer groups such as central bankers and their officials, finance ministers and their deputies, or the regulatory agencies. The diplomatic congress has been replaced by meetings of the G-5 and summits of the G-7. The traditional diplomat has not been the winner.

Anyone who has participated in negotiations with the Japanese government will be familiar with the scene. The foreigner accompanied by a handful of colleagues will face much larger numbers of Japanese officials across the table. In the background will be many more, listening and taking notes. Maybe one or two on the foreigner's side will know Japanese; but half or three-quarters on the Japanese side will know English and will have studied or worked in the USA or Europe. This naturally gives an enormous advantage to the Japanese. There is a good case then for:

1. Training a much larger corps of officials and diplomats to prepare and conduct negotiations on economic and financial matters with the Japanese; strengthening the hand of the diplomat as coordinator to bring together the many different interests involved in relations with Japan and to try to make sense of the many conflicting sources of information.

2. Requiring diplomats to be judged by the same standards as anybody else, that is by their output. Without damage to confidentiality this could be more freely available, both in the country in which the diplomat was stationed and back at home.

Scholars, journalists, diplomats and officials are among the most important mediators between our countries. But there are many others – politicians, businessmen, labour leaders, students, athletes. Recent years have seen an increase in their interaction and exchanges, but the traffic is still too much a one-way affair of Japanese going to the USA and Europe. More could be done to encourage Americans and Europeans to go to Japan.

The aim should be to increase the opportunities for contacts, and to increase the channels of communication. Only then can there be a shift from chance symbols to regular signals; from a limited number of outdated stereotypes to a full range of apposite images; from the capricious and emotional to the fixed and considered.

Nothing can be achieved until the Japanese define more clearly the role they wish to play on the world stage, and having decided it, make massive efforts to be better understood. Nothing can be achieved unless Americans and Europeans, in reacting to external pressures, respond positively with a newly awakened desire to learn the sources of both their own strengths and weaknesses, as well as those of their competitors, principally Japan.

ANNEX

Table 1. Basic Statistics of Japan, the EC and the USA, 1989

		Japan	EC	USA
Population	(million)	123	327	249
GNP	(trillion $)	2.8	5.1	5.2
GNP per capita	($)	23,000	15,600	21,000
Total imports	(billion $)	210	491	454
Imports per capita	($)	1,715	1,500	1,820
Import dependence	(%)	9	10	9
Imports of:				
Food	(%)	15	7	6
Fuels	(%)	20	14	9
Raw materials	(%)	13	9	3
Manufactured goods	(%)	48	68	77
per capita	($)	870	1,025	1,385
Total exports	(billion $)	272	454	330
Exports per capita	($)	2,200	1,392	1,325
Export dependence	(%)	10	9	6

Note: Figures have been rounded to nearest decimal point so that totals may not always add up exactly. Imports divided according to SITC, Revision 3. Imports (exports) of the EC represent imports (exports) of the twelve member countries from outside the EC. It does not include trade between member states. Import (export) dependence equals imports (exports) as a percentage of GNP.

Sources: Bank of Japan, 1990; Eurostat, 1990.

Table 2. Growth Rates in Real GNP of Japan, the EC and the USA, 1961–92

	1961–5	1966–70	1971–5	1976–80	1981–5	86	87	88	89	90	91	92
Japan	10.0	11.3	4.6	5.1	4.3	2.5	4.6	5.7	4.9	4.5	3.6	3.8
EC	4.7	4.4	2.7	3.0	1.2	2.6	2.8	3.8	3.4	2.9	2.2	2.5
USA	4.6	3.0	2.2	3.4	2.3	3.0	3.6	3.9	2.9	1.1	−0.4	2.5

Sources: OECD Economic Outlook. EC forecasts and Consensus Economics, London.

Table 3. Trade in Manufactured Goods (per cent)

	Imports		Exports	
	1962	1989	1962	1989
Japan	1.6	3.6	7.1	9.6
USA	7.8	7.2	2.4	4.6
Germany	5.6	16.3	13.5	25.7
UK	4.4	18.3	11.2	14.3
France	4.1	16.2	4.9	15.1

Note: Imports and exports of manufactured goods (SITC 5–8) measured as a percentage of nominal GNP.
Source: Bank of Japan, 1963–90 and OECD, 1990.

Table 4. Imports of Manufactured Goods from the Asian NICs 1986–9
($ billion)

	1986	(% of GNP)	1987	(% of GNP)	1988	(% of GNP)	1989	(% of GNP)
US	46	(1.10)	58	(1.35)	63	(1.30)	63	(1.22)
EC	15	(0.43)	17	(0.39)	20	(0.43)	28	(0.55)
Japan	11	(0.55)	12	(0.50)	16	(0.56)	19	(0.67)

Source: Comtrade.

Table 5. Trade and Current Account Balances, Japan, the EC and the USA, 1973–92

	Japan		EC		USA	
	Trade balance ($ bn)	Current balance ($ bn)	Trade balance ($ bn)	Current balance ($ bn)	Trade balance ($ bn)	Current balance ($ bn)
1973	− 1	− 0.1	−12	+ 1	− 3	+ 7
1974	− 7	− 5	−31	−11	− 12	+ 2
1975	− 2	− 1	−15	− 1	+ 2	+ 18
1976	+ 2	+ 4	−31	− 6	− 17	+ 4
1977	+10	+11	−21	+ 3	− 39	− 14
1978	+18	+17	−14	+17	− 42	− 16
1979	− 8	− 9	−44	−13	− 40	− 1
1980	−11	−11	−85	−43	− 25	+ 2
1981	+20	+ 5	−55	−21	− 40	+ 6
1982	+18	+ 7	−47	−19	− 41	− 8
1983	+31	+21	−33	+ 3	− 68	− 46
1984	+44	+35	−31	+10	−114	−107
1985	+56	+49	−25	+20	−122	−118
1986	+93	+86	+11	+69	−145	−142
1987	+96	+87	+ 1	+38	−161	−153
1988	+95	+80	−14	+15	−129	−120
1989*	+77	+57	−30	+ 0.2	−115	− 96
1990*	+64	+36	−43	−17	−116	− 93
1991*	+79	+59	−44	−53	−123	−104
1992*	+90	+63	−35	−55	−100	− 89

Figures have been rounded. The EC is the EC of the 12.
Sources: IMF (DOT), 1990; Exports, FOB; Imports, CIF.
*Estimates

Table 6. EC and US Merchandise Trade with Japan, 1970–90 ($ million)

	EC exports to Japan		EC imports from Japan			US exports to Japan		US imports from Japan		
	Rank		Rank		Balance	Rank		Rank		Balance
1970	1.4	9	2.1	6	− 0.7	4.7	2	6.2	2	− 1.5
1971	1.4	11	2.1	7	− 0.8	4.1	2	7.7	2	− 3.6
1972	1.7	10	2.9	5	− 1.3	4.9	2	9.6	2	− 4.7
1973	2.9	6	4.4	5	− 1.6	10.2	2	10.2	2	− 1.9
1974	3.3	10	5.4	7	− 2.1	10.7	2	13.3	2	− 2.6
1975	2.9	15	6.9	6	− 4.0	9.6	2	12.3	2	− 2.7
1976	3.0	15	9.7	6	− 6.6	10.1	2	16.9	2	− 6.8
1977	3.7	13	10.5	5	− 6.9	10.5	2	20.2	2	− 9.7
1978	5.0	11	12.8	4	− 7.8	12.9	2	26.5	2	−13.6
1979	6.8	8	13.4	5	− 6.6	17.6	2	28.1	2	−10.5
1980	6.7	11	19.4	4	−12.8	20.9	2	33.0	2	−12.1
1981	6.6	12	19.3	4	−12.7	21.8	2	39.9	2	−18.1
1982	6.5	10	18.8	3	−12.3	21.0	2	39.9	2	−18.9
1983	6.9	7	19.5	2	−12.7	21.9	2	43.5	2	−21.6
1984	7.4	7	20.3	2	−12.9	23.6	2	60.4	2	−36.8
1985	7.9	7	21.8	2	−13.8	22.6	2	72.4	1	−49.8
1986	11.2	5	32.7	2	−21.5	26.9	2	85.5	1	−58.6
1987	15.7	5	39.9	2	−24.2	28.2	2	88.1	1	−59.9
1988	20.0	5	48.4	2	−28.4	37.8	2	90.2	1	−52.0
1989	23.4	5	50.7	2	−27.3	44.6	2	93.6	1	−51.3
1990*	28.8	5	53.7	2	−24.9	45.3	2	86.8	1	−41.5

Sources: EC (12)–Japan trade, Eurostat; Exports, FOB; Imports, CIF.
USA–Japan trade, IMF (DOT) 1990; Exports, FOB; Imports, CIF.
*Estimates

Table 7. Japan, EC and USA: Shares of Each Other's External Trade, 1960–89

	1960	1970	1980	1985	1986	1987	1988	1989*
Japan's share of EC exports	1.2	2.6	2.2	2.8	3.3	4.0	4.7	5.0
Japan's share of US exports	7.7	12.9	9.4	10.6	12.9	11.2	11.8	11.8
Japan's share of EC imports	1.4	3.4	4.9	7.0	9.9	10.2	10.7	10.2
Japan's share of US imports	7.6	15.1	12.5	20.5	23.2	21.0	20.3	19.8
EC share of US exports	25.8	28.6	24.7	21.5	23.0	21.1	23.7	24.2
EC share of Japan's exports	7.8	9.6	12.8	11.9	14.8	15.7	16.4	17.4
EC share of US imports	24.1	24.3	14.9	20.1	20.9	20.5	19.3	18.1
EC share of Japan's imports	7.0	8.2	5.6	7.0	10.2	11.7	13.0	13.6
US share of EC exports	13.6	18.0	12.8	22.6	22.0	21.2	19.7	18.9
US share of Japan's exports	27.0	31.0	25.0	37.6	38.9	37.0	34.1	34.0
US share of EC imports	20.4	21.7	16.9	16.9	16.9	16.5	17.4	19.4
US share of Japan's imports	35.0	29.0	17.0	20.0	24.3	20.9	22.3	23.1

Note: EC is the EC of the 12.
Source: IMF (DOT) 1989; Exports, FOB; Imports, CIF.
*Estimates

Table 8. Japan's Trade in Passenger Cars with the EC and the USA, 1970–90

	Registration in the EC of cars imported from Japan		Registration in Japan of cars imported from the EC		Registration in the USA of Japanese cars imported from Japan		Registration in Japan of cars imported from the USA	
	Numbers	%	Numbers	%	Numbers	%	Numbers	%
1970	31,923	0.6	11,313	0.7	276,000	3	5,416	0.31
1975	313,645	4.6	25,842	1.0	810,000	9	16,000	0.62
1980	762,719	9.1	32,500	1.1	1,819,000	21	11,058	0.41
1981	703,281	8.3	29,412	1.0	1,761,000	22	7,742	0.29
1982	691,343	8.0	30,889	1.0	1,692,000	23	4,000	0.14
1983	772,720	8.7	31,396	1.0	1,698,000	19	2,646	0.09
1984	789,393	9.1	38,016	1.2	1,852,000	18	2,382	0.06
1985	862,223	9.0	46,171	1.5	2,216,000	20	1,816	0.06
1986	1,039,960	9.9	62,724	2.0	2,348,000	21	2,345	0.06
1987	1,051,669	10.0	88,825	2.7	2,204,653	22	4,006	0.12
1988	1,043,382	8.6	111,806	3.0	2,020,883	23	14,511	0.38
1989	1,113,000	8.4	141,000	3.4	2,588,000	25	20,000	0.50
1990	1,120,000	9.4	178,000	4.1	1,876,055	32	28,000	0.60

Note: Per cent refers to the percentage of new car registrations.
Sources: Japanese passenger cars registered in Europe: Comité de Liaison de la Construction Automobile. EC imports are for the EC of the nine member states for 1970 and 1975, of the ten for 1980–84, and of the twelve from 1986 onwards. EC passenger cars registered in Japan: The Japan Automobile Importers' Association. Cars exported from the EC to Japan are from French, German, Italian and British makers. USA: *Automotive News*.

Table 9. Unemployment as a Percentage
of the Workforce, 1973–92

	Japan	EC	USA
1973	1.3	2.5	4.8
1974	1.4	2.9	5.5
1975	1.9	4.3	8.3
1976	2.0	4.9	7.6
1977	2.0	5.3	6.9
1978	2.2	5.5	6.0
1979	2.1	5.6	5.8
1980	2.0	6.4	7.0
1981	2.2	8.1	7.5
1982	2.4	9.5	9.5
1983	2.6	10.0	9.5
1984	2.7	10.8	7.4
1985	2.6	10.9	7.1
1986	2.8	10.8	6.9
1987	2.8	10.4	6.1
1988	2.5	9.7	5.4
1989	2.3	9.0	5.2
1990	2.1	8.5	5.3
1991*	2.5	8.8	6.1
1992*	2.3	8.8	6.7

Sources: Japan: Economic Planning
Agency, Tokyo; EC (12): Eurostat;
USA: *Current Business Indicators*.
*Forecast

Table 10. The Value of the Yen, 1949–90

Yen per	$	£	DM	ECU
1949–71	360	1,000	98	
1971	349	848	100	364
1972	303	754	98	340
1973	271	663	102	333
1974	292	680	113	347
1975	296	654	121	368
1976	296	531	118	331
1977	268	467	116	306
1978	210	402	105	267
1979	219	463	121	300
1980	226	525	126	315
1981	221	440	96	245
1982	249	435	103	244
1983	238	359	91	211
1984	238	315	85	187
1985	239	309	82	181
1986	169	241	81	165
1987	145	236	78	167
1988	128	228	73	151
1989	139	225	72	150
1990	145	258	90	185

NOTES

Part I The Rise of Japan

1. Using purchasing-power parity rather than market exchange rates, the OECD calculated that in 1988 Japan ranked ninth after the USA, Canada, Switzerland, Norway, Luxemburg, Iceland, Sweden and Germany, in that order, with 70 per cent of the USA's GNP per capita. See the *Economist*, 4 November 1989, p. 127.
2. The Asian Newly Industrializing Countries (NICs) are Hong Kong, Singapore, South Korea and Taiwan. They are also referred to as NIEs (Newly Industrializing Economies). The members of the Association of Southeast Asian Nations (ASEAN) are Brunei, Indonesia, Malaysia, Singapore, Thailand and the Philippines.
3. In 1960, Japan was the EC's 21st largest export market in the world and 23rd largest supplier. In 1989, it was the EC's fifth largest market and second largest supplier. Today about 35 per cent of Japan's exports go to the USA and 17 per cent to the EC. On the other hand, Japan takes 12 per cent of US exports and only 5 per cent of EC exports. The USA has 23 per cent of Japan's imports, the EC 14 per cent.
4. It is wise to remember that this has not always been so. The USA has had friendly relations and harboured favourable images of either Japan or China; rarely both at once. Usually the USA favoured whichever was weaker at the time. Admirers of China were affected by Chinese hostility towards Japan on the principle that my friend's enemy is my enemy too. China experts in the West are rarely Japan experts and vice versa. From 1850 to 1900 the USA was pro-Japan and anti-China; from 1900 to 1945 the USA was pro-China and anti-Japan; from 1946 to 1952 the US occupation of Japan saw the last great flowering of the missionary urge; the success of the occupation was in contrast to the 'loss' of China at that time. The warm feelings lasted well into the seventies. China's opening to the USA in the early seventies coincided with the intensification of economic and trade frictions with Japan. See Johnson, 1988, pp. 8–12.
5. In 1979 a study was made by the Japanese ministry of transport of the speed of walking in different cities of the world. Osaka came out top with a speed of 1.67 metres per second; Tokyo was second with 1.56; Paris attained 1.46. Lee, 1984, p. 186.
6. Macaulay, 1840.
7. Hanabusa, 1979, p. 4.

8. Pons, 1988. See also Chapter 8.
9. For a fascinating account of the successive and overlapping roles of European, US, Japanese and indigenous sources of capital in Southeast Asia, see Yoshihara, 1988.
10. In 1899, Kipling had written *The Ballad of East and West*. Ever since that time he lamented that he had been misquoted. 'Long ago I stated that "East was East and West was West and never the twain should meet". It seemed right, for I had checked by the card, but I was careful to point out circumstances under which cardinal points ceased to exist.' Indeed the next two lines of his poem state, 'There is neither East nor West, Border, nor Breed, nor Birth / When two strong men stand face to face, though they come from the ends of the Earth', Kipling, 1937.
11. Stimulated by the formation of the European Community in 1967, Prime Minister Miki put forward the idea of a Pacific Association, and later in the same year an annual conference of businessmen was launched (Pacific Basin Economic Council). Mr Ohira's 1978 proposal for a Pacific Rim Community eventually merged with an Australian initiative as the Pacific Economic Cooperation Conference, a talk shop including business, government and academe. Mr Nakasone's 1987 proposal for a Pacific Forum for Economic and Cultural Cooperation was not taken up. Mr Takeshita's espousal, in 1989, of a regional dialogue was an effort to tone down a more ambitious Japanese proposal for a Regional Trade Conference and to leave to the Australians the running of the first conference on the Asia Pacific Economic Cooperation (APEC) at the end of the year which brought together twelve Asia Pacific nations.

   US proposals have tended to be more overtly trade-policy oriented, for example the 1979 idea for an Organization for Pacific Trade and Development which was opposed by Japan and the ASEAN. Several US Senators called for a Pacific OECD at the end of the eighties as did the Australian prime minister. Occasional calls from individuals in Washington for a US–Japan Free Trade Agreement were met with less than enthusiasm in Tokyo.

Part II The West as Seen by Japan

1. Sōseki, 1911.
2. Dōi, 1973.
3. Dore, R. P., 'Japan and the Third World', unpublished paper, July, 1979. For a description of the development of the Japanese aid programme, see Chapter 25, note 9.
4. Kato, 1965, pp. 425–46.
5. Tani and Sugase, 1973.
6. Tani and Sugase, 1973.
7. Shiga, 1888, p. 139.
8. On *Rangaku* see Keene, 1969.
9. Sugita, 1815, pp. 38, 43; see also Keene, 1969, pp. 20–24.
10. Sugita, 1815, pp. 16–17.
11. Keene, 1969.
12. French, 1974.
13. Quoted in Keene, 1976, p. 46.
14. Aizawa, Seishisai, 'New Proposals' (*Shinron*), 1825, translated in De Bary *et al.*, 1958, vol. I, pp. 95–6.

15. Shionoya wrote these words in 1859. They are translated in Van Gulik, 1939, pp. 478–545.

16. Fujita, Toko (1806–54), a leading spokesman of the Mito school whose slogan was 'Reverence the Emperor, expel the barbarians', quoted in Chang, 1970, p. 61.

17. Chang, 1970.

18. Fukuzawa, 1899, p. 21.

19. Chang, 1970, p. 184, quoting the *Diary of a Delegation to Washington*, 1861.

20. Fukuzawa, 1899, p. 216.

21. Fukuzawa, 1899, pp. 21, 43.

22. Fukuzawa, 1899, p. 91.

23. Satow, 1865, p. 368.

24. Fukuzawa, 1875, Foreword. On the role of foreign experts in Japan, see Jones, 1980; and on the role played by overseas students, see Watanabe, 1966, pp. 254–93.

25. Nakamura, 1975, pp. 507–8.

26. Deguchi, 1979. On the adaptation of Samuel Smiles to Japan, see Kinmoth, 1981.

27. Hattori, Busshō, *Tokyo Shin Hanjo Ki*, 1874, translated and quoted in Keene, 1956, pp. 34–6.

28. Baelz, 1974, p. 239.

29. Fukuzawa, 1899, p. 175.

30. Fukuzawa, 1899, p. 120.

31. Akutagawa, 1930, pp. 99–122.

32. Natsume, Sōseki, *Bungakuron*, quoted in Yamanouchi, 1978, p. 48. An Englishman who was a Japanese prisoner of war in Indonesia confirms the heavy responsibility of unsympathetic landladies, 'Experience had already taught us, and it was an experience to be confirmed in subsequent years, that, as a general rule, English-speaking Japanese were more evilly disposed towards P.O.W.s than those Japanese who knew no English. This was particularly marked among the English-speaking Japanese who had visited, or lived in, the UK or the USA. Perhaps they had memories of landladies slamming boarding house doors in their faces; perhaps they recalled other insults. Now was their chance to get their own back and they took it in both hands,' Cooke, 1971, p. 91.

33. Nakae, Chōmin, *Kindai Nihon Shiso Taikei*, quoted in Lifton *et al.*, 1979, p. 133.

34. Pyle, 1969, p. 74.

35. Tokutomi, Sōho, *Jiden*, quoted in Pyle, 1969, p. 85.

36. Chamberlain, 1890, p. 263. The view that Europeans were unclean dates back at least to the sixteenth century, when the first Europeans to arrive in Japan were observed to eat with their fingers rather than with chopsticks. Old epithets for Westerners include 'hairy foreigners' or 'stinking of butter'.

37. Morri, 1935, p. 145.

38. Fukuzawa, 1899, p. 335.

39. Okakura, 1906, p. 9.

40. Kawakami, 1917.

41. Mushanokoji, 1958.

42. Tokutomi, Sōho, 'Commentary on the Imperial Rescript Declaring War on the United States and the British Empire', translated in De Bary *et al.*, 1958, p. 293.

43. See Chapter 14 for a discussion of Hitler's views on Japan and Asia.

44. Shillony, 1981, pp. 134–77. The best discussion of Japanese attitudes towards the West during the Pacific War is in Dower, 1986, pp. 203–92.

45. Professor Miller as quoted in Halberstam, 1986, p. 277.

46. Chūo Chōsasha (1964–). This opinion poll has been conducted every three months since 1964.

47. In the 1983 survey, 53 per cent of the respondents believed that the Japanese were 'better than Westerners'. In 1953, only 20 per cent had felt this to be so. 'A Study of the Japanese National Character' (*Nihonjin Kokuminsei no kenkyū*), Tokyo, 1958, 1963, 1968, 1973, 1978 and 1983. This survey is an attempt by the Institute of Statistical Mathematics to quantify how and if Japanese values have been shifting from traditional to modern.

48. Nakagawa, 1979, pp. 5–56. The best-selling author he quotes is Fukada Yasuke (also writing in *Bungei Shunju*, March 1977).

49. Amaya, 1977.

50. Nihonjin, Kenkyukai, 1977. On early Japanese images of Germany, see Opitz, 1980; and on recent images see Zahl, 1980, as well as other articles in the same issue. A fascinating catalogue of an exhibition of pictures of each other's country painted by Japanese and German schoolchildren shows the extraordinary degree to which the most obvious stereotypes are still passed from one generation to the next: *Hakenkreuz*, 1981.

51. Fukada, 1976. Despite the size of the European Community single market, even Japanese books about international economic issues facing Japan, including trade frictions, hardly mention the EC at all. Attention in the external field is focused on the USA or Asia. If the EC is included at all it is often only as a footnote. For example the popular comic on the Japanese economy put out by the *Japan Economic Journal* in 1988 discussed the USA in four separate chapters. The EC gets one paragraph, much less than the Asian NICs, *Nihon Keizai Shimbun*, Tokyo, 1988.

52. The 1967 survey is quoted in Nihonjin Kenkyūkai, 1977, pp. 91–2. The second poll on attitudes towards the French was jointly conducted by *Asahi* and *Le Monde* in 1984; the museum curator was quoted in the *International Herald Tribune*, 31 August 1988.

53. Kanagaki, Rōbun, *Aguranabe* ('The Beefeater'), Tokyo, 1871, translated in Keene, 1956, p. 32.

54. Morri, 1935, p. 120.

55. Kokuminsei Chōsa, 1978, and *Asahi Jyanaru*, vol. XXI, no. 32, 17 August 1979. The 1983 version of this poll showed the highest level of regard for family, filial piety and *ongaeshi* since the 1950s.

56. Ishida, Takeshi, 'Weight of the Past in the Japanese Vision of Europe', unpublished paper, Tokyo, 1979.

57. In 1989, as measured by assets, nine out of the ten largest banks in the world were Japanese. Its biggest brokerage house, Nomura, was five times larger than Merrill Lynch, the largest in the USA. In 1987 Nomura hired more graduates from Oxford and Cambridge than did the British foreign office.

58. Okita, 1987.

59. Apart from the big industrial combines, the LDP is supported by various lobbies whose interests it protects by preventing the opening of the Japanese market. Three of the most important lobbies were agriculture, the small shopkeepers and the construction industry. So powerful was the first of these lobbies that Japanese have often argued that to liberalize too quickly in

agriculture could destabilize the LDP (of the 445 LDP Diet members, 200 belong to the farm lobby). The *Nokyo* (agricultural co-ops), the ministry of agriculture and fisheries, and the Liberal Democratic Party are referred to as the 'iron triangle'. The *Nōkyō* had profits of $15 billion on a turnover of $57 billion in 1987 and it contributes over $100 million to the LDP every year.

The LDP also gained many votes from the small shopkeepers who, until recently, successfully won support from the Party to prevent the rationalization of the distribution system. Finally, the construction industry also provides similar huge sums to the LDP annually which in return strongly resisted opening construction contracts to foreign bidders for many years.

Part III   Japan as Seen by the West

1. On the Western image of the Orient see Martino, 1906; Steadman, 1969; and Said, 1979. On the European and American image of Japan see Ashmead, 1951; Iriye, 1975; Minear, 1980; Johnson, 1988; Mouer and Sugimoto, 1986; and Dower, 1986.
2. Cooper, 1965.
3. Frois was writing in 1585. Lach, 1965, vol. I, pp. 687–8.
4. Alcock, 1863, vol. I, pp. 357–8.
5. Lowell, 1888, pp. 1–2.
6. Lewis, J., in the *Far Eastern Economic Review*, 20 April 1979, p. 70.
7. Chamberlain, 1890, pp. 480–82.
8. Hearn, 1904, pp. 7–8.
9. The *Economist*, London, 31 December 1977, p. 34, and Smith, 1983. The *Economist*'s contrast was taken from Nakane, 1970.
10. Quoted in Cooper, 1965, p. 4. On this period in general see Boxer, 1951.
11. When the first members of the Japanese mission to Europe (1584–6) were received by Philip II of Spain they presented him with a gold screen on which was a map, not of Japan, but of China. See Lach, 1965, p. 693.
12. Quoted in Boxer, 1951, p. 170.
13. Kaempfer (1726–8), vol. III, 1906, p. 301.
14. *Encyclopaedia Britannica*.
15. Review of MacFarlane's *Japan* in the *Christian Remembrance*, vol. XXIV, 1852, p. 448.
16. See Miner, 1958, and Schwartz, 1927. Among the many excellent books on Japanese influences on European painting, see Yamada, 1976, and Wichmann, 1981; *Le Japonisme*, 1988.
17. Dumas, 1887, Act IV, Scene 2.
18. Gilbert and Sullivan, 1885. The song which opens Act 2, Scene 5 was taken by Sullivan from a Japanese song, 'Miyasan, Miyasan' (anon., 1867), which in turn was based on a Western march and rewritten in the major scale minus the fourth and seventh degrees to make it acceptable to Japanese ears. Another example of an unconscious cross-borrowing.
19. De Beauvoir, 1872, p. 160; quoted by Lehmann, 1978.
20. Arnold, 1898, pp. 240–43.
21. Quoted in Cooper, 1965, pp. 64–5.
22. On Loti, see Nishimoto, 1962, and Ono, 1972.
23. Loti, 1887, p. 239.
24. Norman, 1892, p. 239. Thirty pages of quotations from Western authors eulogizing Japanese women can be found in Ashmead, 1951, pp. 400–32.

25. James, 1893, pp. 151–87.
26. I am indebted to Johannes Van Rij for a detailed explanation of the connections between Madame Butterfly and Madam Chrysanthemum. Puccini had a number of operatic predecessors on butterfly themes, the first of whom was Saint-Saëns, whose *La Princesse Jaune*, 1872, tells how a young Dutch scientist – perhaps modelled after the German Japanologist von Siebold – becomes infatuated with a Japanese statuette and under the influence of drugs fancies himself in Japan. Other light operas on butterfly themes include Sidney James, *The Geisha*, 1896, and Pietro Mascagni, *Iris*, 1898.
27. Chéradam, 1906, pp. 3–5. See also Pozdneyev, 1895.
28. Holland, 1895, 1902.
29. Champsour, 1903; Hautemer, 1907; Bouquet, 1925; D'Estray, 1905; Orwell, 1934; Maugham, 1951. The 1906 smash-hit cabaret song *La Petite Tonkinoise* sums up the French–Indochinese version of the Chrysanthemum theme:

Ne pleur' pas si je te quitte/ Petite Anna, p'tite Annamite
Tu m'as donne ta jeunesse/ Ton amour et tes caresses
T'etais ma p'tit' bourgeoise/ Ma Tonkiki, ma Tonkiki, ma Tonkinoise.

(Annam was the old name for Vietnam; Tonkin for the North).
30. Fleming, 1964, pp. 1, 190.
31. Valéry in Preface to Bezombes, 1953, p. vii.
32. Bacon, 1902, p. 262.
33. Kipling, 1920, pp. 408, 442.
34. Bird, 1863, vol. I, p. 236.
35. Morri, 1935, p. 14.
36. Curtis, 1896, vol. I, p. 253.
37. Loti, 1889, pp. 77–106. The German observer was Netto, 1898.
38. Hearn, 1894, vol. I, p. 665; Hearn, *Japanese Letters*, 1922, quoted in Ono, 1972, p. 170. 'The image of Japanese literature that Hearn popularised was of the miniature, the exquisite, the unintellectual', Keene, D., speech reprinted in the *Japan Times*, 4 April 1988. Kipling, 1920, p. 402. For an amusing interpretation of the genius of Japanese culture as being the mastery of the miniature see Lee, 1984.
39. Kipling, 1920, pp. 418–19.
40. Villenoisy, de, 1895.
41. Norman, 1895, p. 2. The fear of a Japanese-led Asia threatening the West became one of the most common themes from that day to this. 'Much of the [Asia Pacific] region is deeply influenced by the same cultural forces that have helped to make Japan so successful. If one adds to this mix the potentially catalytic role of Japanese capital in seeding new industries and accessing remote raw materials, the prospects increase for a Japan-led, Pacific-driven world economy of the future,' Burstein, 1988, p. 250.
42. Pinon, 1904, pp. 191–2, quoted in Lehmann, 1978.
43. *The Times*, 11 February 1904, quoted in Lehmann, 1978, upon whose excellent study I have drawn heavily for this period.
44. Falkenegg, 1905, quoted in Lehmann, 1978.
45. Pinon, 1904, pp. 218–19.
46. Lea's book was reissued and enjoyed a boom in the USA in the year after Pearl Harbor at which time secretary of war Stimpson recorded in his Diary, 'Many times during recent months I have recalled meeting Homer Lea . . .

He was a little humpback man who wrote a book on the Japanese peril . . . In those days the book seemed fantastic. Now the things which he prophesied seem quite possible,' Dower, 1986, p. 344. There were plenty of other popular novels on the same theme after the Russo-Japanese war but Lea's had the widest success and was also much appreciated in Japan. Driant was reissued in 1979.

47. Théry, E., in *Journal*, 11 February 1904.
48. Preface by the diplomat–politician and Nobel Prize winner Estournelles de Constant in Théry, 1901.
49. Pinon, 1904, pp. 194–5.
50. Spencer's letter is quoted in Hearn, 1904, pp. 481–4.
51. On Swedish reactions to the Japanese victory see Burgman, 1965.
52. France, A., *Sur la Pierre Blanche*, Paris, 1904, quoted in Lehmann, 1978, pp. 154–6.
53. Plomer, 1976, pp. 181–2.
54. Pinon, 1904, p. 217.
55. Barrett, 1902.
56. Morri, 1935, p. 18.
57. Kipling, 1920, p. 370.
58. *Evening Standard*, London, 24 September 1937, quoted in Chinese Delegation, 1937.
59. Woodcock, 1969, p. 212; Manchester, 1979, pp. 187–8. By far the best study of racist stereotyping on both sides during the Pacific War is Dower, 1986, who makes the point that the stereotypes applied to the Japanese were very similar to those applied by whites to non-white peoples since at least the sixteenth century – for example, by the Spaniards to the Indian populations of the New World, or during the Indian wars in the United States.
60. Hitler, 1943, pp. 290–91; Hitler, 1953, p. 489; Presseisen, 1963; Martin, 1969.
61. Petit, 1905; Apellius, 1941; Benedict, 1946.
62. *Vision*, Paris, 15 March 1971, pp. 15–16.
63. *Time*, 2 March 1970, pp. 25–6.
64. *EC Bulletin*, 3–1971, pp. 26–7; *Time*, 2 March 1970, p. 29.
65. *Japan Times* questionnaire, 26 June 1979; *Newsweek*, 7 May 1979, p. 4; Iacocca, 1985, p. 315; McKraw, 1987, p. 378.
66. Lustbader, 1980, 1984; Hoover, 1988; Burstein, 1988, pp. 180–81. The Fu Manchu novels were the creation of Sax Rohmer. The first appeared in 1913, the last in 1941. Several were made into movies. Dower remarks that Rohmer drew together the three main strands of an otherwise incohate fear: Asian mastery of Western knowledge and technique, access to mysterious powers, and mobilization of the yellow horde, Dower, 1986, p. 158. Fu Manchu lived on in the next generation in characters such as Dr No of James Bond fame.
67. *Overland Monthly*, July 1896, quoted in Iriye, 1975, p. 75.
68. Guillain, 1969; Scharnagl, 1969; Hedberg, 1970; Jecquier, 1970; Delassus, 1970; Price, 1971; Efimov, 1971.
69. Issei Sagawa was referred to in the French press as the 'cannibal of the Bois de Boulogne'. In 1981 he shot, raped, carved up, refrigerated and ate his French girl friend. On release from psychiatric hospital in 1984 he was asked why he had done so, and replied, 'When I told her I loved her, she burst out

laughing.' Miyazaki Tsutomi admitted in a blaze of publicity in 1989 to murdering three kindergarten-aged girls. He hacked two of them to pieces and filmed the results for his porno collection.

70. The *Economist* Correspondents, 1963. The articles upon which the book is based were written by Norman Macrae, and first appeared in the *Economist* in September 1962; Federation of British Industries, 1934.

71. Kahn, 1970; the *Economist*, 'The Pacific Century, 1975–2075', 4 January 1975, pp. 15–35.

72. US House of Representatives, 1980.

73. *Hansard*, 1977.

74. See Johnson, 1981, Chapter 1, 'Explanations for Japan's success'.

75. For an analysis of the 'Shōgun' phenomenon, see Smith, 1980.

76. One way of tracing the increased knowledge of Japan in Europe is to compare a comprehensive survey of European images of Japan which was conducted as a public opinion poll in the winter of 1977 in England, France, West Germany, Italy and Belgium, and was repeated in 1982, 1986, 1988 and 1989 for the same countries with the addition of Spain.

The contrast between what the pollsters found in 1977 and in 1989 is striking. In 1977 in England, for example, one-third of those polled thought Japan was either a Communist state or a despotism; more than 30 per cent in all five countries thought that Japan had atomic weapons and 50 per cent thought that it either had them or would acquire them. They also thought that Japanese salaries and social welfare were lower than in their own countries. As to Japan's international role they were critical, feeling it was too reactive, and that there was room for it to make positive contributions to the world economy, for example, by increasing development aid. In general, they were not convinced that Japan was reliable.

Unfortunately for the follow-ups to this poll, the pollsters addressed themselves not to the general public, as they had done in the first one, but to leaders of public opinion, so strictly speaking the later polls are not comparable with the first.

Reflecting the better-informed group polled and the improved knowledge of Japan, the 1989 poll reveals a more accurate image of Japan, as a strong economic power deeply influenced by tradition, whose people are hard-working, efficient, cooperative and polite. Many were aware that Japan has a democratic government and a policy of not possessing nuclear weapons, but only in Germany and Italy was it felt that the Japanese standard of living was lower; all the other European countries felt it to be the same or higher. Increasingly the Japanese were considered to work too hard. As to Japan's international role many, especially in Britain, felt Japan should do more, for example, in supporting the world economy, extending aid to developing countries, or in scientific and technological contributions. Ministry of Foreign Affairs, (1978–89).

77. Theroux, 1975, p. 336.

78. Benedict, 1946, p. 2. Glazer, 1975, contains a good discussion of the influence of Benedict whose work grew out of the US wartime 'national-character' studies; on which see 'Primitives, Children, Madmen', Dower, 1986, pp. 118–46.

79. Chamberlain, 1890, p. 303.

80. Johnstone in the *Far Eastern Economic Review*, 19 May 1989; Hollerman, 1988, p. 126.

81. *International Herald Tribune*, 2 August 1988; *Newsweek*, 8 October 1984, p. 10, and 21 January 1974, p. 56; Van Wolferen, 1989.
82. Ballon, 1978, pp. 1–5.

Part IV Open Markets and Double-bolted Doors

1. Ono, 1890, p. 104.
2. Keene, 1969, p. 109.
3. Itō, Hirobumi recording Okubo's words, translated in De Bary *et al.*, 1958, vol. II, pp. 158–9.
4. Fukuzawa, 1899, p. 223.
5. Sugi, Kōji and Nishimura, Shigeki in *Meiroku Zasshi*, no. 24, December 1874, and no. 29, February 1875, quoted in Braisted, 1976, pp. 302–4, 356–8.
6. Spencer's letter of 26 August 1892, which I have quoted from, was published in *The Times* of London on 18 January 1904, just after his death. Its publication did not give rise to a storm of animosity, possibly because the conditions to which Spencer addressed himself had been bypassed by events with Japan's successful renegotiation of the unequal treaties. It is also possible that readers of Spencer's letter could see some sense to his arguments. The letter is reprinted in Hearn, 1904, pp. 481–4.
7. Chamberlain, 1905, p. 261.
8. Norman, 1892, pp. 356–7. Nearly one hundred years later, in 1987, the European Community entered a similar complaint to the General Agreement on Tariffs and Trade (GATT). To quote the annual report:
   'Japanese spirits and wines were labelled in a European style, in a European language and with European symbols. Japanese manufacturers used in their labelling French words, French names, German script and other devices with a clear implication that the product was in some sense of European origin. In the case of wines, only recently did the main label indicate the name of the "producer", maintaining however a degree of ambiguity as to his precise activities', GATT, 1988, pp. 83–127. The GATT ruled that foreign liquors and wines were subject to discriminatory import taxes, but that Japanese labelling did not infringe international agreements on trade marks.
9. Norman, 1895, pp. 380–83.
10. Norman, 1895, p. 383.
11. Murray, David, *Japan*, 1906, pp. 381–2, quoted in Lehmann, 1978, p. 131.
12. Brooks Adams quoted in Iriye, 1967, p. 66.
13. Groupe d'Études du Pacifique, 1930.
14. Federation of British Industries, 1934, pp. 20–21.
15. Storry, 1979.
16. Ministry of War, Tokyo, 1934.
17. Asahi, 1934.
18. Sanders, 1975, p. 70. Note the similarity with the views of Honda Toshiaki (no relative) as quoted in Chapter 5.
19. *New York Times*, 14 December 1954, quoted in Johnson, 1988, p. 96.
20. Ushiba and Hara, 1979, pp. 242, 371; Hanabusa, 1979; Komiya and Itoh, 1988.
21. Mr Dahrendorf was an EC commissioner until 1974 when he became Director of the London School of Economics, *EC Bulletin*, 3–1971, pp. 26–7.

22. The division of Japan's industries into categories such as labour-intensive or knowledge-intensive accords with the cluster pattern of capital, knowledge (two years college and above) and labour inputs when these are plotted on a simple graph. See Wilkinson, 1978.

23. Congressman John Dingell was explaining the reasons that he passionately opposed the export of Alaskan oil to Japan, *Financial Times*, 17 May 1984.

24. The US–Japan discussions came to be termed Market-Oriented, Sector-Selective (MOSS) and covered barriers in many sectors including telecommunications, tobacco, medical equipment, pharmaceuticals, electronics and forest products. The EC Commission conducted similar talks. Some of the main sectors in which NTBs were removed over a ten-year period were: agricultural processed foodstuffs; automobile type approval procedures; automobile exhaust emission regulations; automobile standards; bank operating conditions; chemical and agrochemical standards; cosmetics standards; diesel engine tests; electrical and gas appliance standards; insurance; medical instrument standards; pharmaceutical standards; phytosanitary regulations; sanitary fittings standards; trademarks.

25. In 1979, the head of Japan's defence agency visited NATO headquarters. The first regular contacts between the Japanese Diet and the European Parliament took place in 1977, and they were held annually from 1978 onwards. Regular consultations of the Japanese foreign minister and the chairman of the EC Council were instituted in 1983. In 1974, the EC Commission had opened a permanent diplomatic delegation in Japan, while in 1979, the Japanese foreign ministry was finally allocated the budget, for which it had been vainly asking for years, to open a second mission in Brussels especially to the EC.

26. In 1970, European makers had a 68 per cent share of the foreign car market in the USA while the Japanese had only 28 per cent. By 1980 the tables were turned. The Japanese took a 76 per cent share compared with a European share of 21 per cent.

27. OECD, 1987.

28. Stockman, 1987, p. 403.

29. In this and what follows I have relied heavily on a first-class work of investigative reporting (Funabashi, 1988) which is based on interviews with the main players in the G-5 and G-7 meetings.

30. Amaya, 1987.

31. See the perceptive comments in Vaubel (1982). In discussing the number of hours worked, it pays to remember that what counts is productivity, not the amount of time spent at the work place.

32. Drucker, 1987, p. 935; Iacocca, 1988.

33. *The Economist*, August 1988, January and September 1989. Discussions of informal barriers in Japan are seldom put in perspective by comparing them to NTBs in the EC and the USA, see OECD, 1989, pp. 87–92.

34. The *keiretsu* (large industrial and banking groups) are descendants of the pre-war *zaibatsu*, but the links between companies in the group, although close, are not as close as they had been in the *zaibatsu*. In 1987, the ratio of cross-shareholding in the six top *keiretsu* did not, on average, exceed 10 per cent of total shares, and the dependence on loans from banks in the same group was below 20 per cent of total credit finance, OECD, 1989, p. 51; M. Barre as quoted in *Le Monde*, 11 December 1980, p. 39. On non-tariff barriers in the earlier frictions see Little, 1979, and for a more recent survey,

see Inoguchi and Okimoto, 1988. Lincoln, 1990, gives an excellent summary of the real difficulties that can be posed by Japanese NTBs. Prestowitz, 1988, presents a US trade negotiator's view.

35. *EC–Japan Joint Communiqué*, March 1978, identical in essentials to the later Strauss–Ushiba Agreement. Japan's import structure is examined in Chapter 25, under 'Japanese Actions'.

36. Lincoln, 1988.

37. Smith, 1983.

38. Halberstam, 1986, p. 47.

39. *The Economist*, December 1987; and Drucker in the *Economist*, 21 October 1989, p. 21. On the 'revisionist' view see *BusinessWeek*, 1989.

40. Lincoln, 1988, pp. 230–33.

41. William Verity quoted in the *International Herald Tribune*, 12 September 1988.

42. In some years there was upwards of a 50 per cent difference between the two sets of statistics. Over a longer period the trend lines were the same, but the timing of changes in the trends could differ considerably. Which currency to use to measure trade flows is another question upon which agreement should be reached before mutual accusations are exchanged.

   The situation was even worse when it came to estimating invisible trade (payments, transfers, transport and tourism) and direct investments, about which there are still no internationally agreed definitions. For example, according to the US department of commerce, US cumulative direct investment in Japan as of December 1988 was $16.8 billion. According to Japanese figures the amount was $6.4 billion. The reasons for the disparity in this case appear to be that the Japanese figures do not include cash loans, and loans from parent companies to subsidiaries were only included from 1985. This would account for up to 30 per cent of the difference. Branches set up by foreign companies in Japan or land purchased by them are also not included in the Japanese statistics. The $2 billion European investment in Japan recorded by the Japanese authorities therefore probably seriously underestimates the total amount which is closer to $3 billion.

43. Kolko, 1988, p. 233.

44. *Asian Wall Street Journal*, 4 May 1988.

45. Wilkinson, 1977.

46. Wilkinson, 1977. For a report which reached similarly gloomy conclusions see EC Commission, 1982 and 1989.

47. *Asahi Shimbun*, 10 December 1979; *Japan Economic Journal*, 7 July 1979, p. 6; *Asahi Shimbun*, 26 June 1979, pp. 1, 12, 13. Average floor area of dwellings in the mid-eighties according to JETRO were (in square metres): US (135); Germany (94); France (86) and Japan (81), the *Economist*, December 1988.

48. Asahi, 1934. In 1988 the decision was taken to open Japanese post offices for only five days in the week starting from 1989.

49. Amaya, 1977.

50. The numbers of missionaries and businessmen from the EC in Japan were computed from the statistics of visas issued by the Visa Department, Ministry of Justice, Tokyo.

51. Richard Smith writing in the *International Herald Tribune*, 2 October 1989.

Part V Conclusions

1. Johnson and Packard, 1981; Satoh, 1982; Mendl, 1984. The only agreement directly between Europe and Asia is the Five Power Defence Arrangement (1971) linking Australia, New Zealand, the UK, Malaysia and Singapore. It was reactivated in the late eighties because of worries over US commitment and uncertainties over the US bases in the Philippines.

2. There are several ways of measuring a country's dependence on imports of a given product. The most accurate is to calculate the ratio of imports to total apparent consumption of the product (total domestic production plus imports, minus exports). The result is the import penetration ratio of that product. The OECD has calculated for all its member countries their import penetration ratios both for total manufactured products and for individual industrial sectors over the period 1970–85, OECD, 1988 and 1989; EC Commission, 1989. It is these findings which are quoted in the text.

   Another commonly used but less accurate method is to calculate the ratio of imports to GNP. By this measure of import dependence Japan also scores lowest of all the OECD countries (see Annex, Table 3).

   A third even less useful method is to calculate the ratio of manufactured imports to total imports. This method was used for many years by EC and US trade negotiators with Japan who requested that Japan increase its ratio of imports of manufactures to total imports. One of the weaknesses of this method is that it takes no account of the fact that Japan's total imports as a percentage of GNP were already unusually low. Another weakness that it ignores is that, in the case of Japan, the relative value of imports of manufactures is largely a function of the cost of imported fuel. When the price of oil dropped in 1986–7, Japan's fuel imports, measured in dollar terms, halved (although in volume terms they remained at the same level) and the percentage of manufactured imports surged.

   The OECD has also calculated the export performance in manufactured goods of its members as measured by the ratio of exports to apparent consumption (total domestic production of manufactures plus imports). Between 1970 and 1985 Japan increased its export performance for manufactures from 10 to 15 per cent; the USA from 6 to 7 per cent. Germany has a high import penetration ratio (20 per cent in 1970, 39 per cent in 1985) together with a high export performance (22 per cent in 1970, 36 per cent in 1985), OECD, 1988.

3. The biggest difference in resource endowment between Japan on the one hand and the EC and the USA on the other lies in Japan's lack of primary energy. Taking into account all energy sources including coal, crude oil, natural gas, hydro-electric and nuclear electric power, the EC, with Britain's North Sea oil, Holland's natural gas and Germany's coal, produced per capita four times more energy than Japan. The USA produced per capita three times more than the EC and twelve times more than Japan. Japan and the EC consume per capita roughly equivalent amounts of energy, but Japan in the late eighties produced only 10 to 15 per cent of total energy consumption while the EC was able to meet 40 to 50 per cent of its energy requirements and the USA about 70 per cent. In other words Japan's dependence on imported energy is far higher than that of either the EC or the USA.

4. *Economic Management within a Global Context*, Tokyo, 1988. For the further provisions of the mid-term plan see Chapter 22.
5. Lincoln, 1988, p. 223.
6. See Annex, Table 4.
7. Headlines such as 'Japan Buys Up America' were out of all proportion to the size of the investments. Both the UK and Holland for example invested more in the USA than did Japan, but they had been doing so for a long time and their investments had not been accumulated at such a speed as those of Japan.

   In October 1988 *Le Nouvel Observateur* had a special feature on the Japanese in France; the opening headline used the same old journalistic technique to attract attention, namely the centrality of the reader's own country (in this case France) and the military nature of the Japanese advance, '. . . to affirm their economic leadership, Japanese enterprises are investing in Europe. The great financial and industrial groups aided by Japanese high technology have put into place a plan of attack in which France is the focal point. Watch out for the shock!'
8. Farmers in Japan are by no means a poor group in society: they earn 80 per cent of their incomes from non-farm activities. The Japanese consumer pays six to eight times the world price of rice and four times the world price of beef. However, there are powerful vested interests preventing a reform of agricultural policy, notably the 'iron triangle' of *Nōkyō* (agricultural co-ops), the ministry of agriculture and fisheries, and the Liberal Democratic Party, Hayami, 1988. See also Part II, note 59.
9. From 1954 to 1964, Japan provided reparations to those Asian countries which it had attacked during the war. It became an aid donor in 1965 when it joined the Development Assistance Committee (DAC) of the OECD. Its programme was intended to cultivate goodwill in Washington. Ten years later in 1974 Japanese aid was criticized in the DAC as consisting mainly of tied aid serving Japanese commercial interests. Loans far outweighed grants. 'Tied aid' means the recipient country is obliged to purchase goods or services from specific countries, usually the donor country. The proportion of Japanese aid which is tied has been reduced in recent years. The grant element, although currently about 30 per cent of the total, is less than that of other donors. Under the fourth medium-term target covering 1988 to 1992, the government aims to disburse the enormous sum of $50 billion. Despite the very large increases, Japan's ODA in relative terms as a percentage of GNP at 0.32 in 1988 was still below the DAC average of 0.35 per cent (compare the EC with 0.47 per cent and the USA with 0.29 per cent).

   Japan could no doubt do more for refugees and minorities. It only became a full member of the 1951 International Convention on the Status of Refugees in 1981. The Convention allows refugees, once they have been accepted for residence, the same benefits as citizens. Seven hundred and fifty thousand Koreans in Japan are currently denied such benefits although many of them are second-generation immigrants entirely brought up in Japan and speaking only the Japanese language. The small number of refugees from Indo-China who have been allowed Japanese citizenship (35), permanent residence (500) or even temporary asylum (6,000) is another indication that the Japanese, like the Swiss, enjoy visitors but prefer to keep most foreigners, especially Asians, in their place.

10. For an interesting discussion of *honne* and *tatemae* see Dōi, 1985. Mr Takeshita was quoted in the *Economist*, 12 March 1988.
11. Saji Keizo, 1980. Mr Saji is the President of Suntory and of the Suntory Foundation.
12. Schwantes, 1974. On the earlier period see Valliant, 1972.
13. In December 1980, to take another example, a month after a Council of Foreign Ministers of the EC had called once again for a united strategy towards Japan, the co-ordinator of French policy on Japan who had been specially appointed by the French President stated to the press that 'the French government has chosen to negotiate bilaterally with Japan . . . because the different European countries have chosen such different positions'. And in case anybody had failed to get the message, he added, 'The Commission in Brussels wants to negotiate on appearances, but I wish to negotiate on the basis of realities.' *Le Monde*, 6 January 1981.
14. School of Oriental and African Studies (1955–6). Sansom was a British diplomat who served as commercial counsellor in the embassy in Tokyo in the thirties. His reports on the Japanese economy and market conditions were available for sale to the general public in London. After the war he became a professor at Columbia University in New York.

REFERENCES

Akutagawa, Ryūnosuke, 'The Ball', in *Short Stories by R. Akutagawa*, translated by Shaw, G. W., Tokyo, 1930, pp. 99–122.

Alcock, R., *The Capital of the Tycoon, A Narrative of Three Years Residence in Japan*, 2 vols., New York, 1863.

Amaya, Naohirō, 'Ushiwakamaru Strategy for Trade Frictions' (*Kancho Nyusu Jihyo*), January 1977.

Amaya, Naohirō, 'Trade Frictions,' *Journal of Japanese Trade and Industry*, No. 5, 1987.

Asahi, Isoshi, *The Secret of Japan's Trade Expansion*, Tokyo, 1934.

Apellius, M., *Cannoni e ciliegi in fiore*, Rome, 1941.

Arnold, E., *Seas and Lands*, London, 1898.

Asahi, Isoshi, *The Secret of Japan's Trade Expansion*, Tokyo, 1934.

Ashmead, J., *The Idea of Japan: 1853–1895, Japan as Described by American and Other Travellers from the West*, unpublished Ph.D. thesis, Harvard University, 1951.

Bacon, A. M., *Japanese Girls and Women*, Boston, 1902.

Baelz, E., *Awakening Japan: The Diary of a German Doctor*, Bloomington, 1974.

Balassa, B., and Noland, M., *Japan in the World Economy*, Washington, 1988.

Ballon, R., 'A European Views the Japanese', *The Wheel Extended*, Special Supplement, No. 2, Tokyo, 1978, pp. 1–5.

Bank of Japan, *Comparative Economic and Financial Statistics, Japan and Other Major Countries*, (annual), Tokyo, 1989.

Barrett, J., 'New Japan, Schoolmaster of Asia', *Review of Reviews*, December 1902.

Benedict, R., *The Chrysanthemum and the Sword*, Boston, 1946.

Bezombes, R., *L'Exotisme dans l'Art et la Pensée*, Paris, 1953.

Bird, I. L., *Unbeaten Tracks in Japan*, New York, 1863.

Bouquet, *Poupée Parfumée*, Paris, 1925.

Boxer, C. R., *Jan Campagnie in Japan, 1600–1850*, The Hague, 1950.

Boxer, C. R., *The Christian Century in Japan, 1549–1650*, Berkeley, 1951.

Braisted, W. R., *Meiroku Zasshi*, Tokyo, 1976.

Burgman, T., *Svensk Opinion Och Diplomat Undur Rysk – Japanska Kriget 1904–1905*, Stockholm, 1965.

Burstein, D., *Yen! Japan's New Financial Empire and its Threat to America*, New York, 1988.

Buruma, I., *A Japanese Mirror*, London, 1984.

BusinessWeek, 'Rethinking Japan', 7 August 1989, pp. 44–52.

Chamberlain, B. H., *Things Japanese*, London and Tokyo, 1890.

Chang, R. C., *From Prejudice to Tolerance: A Study of the Japanese Image of the West, 1862–1864*, Tokyo, 1970.

Chéradam, A., *Le Monde et la Guerre Russo-Japonaise*, Paris, 1906.

Chinese Delegation, Press Bureau, *Japanese Aggression and World Opinion*, Geneva, 1937.

Chūo Chōsasha, 'Countries liked and disliked' (*Suki na Kuni, Kirai na Kuni*), Tokyo, 1964–.

Cooke, J. F., *The Emperor's Guest*, London, 1971.

Cooper, M., *They Came to Japan; an Anthology of European Reports on Japan, 1543–1640*, Berkeley, 1965.

Curtis, W. E., *The Yankees of the East*, New York, 1896.

De Bary, W. T., Tsunoda, R., and Keene, D., *Sources of Japanese Tradition*, New York, 1958.

De Beauvoir, *Pékin, Yeddo, San Francisco, Voyage autour du Monde*, Paris, 1872 (quoted in Lehmann).

Deguchi, Kazuō, 'A study of publishing' (*Shuppan o manabu hito no tame ni*), Tokyo, 1979.

Delassus, L., *Japan: Monster or Model*, Lausanne, 1970.

D'Estray, *Thisen, La Petite Amie Exotique*, Paris, 1905.

Dōi, Takeo, *The Anatomy of Dependence*, Tokyo, 1973.

Dōi, Takeo, *The Anatomy of Self*, Tokyo, 1985.

Dower, J. W., *War Without Mercy: Race and Power in the Pacific War*, New York, 1986.

Driant (pseudonym of Capitaine Danrit), *The Yellow Invasion*, 3 vols., Paris, 1905; reissued 1969.

Drifte, R., 'The Internationalization of Japan', Fukuoka UNESCO, *Proceedings of the 6th Kyushu International Cultural Conference, 1987*, Fukuoka, 1988.

Drucker, Peter, 'Japan's Choices', *Foreign Affairs*, Summer 1987, vol. 65, p. 5.

Dumas, Alexandre, *Francillon*, Paris, 1887.

EC Commission, 'The Competitiveness of European Industry', Brussels, March 1982.

EC Commission, 'The Community's industrial competitiveness and international trade in manufactures', *European Economy*, vol. 39, 1989, pp. 33–46.

Economic Planning Agency, Long Term Outlook Committee, *Japan in the Year 2000*, Tokyo, 1983.

Economic Planning Agency, Long Term Outlook Committee, 'Outlook for the world economy to the year 2000' (*Nisen nen e no sekai keizai danbō*), Tokyo, 1987.

Economist Correspondents, *Consider Japan*, London, 1963.

Efimov, J., *Stop the Japanese Now*, Paris, 1971.

Eguchi, Takashi and Matsuda, Manabu, 'Trade friction: invisible war' (*Boeki masatsu: mienai sensō*), Tokyo, 1987.

Emmott, Bill, *The Sun Also Sets*, London, 1989.

Encyclopaedia Britannica, 1st edition, 1771, vol. II, p. 210; 2nd edition, 1780, vol. V, pp. 3816–20; 6th edition, 1823, vol. V, pp. 33–40.

Eurostat, *Basic Statistics of the Community*, Luxemburg, 1989.

Eurostat, *External Trade*, Luxemburg, monthly.

Falkenegg, Von, *Japan, die Neue Weltmacht*, Berlin, 1905 (quoted in Lehmann).

Federation of British Industries, *Report of Mission to the Far East, August to November 1934*, London, 1934.

Fleming, I., *You Only Live Twice*, London, 1964.

France, A., *Sur la Pierre Blanche*, Paris, 1904 (quoted in Lehmann).

French, G. L., *Shiba Kōkan*, New York, 1974.

Frost, Ellen L., *For Richer, For Poorer, The New US–Japan Relationship*, New York, 1987.

Fukada, Yusuke, 'New Conditions in the West' (*Shin, Seiyō-jijō*), Tokyo, 1976.

Fukada, Yusuke, 'Conditions in the West' (*Seiyō-jijō*), Tokyo, 1866.

Fukuzawa, Yukichi, *The Autobiography of Fukuzawa Yukichi*, New York, 1966 (first published 1899).

Fukuzawa, Yukichi, 'Foreword' to *An Outline Theory of Civilization*, Tokyo, 1973 (first published 1875).

Funabashi, Yoichi, *Managing the Dollar: From the Plaza to the Louvre*, Washington, 1988.

GATT (General Agreement on Tariffs and Trade), *Basic Instruments and Selected Documents, 1986–7*, Geneva, 1988.

GATT (General Agreement on Tariffs and Trade), *International Trade, 1988–9*, vol. 2, Geneva, 1989.

Gilbert and Sullivan, *The Mikado*, London, 1885.

Gilpin, R., *The Political Economy of International Relations*, Princeton, 1987.

Glazer, N., 'From Ruth Benedict to Herman Kahn: The Postwar Japanese Image in the American Mind', in Iriye, 1975, pp. 138–68.

Griffis, W., *The Mikado's Empire*, Boston, 1872.

Groupe d'Études du Pacifique, *Les Conséquences du Développement Économique du Japon pour l'Empire Français*, Paris, 1930.

Guillain, R., *The Japanese Challenge*, Paris, 1969.

Hakenkreuz und Butterfly, Japanische Schuler sehen uns, Deutscher Schuler sehen Japan, Stuttgart, 1981.

Halberstam, D., *The Reckoning*, New York, 1986.

Hanabusa, Masamichi, *Trade Problems between Japan and Western Europe*, London, 1979.

Hansard, 'Proceedings of Parliamentary Committee on Science and Technology (Japan Sub-Committee)', 14 July 1977, pp. 71–88.

Hautemer, *Petite Mousmé*, Paris, 1907.

Hayami, Yujirō, *Japanese Agriculture under Siege*, London, 1988.

Hearn, L., *Glimpses of Unfamiliar Japan*, Boston, 1894.

Hearn, L., *Japan, an Attempt at Interpretation*, Boston, 1904.

Hedberg, S., *The Japanese Threat*, Paris, 1970.

Henderson, D., *Innocence and Design*, London, 1985.

Hitler, A., *Mein Kampf*, English translation, Boston, 1943.

Hitler's Table Talk, 1941–1944, London, 1953.

Holbrooke, R., MacFarquar, R., and Nukuzawa, K., *East Asia in Transition: Challenges for the Trilateral Countries*, New York, 1988.

Holland, C. (pseud. of C. J. Hankinson), *My Japanese Wife*, London, 1895.

Holland, C. (pseud. of C. J. Hankinson), *Mousmé*, London, 1902.

Hollerman, L., *Japan Disincorporated*, Stanford, 1988.

Hoover, T., *The Samurai Strategy*, London, 1988.

Iacocca, L., *An Autobiography*, New York, 1985.

Iacocca, L., *Talking Straight*, New York, 1988.

IMF (DOT), *Direction of Trade Statistics*, International Monetary Fund, Yearbook, Washington, 1989.

IMF (IFS), *International Financial Statistics*, International Monetary Fund, Yearbook, Washington, 1989.

Inoguchi, Takahashi and Okimoto, Daniel I., (eds.) *The Political Economy of Japan, Volume 2, The Changing International Context*, Stanford, 1988.

Iriye, Akira, *Across the Pacific*, New York, 1967.

Iriye, Akira, *Mutual Images: Essays on American–Japanese Relations*, Cambridge, 1975.

Ishinomori, Shōtarō, *Japan Inc.*, California, 1988.

James, H., 'Pierre Loti', in *Essays in London and Elsewhere*, New York, 1893.

Japan Times, Japan's Economy and Japan– US Trade, Tokyo, 1982.

Japan Times, Japan's Economy and Japan– EC Trade, Tokyo, 1982.

Japan– US Economic Relations Group, 'Report', *Japan Economic Journal*, 9 June 1981, pp. 30–32.

Jecquier, C., *The Japanese Industrial Challenge*, Lausanne, 1970.

JETRO, *1989 White Paper on World Direct Investment*, Tokyo, 1989.

Johnson, C., *MITI and the Japanese Miracle*, Chapter 1, 'Explanations for Japan's success', California, 1981.

Johnson, Sheila K., *The Japanese Through American Eyes*, Stanford, 1988.

Johnson, U. A., and Packard, G. R., *The Common Security Interests of Japan, the United States, and NATO*, Cambridge, Mass., 1981.

Jones, H. L., *Live Machines: Hired Foreigners and Meiji Japan*, Seattle, 1980.

Kaempfer, E., *History of Japan*, London, 1726–8; reprinted 3 vols., Glasgow, 1906.

Kahn, H., *The Emerging Japanese Superstate*, New York, 1970.

Kamata, Satoshi, *Japan in the Passing Lane*, London, 1983.

Kato, Shuichi, 'Japanese Writers and Modernization', in Jansen, M. (ed.), *Changing Japanese Attitudes towards Modernization*, Princeton, 1965, pp. 425–46.

Kawakami, Hajime, 'Tales of poverty', *Binbō Monogatari*, Tokyo, 1917.

Keene, D., *Modern Japanese Fiction*, New York, 1956.

Keene, D., *The Japanese Discovery of Europe, 1720–1830*, Stanford, 1969.

Keene, D., *World within Walls, Japanese Literature of the Premodern Era, 1660–1867*, Tokyo, 1976.

Kikuchi, Makoto, *Japanese Electronics*, Tokyo, 1983.

Kinmoth, E. J., *The Self-Made Man in Meiji Japan: From Samurai to Salaryman*, Berkeley, 1981.

Kipling, R., *From Sea to Sea*, vol. XIII of *Writings in Prose and Verse of Rudyard Kipling*, New York, 1920.

Kipling, R., *Something of Myself*, London, 1937.

Kolko, Joyce, *Restructuring the World Economy*, New York, 1988.

Komine, Takao, *Economic Friction (Keizai masatsu)*, Tokyo, 1986.

Komiya, Ryutarō and Itoh, Motoshige, 'Japan's International Trade and Trade Policy, 1955–84', in Inoguchi, Takahashi and Okimoto, Daniel I., (eds.) *The Political Economy of Japan*, vol. 2; *The Changing International Context*, Stanford, 1988, pp. 173–224.

Lach, D., *Asia in the Making of Europe*, vol. I: *The Age of Discovery*, Chicago, 1965.

Lea, Homer, *The Valor of Ignorance*, New York, 1909.

Le Japonisme, Exposition au Grand Palais, 17 mai–15 août, Paris, 1988.

Lee, O-Young, *Smaller is Better*, Tokyo, 1984.

Lehmann, J. P., *The Image of Japan, From Feudal Isolation to World Power, 1850–1905*, London, 1978.

Lifton, R. J., Kato, S., and Reich, M. R., *Six Deaths*, New Haven, 1979.

Lincoln, E. J., *Japan: Facing Economic Maturity*, Washington, 1988.

Lincoln, E. J., *Japan's Unequal Trade*, Washington, 1990.

Little, A. D., Inc., *The Japanese Non-tariff Barrier Issue: American Views and the Implications for Japan– US Trade Relations*, Tokyo, 1979.

Loti, P., *Madame Chrysanthème*, Paris, 1887.

Loti, P., 'Un Bal à Yeddo', in *Japoneries d'Automne*, Paris, 1889.

Lowell, P., *The Soul of the Far East*, Boston, 1888.

Lustbader, E., *The Ninja*, New York, 1980.

Lustbader, E., *The Miko*, New York, 1984.

Macaulay, T. B., 'Von Ranke', *Edinburgh Review*, October 1840.

Manchester, W., *American Caesar, Douglas MacArthur, 1880–1964*, New York, 1979.

Martin, B., *Deutschland und Japan im Zweiten Weltkrieg*, Gottingen, 1969.

Martino, P., *L'Orient dans la Littérature Française au XVIIe et au XVIIIe siècle*, Paris, 1906.

Masuzoe Yōichi (ed.), 'Japan and the World in the 1990s – 8 Issues' (*Nihon to Sekai*), Tokyo, 1988.

Maugham, W. S., 'Masterson' in *Complete Short Stories*, vol. IV, London, 1951, pp. 266–75.

McKraw, T., *America versus Japan*, New York, 1987.

Mendl, W., *Western Europe and Japan between the Super Powers*, London, 1984.

Minear, R. H., 'Orientalism and the Study of Japan', *Journal of Asian Studies*, XXXIX, 3, May 1980, pp. 507–17.

Miner, E. R., *The Japanese Tradition in British and American Literature*, Princeton, 1958.

Ministry of Foreign Affairs, Tokyo, 'Survey of public opinion towards Japan in five EC countries' (*EC gokakoku tai Nichi seiron chōsa*),

Tokyo, 1978, 1982, 1986, 1988 and 1989. The two most recent polls in this series cover seven countries in the EC.

Ministry of War, Tokyo, 'The Essence of National Defence and Proposals for Strengthening It' (*Kokubo-no Hongi to Sono Kyōka no Teisho*), October 1934.

MITI, 'White Paper on International Trade' (*tsusho hyakusho*), Tokyo, annual.

Morita, A., and Ishihara, S., *The Japan That Can Say 'No'*, (*'No' to ieru Nihon*), Tokyo, 1989.

Morri, Yasotarō, *Sunrise Synthesis, Aspects of Changing Japan*, Tokyo, 1935.

Mouer, Ross and Yoshio, Sugimoto, *Images of Japanese Society*, London, 1986.

Mushanokoji, Saneatsu, *Love and Death*, translated by Marquandt, W. F., New York, 1958.

Nakagawa, Yatsuhirō, 'Japan, the Welfare Superpower', *Journal of Japanese Studies*, vol. V, no. 1, 1979, pp. 5–56.

Nakamura, Hajime, *Parallel Developments*, Tokyo, 1975.

Nakane, Chie, *Japanese Society*, London, 1970.

Natsume, Sōseki, 'The Enlightenment of Modern Japan' (*Gendai Nihon no Kaika*), a talk given in 1911, quoted in Yamanouchi, 1978, p. 77.

Netto, C., *Papierschmetterlinge aus Japan*, Hamburg, 1898.

Neustupny, J. V., 'Communication with the Japanese', *The Wheel Extended*, Tokyo, III, 1, 1983.

Nicolson, Harold, *Public Faces*, London, 1932.

Nihon Shimbun Kyōkai, *The Japanese Press*, Tokyo, 1982, 1988.

Nihonjin Kenkyūkai (eds.), 'Japanese attitudes towards foreign countries' (*Nihonjin no tai gaikoku taidō*), Tokyo, 1977.

Nihonjin Kokuminsei no kenkyū (*A Study of the Japanese National Character*), Tokyo, 1958, 1963, 1968, 1973, 1978 and 1983.

Nippon Research Centre, 'A Research Report on the Study of Japanese Attitudes towards the European Communities', Tokyo, 1979.

Nishimoto, K., *Loti en Face du Japon*, Quebec, 1962.

Nomura Research Institute, 'Excerpts and Analysis of European and American criticisms of Japan' (*OuBei no tai Nichi hihann no bunrui, bunseki*), Keizai Koho Centre, Tokyo, 1980.

Norman, H., *The Real Japan*, London, 1892.

Norman, H., *The People and Policies of the Far East*, London, 1895.

OECD, *The Costs of Restricting Imports, The Automobile Industry*, Paris, 1987.

OECD, 'The OECD Compatible Trade and Production Data Base,

1970–1985', Department of Economics and Statistics, Working Paper No. 60, Paris, 1988.

OECD, *Japan, 1988–1989 Annual Survey*, Paris, 1989.

Ōgura, K., 'Japan–US Economic Frictions' (*Nichibei keizai masatsu*), Tokyo, 1982.

Ohmae, Kenichi, *Beyond National Borders*, Tokyo, 1987.

Okakura, Tenshin, *The Book of Tea*, Boston, 1906.

Okita, Saburo, 'The Problem of the Japan Problem', *Journal of Japanese Trade and Industry*, 5/1987.

Ono, S., *A Western Image of Japan: What Did the West See through the Eyes of Loti and Hearn?*, Geneva, 1972.

Ono, Yeijirō, *The Industrial Transition in Japan*, Boston, 1890.

Opitz, F., 'Die Entwicklung des japanischen Deutschlandbildes', *Zeitschrift für Kulturaustausch*, no. 2, Stuttgart, 1980.

Orwell, G., *Burmese Days*, London, 1934.

Packard, George R., 'The Coming US–Japan Crisis', *Foreign Affairs*, vol. 66, 2, 1987, pp. 348–67.

Parabellum, *Bansai!*, Leipzig, 1905.

Petit, L., *Pays de Mousmé! Pays de Guerre!*, Paris, 1905.

Phillipps, K. R., *Staying on Top: Winning the Trade War*, New York, 1986.

Pinon, R., 'La Guerre Russo-Japonaise et l'Opinion Européenne', *Revue des Deux Mondes*, vol. XXI, May 1904 (quoted in Lehmann).

Plomer, W., *Autobiography*, New York, 1976.

Pons, P., 'M. Takeshita en Europe', *Le Monde* editorial, 30 April 1988.

Pozdneyev, D. M., *Japan, Present and Future, in the Eyes of Western Writers*, St Petersburg, 1895.

Preskowitz, C. V., *Trading Places – How We Allowed Japan to Take the Lead*, New York, 1988.

Presseisen, E. L., 'Le racisme et les Japonais: un dilemme Nazi', *Revue d'Histoire de la Deuxième Guerre Mondiale*, vol. XIII, 4 July 1963.

Price, V., *The Japanese Miracle and Peril*, New York, 1971.

Pyle, K. B., *The New Generation in Meiji Japan, Problems of Cultural Identity*, Stanford, 1969.

Said, E. W., *Orientalism*, London, 1979.

Saji, Keizo, 'Introduction', International Symposium, *Japan Speaks*, Osaka, 1980.

Sanders, S., *Honda, The Man and His Machines*, Tokyo, 1975.

Satoh, Yukio, *The Evolution of Japanese Security Policy*, Adelphi Papers, London, 1982.

Satow, E., 'Diary of a Member of the Japanese embassy to Europe, 1862–1863', *The Chinese and Japanese Repository*, XXIV, 1865.

Scharnagl, M., *Japan: The Planned Aggression*, Munich, 1969.

Schmiegelow, H., *Japans Aussenwirtschaftspolitik: Merkantilistisch, liberal oder funktionell?*, Hamburg, 1981.

School of Oriental and African Studies, *Report of the Governing Body*, University of London, 1955–6.

Schwantes, R. S., 'Japan's Cultural Policies', in Morley, J. W. (ed.), *Japan's Foreign Policy, 1868–1941: A Research Guide*, New York, 1974, pp. 178–9.

Schwartz, W. L., *The Imaginative Interpretation of the Far East in Modern French Literature*, Paris, 1927.

Scidmore, *Jinrikshaw Days in Japan*, New York, 1902.

Shibaguchi, K., Trevor, M., and Abo, T., *Japanese and European Management*, Tokyo, 1989.

Shibusawa, Masahide, *Japan and the Asia Pacific Region*, London, 1984.

Shiga, Shigetaka, *History of Nations*, Tokyo, 1888.

Shillony, Ben-Ami, *Politics and Culture in Wartime Japan*, Oxford, 1981.

Smith, Henry, III, *Learning From Shogun, Japanese History and Western Fantasy*, Santa Barbara, 1980.

Smith, T. S., *Japanese Society*, Cambridge, 1983.

Standish, R. (pseudonym of D. G. Gerahty), *The Three Bamboos*, London, 1943; 9th edition, Tokyo, 1970.

Steadman, J. M., *The Myth of Asia*, New York, 1969.

Stockman, D., *The Triumph of Politics*, London, 1987.

Storry, R., 'The English-language presentation of Japan's case during the China Emergency of the late nineteen-thirties', in Nish, I. and Dunn, C. (eds.), *European Studies of Japan*, Tenterden, 1979, pp. 140–8.

Sugita, Genpaku, *Dawn of Western Science in Japan*, 1815; English translation, Tokyo, 1969.

Tani, Shinichi and Sugase, Tadashi, *Nanban Art*, New York, 1973.

Taylor, J., *Shadows of the Rising Sun*, Tokyo, 1983.

Theroux, P., *The Great Railway Bazaar*, London, 1975.

Théry, E., *Le Péril Jaune: La Transformation du Japon*, Paris, 1901.

US Congress, *International Competition in Advanced Industrial Societies*, Washington, 1982.

US Department of Commerce, *Historical Statistics of the United States*, Part 1, Washington, 1975.

US House of Representatives, 'Preface' to *Report on Trade with Japan of the Subcommittee on Trade of the Committee on Ways and Means*, Washington, 5 September 1980.

Ushiba, Nobuhiko and Hara, Yasushi, 'The tradition of Japanese economic diplomacy' (*Nihon Keizai Gaikō no Keifu*), Tokyo, 1979.

Valliant, R. B., 'The Selling of Japan: Japanese Manipulation of Western Opinion, 1900–1905', *Monumenta Nipponica*, XXIX, 4, 1972, pp. 415–38.

Van Gulik, R., 'Kakkaron: A Japanese Echo of the Opium War', *Monumenta Serica*, 1939, vol. IV, pp. 478–545.

Van Wolferen, K., *The Enigma of Japanese Power*, London, 1989.

Villenoisy, F. de, *La Guerre Sino-Japonaise, ses Consequences pour l'Europe*, Paris and Limoges, 1895.

Vogel, E., *Japan as Number One*, Cambridge, Massachusetts, 1979.

Vogel, E., 'Pax Nipponica', *Foreign Affairs*, vol. 64, 4, Spring 1986, pp. 752–67.

Watanabe, M., 'Japanese Students Abroad and the Acquisition of Scientific and Technical Knowledge', *Journal of World History*, vol. IX, no. 1, 1966, pp. 254–93.

White, M., and Trevor, M., *Under Japanese Management*, London, 1983.

White, T., 'The Danger from Japan', *New York Times Magazine*, 28 July 1985.

Wichmann, S., *Japonisme*, London, 1981.

Wilkinson, Endymion (under *nom de plume* George Staunton), 'Tokyo: aller au fond des choses', *Le Monde*, 12 December 1977.

Wilkinson, Endymion, 'Changement de Structure des Exportations du Japon, 1955–1976 et Ses Implications pour la Communauté Européenne, *Chroniques d'Actualité de la S.E.D.E.I.S.*, Paris, vol. XVIII, no. 8, April 1978, pp. 244–65.

Woodcock, G., *The British in the Far East*, London, 1969.

Woolf, M., *The Japanese Conspiracy*, New York, 1984.

World Bank, *World Development Report 1988*, Oxford, 1989.

Yamada, C. F., *Dialogue in Art, Japan and the West*, Tokyo, 1976.

Yamanouchi, Hisaki, *The Search for Authenticity in Modern Japanese Literature*, Cambridge, 1978.

Yoshihara, Kunio, *The Rise of Ersatz Capitalism in Southeast Asia*, Singapore, 1988.

Zahl, K. F., 'Die Deutschen – in den Augen der Japaner', *Zeitschrift für Kulturaustausch*, no. 2, Stuttgart, 1980.

NAME INDEX

GENERAL INDEX

Administrative guidance, 139
Aid (official development
    assistance), 4, 41, 167, 198,
    201, 207–8, 240, 277
  to Asia Pacific, 21–2, 24
Aircraft industry, 174, 194, 227, 232
Amae (the desire to be loved), 40–41
Anti-dumping, 180, 238
Arms industry, 194–5, 227
Asia Pacific region, *see also* Japan,
    and Asia Pacific region
  cooperation in, 27–9, 266
  defined, 18
Association of Southeast Asian
    Nations (ASEAN), 22, 26, 28,
    265; *see also* Indonesia,
    Malaysia, Singapore, the
    Philipines and Thailand
Atlantic, 6, 11–22, 91
Australia, 29, 79, 266
Automobile industry, 22–3, 175,
    179, 182–9, 232, 262
  decline in Europe, 183
  EC trade with Japan, 182–9
  effects of VERAs, 185–7
  growth in Japan, 182–3
  investments in, 187–8
  productivity in, 188–9
  protection in EC, 185, 212
  protection in Japan, 202–3
  US, EC and Japanese market
    shares; measured in units,
    183–4, 262; measured in value,
    184, 232
  US trade with Japan, 184–7
  wages in, 185

Bakufu, 55–6, 62
Banks, 191, 193, 204–6, 221, 232
Bearings, 156, 170, 178
Beef, 47, 85
Best-sellers in Japan,
  in Meiji period, 58–9
  1939–45, 73
  1946–88, 81–5
Biotechnology, 232
Buddhism, 47, 50, 104, 128
'Bullet' train (*shinkansen*), 88, 139,
    246
Bureaucracy
  language, 216, 248–9
  procedures, 196, 213, 248, 253–5
Burma, 18, 26, 74

Cameras, 170, 233
Canada, 6, 135
Ceramics industry, 128, 170
China and the Chinese, 10, 21, 26,
    28, 67–8, 76, 97, 99
  as market for Japan, 21, 165–6
  as model for Japan, 39
  confused with Japan, 31, 99
  discarded as model by Japan,
    41–4, 50–53, 55–6, 67–8, 92
  Japanese atrocities in, 27–8, 130
  Japanese contempt for, 67–8, 108
  Sino-Japanese War, 67–8
  Western attitudes towards, 97–8,
    122–3
Chinese Exclusion Act, 68–9
Cigarettes, exports, 175, 205
Clothing styles, 47–8, 53, 60–61, 63,
    71, 85–6, 89, 121–3, 232, 243

FOR THE BEST IN PAPERBACKS, LOOK FOR THE 🐧

In every corner of the world, on every subject under the sun, Penguin represents quality and variety – the very best in publishing today.

For complete information about books available from Penguin – including Puffins, Penguin Classics and Arkana – and how to order them, write to us at the appropriate address below. Please note that for copyright reasons the selection of books varies from country to country.

In the United Kingdom: Please write to *Dept E.P., Penguin Books Ltd, Harmondsworth, Middlesex, UB7 0DA.*

If you have any difficulty in obtaining a title, please send your order with the correct money, plus ten per cent for postage and packaging, to *PO Box No 11, West Drayton, Middlesex*

In the United States: Please write to *Dept BA, Penguin, 299 Murray Hill Parkway, East Rutherford, New Jersey 07073*

In Canada: Please write to *Penguin Books Canada Ltd, 2801 John Street, Markham, Ontario L3R 1B4*

In Australia: Please write to the *Marketing Department, Penguin Books Australia Ltd, P.O. Box 257, Ringwood, Victoria 3134*

In New Zealand: Please write to the *Marketing Department, Penguin Books (NZ) Ltd, Private Bag, Takapuna, Auckland 9*

In India: Please write to *Penguin Overseas Ltd, 706 Eros Apartments, 56 Nehru Place, New Delhi, 110019*

In the Netherlands: Please write to *Penguin Books Nederland B.V., Postbus 195, NL–1380AD Weesp*

In West Germany: Please write to *Penguin Books Ltd, Friedrichstrasse 10–12, D–6000 Frankfurt/Main 1*

In Spain: Please write to *Longman Penguin España, Calle San Nicolas 15, E–28013 Madrid*

In Italy: Please write to *Penguin Italia s.r.l., Via Como 4, I-20096 Pioltello (Milano)*

In France: Please write to *Penguin Books Ltd, 39 Rue de Montmorency, F-75003 Paris*

In Japan: Please write to *Longman Penguin Japan Co Ltd, Yamaguchi Building, 2–12–9 Kanda Jimbocho, Chiyoda-Ku, Tokyo 101*

FOR THE BEST IN PAPERBACKS, LOOK FOR THE 🐧

PENGUIN BUSINESS

Great management classics of enduring relevance, business texts with a proven track record, and exciting new titles – books for all the diverse needs of today's businesses.

FOR THE BEST IN PAPERBACKS, LOOK FOR THE 🐧

PENGUIN POLITICS AND SOCIAL SCIENCES

Political Ideas David Thomson (ed.)

From Machiavelli to Marx – a stimulating and informative introduction to the last 500 years of European political thinkers and political thought.

On Revolution Hannah Arendt

Arendt's classic analysis of a relatively recent political phenomenon examines the underlying principles common to all revolutions, and the evolution of revolutionary theory and practice. 'Never dull, enormously erudite, always imaginative' – *Sunday Times*

The Apartheid Handbook Roger Omond

The facts behind the headlines: the essential hard information about how apartheid actually works from day to day.

The Social Construction of Reality Peter Berger and Thomas Luckmann

Concerned with the sociology of 'everything that passes for knowledge in society' and particularly with that which passes for common sense, this is 'a serious, open-minded book, upon a serious subject' – *Listener*

The Care of the Self Michel Foucault
The History of Sexuality Vol 3

Foucault examines the transformation of sexual discourse from the Hellenistic to the Roman world in an inquiry which 'bristles with provocative insights into the tangled liaison of sex and self' – *The Times Higher Educational Supplement*

A Fate Worse than Debt Susan George

How did Third World countries accumulate a staggering trillion dollars' worth of debt? Who really shoulders the burden of reimbursement? How should we deal with the debt crisis? Susan George answers these questions with the solid evidence and verve familiar to readers of *How the Other Half Dies*.

Comparative Government   S. E. Finer

'A considerable *tour de force* ... few teachers of politics in Britain would fail to learn a great deal from it ... Above all, it is the work of a great teacher who breathes into every page his own enthusiasm for the discipline' – Anthony King in *New Society*

Karl Marx: Selected Writings in Sociology and Social Philosophy
T. B. Bottomore and Maximilien Rubel (eds.)

'It makes available, in coherent form and lucid English, some of Marx's most important ideas. As an introduction to Marx's thought, it has very few rivals indeed' – *British Journal of Sociology*

Post-War Britain   A Political History   Alan Sked and Chris Cook

Major political figures from Attlee to Thatcher, the aims and achievements of governments and the changing fortunes of Britain in the period since 1945 are thoroughly scrutinized in this readable history.

Inside the Third World   Paul Harrison

From climate and colonialism to land hunger, exploding cities and illiteracy, this comprehensive book brings home a wealth of facts and analysis on the often tragic realities of life for the poor people and communities of Asia, Africa and Latin America.

Housewife   Ann Oakley

'A fresh and challenging account' – *Economist*. 'Informative and rational enough to deserve a serious place in any discussion on the position of women in modern society' – *The Times Educational Supplement*

The Raw and the Cooked   Claude Lévi-Strauss

Deliberately, brilliantly and inimitably challenging, Lévi-Strauss's seminal work of structural anthropology cuts wide and deep into the mind of mankind, as he finds in the myths of the South American Indians a comprehensible psychological pattern.

FOR THE BEST IN PAPERBACKS, LOOK FOR THE

A CHOICE OF PENGUINS

Better Together Christian Partnership in a Hurt City
David Sheppard and Derek Warlock

The Anglican and Roman Catholic Bishops of Liverpool tell the uplifting and heartening story of their alliance in the fight for their city – an alliance that has again and again reached out to heal a community torn by sectarian loyalties and bitter deprivation.

Fantastic Invasion Patrick Marnham

Explored and exploited, Africa has carried a different meaning for each wave of foreign invaders – from ivory traders to aid workers. Now, in the crisis that has followed Independence, which way should Africa turn? 'A courageous and brilliant effort' – Paul Theroux

Jean Rhys: Letters 1931–66
Edited by Francis Wyndham and Diana Melly

'Eloquent and invaluable … her life emerges, and with it a portrait of an unexpectedly indomitable figure' – Marina Warner in the *Sunday Times*

Among the Russians Colin Thubron

One man's solitary journey by car across Russia provides an enthralling and revealing account of the habits and idiosyncrasies of a fascinating people. 'He sees things with the freshness of an innocent and the erudition of a scholar' – *Daily Telegraph*

They Went to Portugal Rose Macaulay

An exotic and entertaining account of travellers to Portugal from the pirate-crusaders, through poets, aesthetes and ambassadors, to the new wave of romantic travellers. A wonderful mixture of literature, history and adventure, by one of our most stylish and seductive writers.

The Separation Survival Handbook Helen Garlick

Separation and divorce almost inevitably entail a long journey through a morass of legal, financial, custodial and emotional problems. Stripping the experience of both jargon and guilt, marital lawyer Helen Garlick maps clearly the various routes that can be taken.